FIX Protocol in Plain English

Order Flow, Drop Copy, and Stable Sessions

Thomas V. Trex

Published by NobleTrex Press

For permissions and other inquiries, write to:
P.O. Box 3132, Framingham, MA 01701, USA

Contents

Introduction

Electronic trading is a system of promises made and kept at machine speed. Each promise-a quote published, an order accepted, a fill acknowledged-must be captured precisely, carried reliably, and rendered unambiguous long after the market closes. The Financial Information eXchange (FIX) Protocol is the common language behind these promises. It is at once simple in spirit and intricate in practice: a terse tag-value wire format that, when disciplined by sequencing, clocks, and operational hygiene, delivers trustworthy business outcomes. This book, FIX Protocol in Plain English: Order Flow, Drop Copy, and Stable Sessions, aims to make that discipline intelligible and repeatable.

You will not find here a mere catalog of tags. Instead, we start from the business events you must express and the failure modes you must survive. The emphasis is practical: how to design order flows that are easy to reason about, how to construct sessions that recover deterministically, and how to operate systems that remain calm when links falter or latency spikes. The intended reader includes developers implementing FIX engines or adapters, site reliability engineers responsible for production health, architects designing venue and broker connectivity, and risk, surveillance, or middle-office teams consuming drop copy.

We begin with the foundations that explain why FIX looks the way it does. The opening chapter maps the electronic trading ecosystem-buy side, sell side, venues, and service providers-and shows how their responsibilities drive connectivity patterns and message choreography. We revisit order types and states, translating market, limit, and stop logic into the corresponding FIX events so that your internal order state machine aligns with what the street will send you. Because transport choices shape reliability, we review TCP behavior, buffering, and TLS or mutual TLS considerations, highlighting what actually matters for throughput and tail latency. Time is a first-class dependency: we discuss NTP and PTP discipline, drift monitoring, and timestamp precision, because sequencing, duplicate detection, and regulatory audit all rest on sound clock hygiene. We close the groundwork by clarifying symbology-symbols, SecurityID schemes, and MIC codes-so that an order is never ambiguous about what it addresses.

With those prerequisites, we turn to FIX architecture and message modeling. You will trace the version lineage from 4.x to 5.0 SP2 and FIX Latest, and see how the FIXT transport decouples session from application concerns. We dissect a FIX message-header, body, trailer, SOH delimiters, length and checksum-and connect field data types and enumerations to validation rules and interoperability pitfalls. Reusable components and repeating groups teach you to model arrays and nested structures without inventing ad hoc conventions. Finally, we introduce FIX Orchestra as a machine-readable contract: how to encode conditional rules, generate code safely, and accelerate certification with fewer surprises.

Sessions are where reliability becomes concrete. We cover logon and logout semantics, CompIDs, heartbeat intervals, and the meaning of a clean versus reset logon. Persistent sequence numbers, durable storage, and out-of-sequence handling form the spine of exactly-once business flow. You will practice gap recovery with ranged ResendRequest and SequenceReset, learn pacing strategies that avoid amplifying incidents, and implement duplicate detection using PossDupFlag and OrigSendingTime so that recovery never repeats a business action. Scheduling windows, daylight saving transitions, and planned sequence resets round out a complete operating model.

Armed with robust sessions, we build order flow. You will encode accounts and parties for accurate routing, craft NewOrderSingle with minimum yet sufficient fields, and design safe cancel/replace choreography that resists race conditions through disciplined use of OrigClOrdID. We interpret ExecutionReport streams-ExecType and OrdStatus in particular-to maintain a faithful internal state. Mass actions demonstrate how to implement bulk controls for risk limits, trading halts, and end-of-day cleanup.

Real-time drop copy gets a dedicated treatment because risk, surveillance, and reconciliation depend on it. We compare ExecutionReport and TradeCaptureReport for downstream needs, design dedicated session and routing topologies, and engineer sequencing and latency so that consumers receive a coherent, timely mirror of trading activity without entangling production order flow.

Reliability under stress requires more than correct code. We present resilience engineering for stable sessions: durable message stores for deterministic restarts, recovery playbooks for disconnections, high availability patterns that preserve single-writer sequencing, and cancel-on-disconnect protections that shrink worst-case exposure. We conclude with operating guidance: choosing and tuning engines, onboarding and certification practices that surface incompatibilities early, observability that turns logs and metrics into actionable alerts, and security with TLS or mTLS, credential rotation, and fine-grained entitlements.

Throughout, examples favor clarity over cleverness. Message types appear by their common codes (for example, 35=D), fields by tag and well-known names, and wire artifacts such as SOH (0x01) are explained where relevant. Callouts mark production cautions and testing tips. By the end, you will not only speak FIX-you will use it to design order flow that is auditable, drop copy that is coherent, and sessions that remain stable when it matters most.

Chapter 1

Foundations of Electronic Trading and FIX

Before you can read a single FIX tag with confidence, you need to see the battlefield it lives in: traders, algos, venues, networks, clocks, and symbols all colliding in microseconds. This chapter walks you through that world in plain English, so that when we finally crack open a FIX message, every field already has a story, a business reason, and a place in your mental map.

1.1 The Electronic Trading Ecosystem & Market Roles

In earlier chapters we treated FIX mainly as a messaging standard: tags, fields, sessions, and the basic idea of sending orders and receiving executions. To make FIX truly understandable in practice, we now have to shift perspective.

FIX is not just "a protocol on the wire." It is the wiring diagram of the trading business itself. Who you are in the market—your role, your obligations, your risk appetite—largely determines:

- whom you connect to,
- which direction information flows,
- how many FIX sessions you need, and
- what each session is allowed (and not allowed) to do.

This section introduces the main actors in the electronic trading ecosystem and then shows how their business relationships naturally map into FIX connectivity patterns. Once you see that mapping, many design decisions in real FIX infrastructures will feel obvious rather than arbitrary.

Four Core Role Families

Most electronic trading ecosystems can be explained in terms of four broad groups:

- **Buy-side**: investors and proprietary traders who ultimately decide what risk to take.
- **Sell-side**: broker-dealers and prime brokers who intermediate between clients and markets.
- **Execution venues**: the "places of execution" where orders actually match and become trades.
- **Service providers**: firms that support trading (data, software, connectivity, clearing, etc.) but typically do not trade on their own account with you via FIX.

These labels describe commercial and regulatory roles, not technologies. A single legal entity can wear multiple hats (for example, a large bank that is both a sell-side broker and a venue operator), but for clarity we will treat them separately.

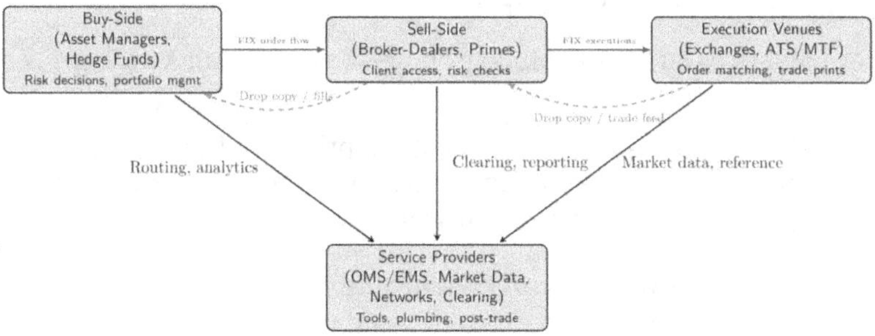

Right after introducing these roles, it is useful to visualize how they connect.

Keep this picture in mind as we go through each role in more detail. We will constantly relate their business imperatives back to concrete FIX session patterns.

Buy-Side: The Origin of Investment Intent

Who is the buy-side?

On the buy-side we find:

- **Asset managers**: mutual funds, pension funds, insurance portfolios.
- **Hedge funds**: often more active, using leverage and derivatives.
- **Proprietary trading firms**: trading their own capital, sometimes very high-frequency.
- **Wealth managers and family offices**: managing money for individuals or families.

What unites them is that they represent (or are) the ultimate owners of risk. Their job is to decide *what* to own or short, in what quantities, and on what time horizon.

Commercial incentives and constraints

Key incentives and constraints for buy-side participants include:

- **Best execution**: achieving good prices and low trading costs for their investors, often measured relative to benchmarks or volume-weighted average prices.
- **Minimal operational risk**: avoiding fat-finger errors, missing fills, or misbooked trades that could damage investor trust.
- **Confidentiality**: protecting trading intentions from leaking to the broader market.
- **Regulatory obligations**: complying with reporting rules, investor disclosure, and sometimes explicit best-execution regulation.

These factors influence how they use FIX. Most buy-side firms do not connect directly to every exchange. Instead, they rely on sell-side brokers and service providers.

Typical workflows

From the buy-side perspective, a trading day often looks like:

- A portfolio manager decides to buy or sell a basket of instruments.
- Orders are entered into an **Order Management System (OMS)** or an **Execution Management System (EMS)**.
- The OMS/EMS routes child orders to one or more brokers via **FIX order-entry sessions**.
- Execution reports, fills, and status updates flow back on the same or closely related FIX sessions.
- At the end of the day, the buy-side reconciles positions and cash using its own records plus **drop copies** and end-of-day reports from brokers and custodians.

FIX connectivity seen from the buy-side

A typical medium-sized asset manager might have:

- Several **FIX order-entry sessions** from its EMS to different brokers. Each session is usually:
  - one-way from the perspective of intent (orders go out, reports come back),
  - bilateral in protocol terms (both sides send and receive FIX messages).
- Separate **drop copy sessions** from brokers (or a broker hub) into the buy-side back office for independent trade capture and compliance.

Sometimes the drop copy flows are combined with order-entry flows in a single FIX session, but many institutional setups prefer to keep them separate so that:

- trading can continue even if back-office systems are offline, and
- back-office and compliance teams can access a feed tailored to their needs without impacting front-office latency.

In other words, buy-side firms naturally create at least two layers of FIX conversations: *trading intent* (orders) and *evidence of what actually happened* (drop copy and post-trade).

Sell-Side: The Intermediating Gatekeeper

Who is the sell-side?

Sell-side firms are typically:

- **Broker-dealers**: executing client orders on venues, either as agents or principals.
- **Prime brokers**: providing financing, custody, and access to multiple executing brokers and venues.

- **Market-making firms** with direct client relationships.

In many markets, only licensed broker-dealers can connect directly to certain exchanges. This makes the sell-side a mandatory gateway for a large portion of buy-side flow.

Commercial incentives and regulatory obligations

The sell-side sits at the intersection of clients and markets, so its incentives and constraints are rich:

- **Client service and revenue**: they earn commissions and fees by providing execution services, liquidity, and research.
- **Risk management**: they are exposed to credit, market, and operational risk from client activity.
- **Regulatory duties**: know-your-customer rules, trade reporting, market-abuse monitoring, and capital requirements.
- **Technology differentiation**: sponsoring direct market access, smart order routing, and algorithmic strategies to attract flow.

These demands directly shape the structure of their FIX networks.

Typical workflows

From the sell-side angle, a single buy-side order can generate a flurry of internal activity:

- The broker receives a **NewOrderSingle** (for example, buy 100,000 shares of XYZ at limit 10.00).
- Internal **risk checks** and compliance checks are run (credit exposure, fat-finger, restricted list).
- The order may be:
  - sent directly to a venue,
  - worked by an internal trader,
  - sliced and sent to multiple venues via **smart order routing**, or

  - internalized against the broker's own inventory, depending on local rules.

- Each child order to a venue generates its own stream of acknowledgements and executions.
- The broker **aggregates** venue-level executions and sends appropriate execution reports back to the client.
- In parallel, the broker sends **drop copies** to risk, compliance, clearing, and—if agreed—to the client's back office.

FIX connectivity seen from the sell-side

Because of that middleman position, the sell-side usually maintains:

- Many **client-facing FIX sessions** (buy-side $\leftrightarrow$ broker) for order flow and client drop copy.
- Many **venue-facing FIX sessions** (broker $\leftrightarrow$ exchange or ATS) for market access and trade capture.
- Internal **drop copy hubs** and reporting feeds (sometimes also FIX) for risk, surveillance, and clearing.

This star-shaped pattern—many clients on one side, many venues on the other—is what makes sell-side firms major FIX infrastructure operators.

A key design question for each client-broker pair is: *How many FIX sessions do we need, and what does each represent?* Some common patterns include:

- A single **multi-account session** that carries orders for many client accounts, distinguished by account tags.
- Separate sessions per **business unit or strategy**, for example, one for high-touch cash equities and another for low-latency DMA.
- A dedicated **drop copy session** streaming all executions in near real-time for post-trade systems, distinct from the lower-latency order-entry sessions.

The choices reflect a balance among technology cost, operational simplicity, risk isolation, and client preference.

Execution Venues: Where Orders Become Trades

Types of execution venues

Execution venues are where matching takes place. Examples include:

- **Central limit order book exchanges**: the classic exchange model with transparent bid/ask books.
- **Alternative trading systems / multilateral trading facilities (ATS/MTFs)**: often competing with primary exchanges, sometimes with different rules or fees.
- **Dark pools and internalizers**: venues where orders are not displayed in the public quote but can be matched, often run by banks or brokers.
- **Systematic internalisers or single-dealer platforms** in some markets: quote-driven execution using a dealer's own balance sheet.

The common thread is that they have *matching logic* and *trade reporting obligations*.

Venue incentives and obligations

Venues care about:

- **Throughput and fairness**: handling large volumes with deterministic latency and fair matching rules.
- **Market quality**: tight spreads, deep liquidity, and reliable price formation.
- **Regulatory compliance**: ensuring that trading rules are enforced and trades are reported correctly.
- **Revenue**: fees on trades, listings, connectivity, and market data.

From a FIX perspective, this means venues must:

- provide robust **order-entry sessions** to members and participants,
- send reliable **execution reports and trade updates**,
- often offer a **drop copy or back-up feed** for risk and surveillance systems.

FIX connectivity seen from venues

Venues typically connect *only* to their members (for example, broker-dealers), not directly to most buy-side firms. Their FIX topologies usually include:

- One or more **production FIX gateways** where members connect for live trading.
- **Test or certification environments** (also FIX) where new participants can validate their setups.
- Sometimes separate gateways or sessions for:
  - different asset classes,
  - sponsored access / low-latency participants,
  - drop copy or "regulatory-only" feeds.

From the venue's point of view, FIX is the way they expose their matching engine to the outside world. Every choice about sessions, sequence numbers, and heartbeat intervals is made with reliability, capacity, and fairness in mind.

Service Providers: The Supporting Infrastructure

Who are the service providers?

Service providers surround the core triangle of buy-side, sell-side, and venues. They include:

- **OMS/EMS vendors**: software platforms used by traders to manage and route orders.
- **Network and connectivity providers**: offering private lines, cross-connects, and FIX hubs.
- **Market data vendors**: distributing price feeds and reference data.
- **Clearing houses and central counterparties**: handling post-trade netting and risk.
- **Custodians and administrators**: safeguarding assets and managing corporate actions.

Many of these firms are not trading against you; they are enabling your trading.

Incentives and responsibilities

Service providers focus on:

- **Stability and performance**: uptime, latency, scalability.
- **Interoperability**: connecting many different clients and venues with varying FIX dialects.
- **Operational tooling**: monitoring, logging, replay, and support.

Because of this, they often sit logically "between" actors in ways that strongly influence real FIX connectivity but are invisible in simple high-level diagrams.

FIX connectivity involving service providers

Common patterns include:

- An EMS vendor running a **FIX hub**: buy-side clients connect to the hub, and the hub maintains FIX connections to many brokers and venues. The hub can translate formats, normalize symbology, and centralize monitoring.

- A network provider offering a **managed FIX network**: your FIX sessions terminate at their edge; they handle routing and performance across a private backbone.
- Clearing houses and custodians consuming **post-trade FIX flows** (or similar formats) to automate allocation and settlement.

In all these cases, FIX sessions are still between identifiable legal entities, but the logical path from a trader's click to an exchange can now pass through several technical and commercial layers.

From Business Roles to FIX Session Topologies

With the ecosystem roles established, we can now focus on how typical business relationships turn into concrete FIX session patterns.

Direct market access vs. sponsored access

A useful distinction is how a buy-side firm reaches a venue:

- **Direct Market Access (DMA):** The buy-side sends its orders to a broker, but those orders are forwarded *unaltered* (or nearly so) to the venue's order book under the buy-side's own identifiers. The broker still performs risk checks but aims to be a thin, low-latency pass-through.
- **Sponsored Access:** The buy-side gains near-direct connectivity to the venue, sometimes even using its own physical line, but trades under the sponsorship and regulatory responsibility of a broker. From the venue's standpoint, the broker is still the accountable member.

In FIX terms:

- For **DMA**, the primary order-entry FIX session is between buy-side and broker; the broker then has its own order-entry sessions to venues. The two layers are distinct, and each has its own sequence numbers and session state.

- For **Sponsored access**, the buy-side might still technically connect to the broker's infrastructure, but the routing is extremely direct. In some implementations, the broker acts almost like a gate or risk-check appliance in front of the venue FIX gateway.

In both cases, the legal roles (who is responsible to regulators) and the commercial roles (who is providing the service) explain why you see separate FIX sessions instead of some mythical universal connection.

Broker hubs and vendor "stars"

Another common pattern is the **hub-and-spoke** topology:

- A buy-side connects its EMS to a *single* vendor-run hub via one or a few FIX sessions.
- The hub then fans out orders to many brokers or venues over numerous FIX sessions it maintains.

The motivations are:

- **Simplicity for the buy-side**: fewer sessions to manage, fewer dialects of FIX to handle.
- **Economies of scale for the vendor**: they specialize in running large FIX networks, monitoring, and translation.

Here the vendor is a service provider, but it owns many of the *technical* FIX sessions, while the commercial relationships remain between buy-side and brokers. Legal agreements and allocation instructions ensure that trades are still attributed correctly, even though the technical plumbing runs through a third party.

Separate sessions for order flow, drop copy, and back-office

We have already hinted that different kinds of conversations often get their own sessions. This is not an arbitrary preference; it follows from the roles and responsibilities we have outlined:

- **Order-entry sessions** (front office): low-latency, strictly controlled, used by traders or algorithms. Outages here directly stop new trading.

- **Drop copy sessions** (risk and compliance): high-volume, may repeat or mirror fills from many sources, often consumed by surveillance or real-time risk systems. Slightly different latency and reliability priorities.
- **Back-office sessions** (operations and settlement): focused on allocations, confirmations, and corrections; can be more tolerant of latency but must be complete and auditable.

Different business users—trading desks, risk managers, operations—want to be able to manage and monitor these flows independently. A risk team may require a drop copy feed even if a particular trading strategy is paused or reconfigured. An operations team may need to reconnect and replay overnight messages without disturbing live trading sessions.

FIX supports this naturally: sessions are cheap to create logically, and sequence numbers allow each session's history to be tracked separately.

Seeing FIX as a Reflection of the Business

By now, several patterns should be clear:

- **Roles define conversations.** The buy-side expresses investment intent; the sell-side intermediates and manages risk; venues match orders; service providers enable and monitor. Each distinct conversation—client-to-broker, broker-to-venue, broker-to-clearing, broker-to-client drop copy—maps cleanly to one or more FIX sessions.
- **Regulation and risk shape topology.** Rules about membership, best execution, transparency, and surveillance almost force FIX networks to have layered structures: clients to brokers, brokers to venues, and separate flows for audit and reporting.
- **Operational needs encourage separation.** Front office, risk, and back office have different latency and stability requirements. It is easier to meet those if their FIX flows run on different sessions, even if they ultimately concern the same trades.

In the chapters that follow, when we dive deeper into specific FIX message types and session behaviors, keep this ecosystem view in mind. When you encounter a particular session configuration or message flow, ask yourself:

> "Which roles are talking to each other right now, and what business problem are they solving?"

Almost always, the answer will explain *why* the FIX connection looks the way it does.

1.2 Order Types, States, and Execution Basics

In the previous section we looked at *who* talks to whom in the electronic trading ecosystem: buy-side firms, sell-side brokers, execution venues, and service providers, all wired together by FIX sessions. We now zoom in on the core object that flows across those wires: the *order*.

To understand FIX messages in a realistic way, you need a clear, operational model of what an order is, which kinds of orders traders actually use, and how an order evolves over time inside a broker or an exchange. Once you can picture an order's life-cycle as a sequence of states, it becomes much easier to understand which FIX messages you should expect to see, and in what order.

This section therefore has three goals:

- Introduce the main order types and what they really guarantee.
- Build an intuitive state machine for an order's life-cycle.
- Connect state changes to typical FIX events and execution reports.

We will keep the focus on equities for simplicity, but the same ideas apply, with minor variations, to futures, options, and other asset classes.

Core Order Types and Their Behaviour

Think of an order as a *conditional instruction*: "If market conditions look like X, then buy or sell Y units of instrument Z." Different order types encode different conditions and priorities about price and timing.

We will start with the basic building blocks that appear in almost every market.

Market Orders: Priority on Immediate Execution

A **market order** says: *"Trade this quantity as soon as possible at the best price currently available."*

Key characteristics:

- **Execution certainty is high.** As long as there is enough liquidity on the opposite side of the book, the order will fill quickly.
- **Price certainty is low.** You do not specify a limit. If the visible best price moves while you are trading, your executions will follow the new prices.
- **No resting in the book.** A genuine market order does not sit and wait; it crosses the spread and consumes existing resting liquidity.

In practice, a trader who submits a buy market order for 10,000 shares in a thinly traded stock is accepting the risk that the average execution price might be significantly worse than the price they saw a moment ago. Many firms therefore wrap market orders in extra protection, such as explicit price bands or "market with protection" logic at the broker.

From a FIX perspective, the *order type* field determines that this is a market order. Execution reports that follow will show the actual prices where fills occurred, which might span multiple levels of the book.

Limit Orders: Priority on Price

A **limit order** says: *"Trade this quantity, but only at a price at least as good as this limit."*

For a buy limit order:

- The limit price is the *maximum* you are willing to pay.
- The order will only execute at or below this price.

For a sell limit order:

- The limit price is the *minimum* you are willing to accept.
- The order will only execute at or above this price.

Key characteristics:

- **Price certainty is high.** You will never do worse than your limit.
- **Execution certainty is limited.** If the market never trades at your limit or better, your order will not fill.
- **Orders can rest.** A limit order that does not find an immediate match will often rest in the order book, visible to other participants.

Because limit orders can rest, they go through more states than market orders: new, accepted, resting, partially filled, fully filled, or eventually canceled or expired. This richer life-cycle will be central to our state machine later.

Stop Orders: Triggered by the Market

A **stop order** adds a *trigger condition* based on the market price. It says, informally:

"Watch the market. When the price crosses a certain threshold, then submit another order (usually a market order)."

Common use cases include:

- A **sell stop** below the current price to limit downside risk (a stop-loss).
- A **buy stop** above the current price to enter after confirming upward momentum.

Until the trigger price is reached, the stop order is usually not visible in the public book. Once triggered, it transforms internally into an active order type:

- A *stop-market* becomes a market order when triggered.
- A *stop-limit* becomes a limit order with a specified limit price.

This two-stage behaviour (monitoring, then conversion) means that stop orders have their own mini life-cycle before they even join the regular order state machine.

Stop-Limit Orders: Combining Triggers with Price Protection

A **stop-limit** order adds both a trigger price and a limit price. For example:

- Trigger (stop) price: 95.00
- Limit price: 94.50

For a sell stop-limit:

- If the market trades at or below 95.00, the stop triggers.
- A limit sell order with limit 94.50 is then submitted.
- The order will execute at 94.50 or better, but never below 94.50.

You gain some protection against extreme price gaps, but at the cost that, in a fast move, the market might skip past your limit, leaving you unfilled.

In FIX and venue implementations, the exact definitions of "trigger" (trade price vs. quote vs. mid) can vary, so in production systems you must always check the venue's rulebook.

Iceberg and Hidden Orders: Controlling Displayed Size

An **iceberg order** (also called a reserve order) exposes only part of its total size to the public book. For example:

- Total quantity: 50,000 shares.
- Display quantity: 5,000 shares.

The visible 5,000 shares rest in the book like a normal limit order. When that portion fills, the venue automatically refreshes another 5,000 from the hidden reserve, often receiving a new time priority.

Related ideas:

- **Fully hidden orders** do not display any size but can still interact with visible liquidity.
- **Discretionary orders** show a limit price but may execute at a better price within a hidden discretionary range.

From the outside, you still see regular partial fills and order state changes. The complexity is in how the venue manages the resting and refreshing of the visible slice.

From Order Types to Order States

Order types describe *rules of behaviour*, but they do not tell you what is happening to a specific order right now. For that we need an order *state* model: a clear vocabulary for the stages an order passes through, from the moment the trader clicks "Send" to the time the order is finally complete.

A useful way to think about this is as a state machine where:

- each state represents a distinct condition of the order, and
- transitions between states correspond to observable events, usually accompanied by FIX messages.

Before drawing the diagram, we will build the main states conceptually.

Key Order States

While different venues and brokers may use slightly different labels, the following core states appear everywhere:

- **New / Created:** The order has been created in the client system (for example, an OMS) but has not yet been accepted by the broker or venue.
- **Accepted / Working:** The order has passed initial checks and is now being worked by the broker or resting on the venue book.
- **Partially Filled:** Some, but not all, of the requested quantity has traded.
- **Filled:** The entire requested quantity has traded; the order is complete in terms of execution.
- **Canceled:** Remaining quantity (if any) has been canceled at the client's request or due to some rule (for example, end-of-day).
- **Rejected:** The order has been refused before it could start working (for example, due to a risk limit or invalid symbol).
- **Expired:** The order has reached its time limit (for example, good-for-day) without being fully filled; any resting portion is removed.

There are also *intermediate* states such as "pending new" or "pending cancel" that represent requests in transit. For a conceptual understanding, it is enough to know that:

- when you send a new order or cancel request, there is usually a brief period where you are waiting for the broker or venue to confirm that action, and
- these pending states help explain why the next message could be either an acceptance or a rejection.

A Canonical Order Life-Cycle

Putting these states together gives us a canonical life-cycle that most regular limit and market orders follow.

Right after we have introduced the states, it is helpful to see them visually.

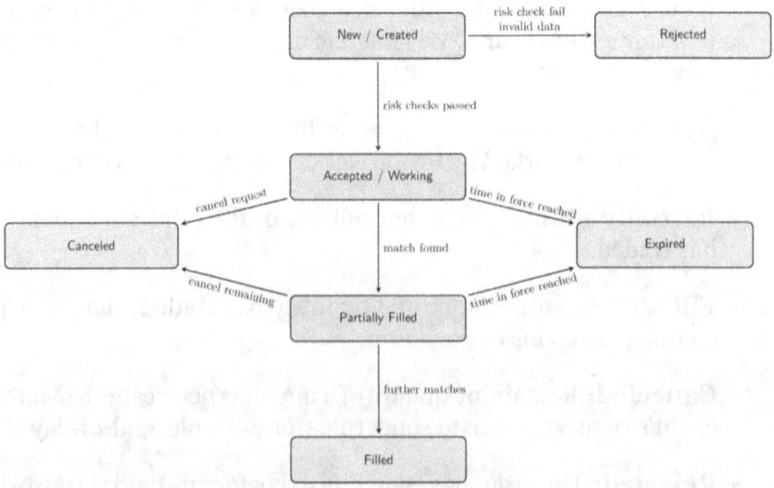

You can walk an order's life by following the arrows:

- *Happy path*: New → Accepted → Partially Filled (one or more times) → Filled.
- *Early rejection*: New → Rejected (never becomes active).
- *Canceled working order*: New → Accepted → Canceled.
- *Expired order*: New → Accepted → Expired.

Later, when we map these transitions to specific FIX messages, this picture will help you reason about what your application should expect next.

What Happens Inside the Broker or Venue?

To make these states feel concrete, imagine a simple limit buy order as it travels from a buy-side EMS, through a broker, into a venue.

Creation and Routing

A trader clicks "Buy 10,000 XYZ @ 10.00 limit." The EMS:

- constructs a new order object in its own memory or database (state: *created* locally),
- chooses which broker and algorithm to use (routing decision),
- sends a FIX *new order* message to the broker.

At this point, from the point of view of the broader market, the order does not exist yet. The only evidence is the outgoing FIX message on the client-to-broker session.

Risk Checks and Acceptance

The broker receives the new order and performs checks:

- Is the symbol valid and tradable?
- Is the account allowed to trade this instrument?
- Is the quantity reasonable (no extra zeros)?
- Does the order fit within credit, margin, and risk limits?

If the order fails these checks, the broker rejects it. In state terms: *New* at the broker transitions *directly* to *Rejected*. A FIX rejection message goes back to the client, and the order never reaches the matching engine.

If the order passes, the broker acknowledges it, and the order becomes *Accepted / Working*. This is usually confirmed back to the client via an execution report or acknowledgement message.

Resting and Matching

Once the order is accepted and forwarded to the venue, the matching engine:

- compares the buy order's limit price against current sell orders,
- executes any immediate matches that satisfy both price and time priority,
- if some quantity remains unfilled, posts that remainder to the book as a resting limit order.

This is where partial fills arise: your 10,000 share order may only find 3,000 shares to trade at or better than 10.00 at that moment. So:

- 3,000 shares move to *Filled*,
- 7,000 shares remain *Accepted / Working* (resting in the book).

Over time, as new sell orders arrive that match your price, more partial fills occur until either:

- the full 10,000 shares are filled, or
- time runs out (end of day or time-in-force limit), or
- someone cancels the remaining quantity.

Every fill, even if small, is usually reported back through the broker to the client via FIX execution reports, each one updating the cumulative filled quantity and remaining open quantity.

Common Non-Happy Paths

Several other important scenarios also fit into the same state framework:

Fat-finger rejections.

If a trader accidentally enters a price of 1000.00 instead of 10.00, a broker-side risk check may detect that the order is too far from the current market price and reject it. This is a transition from *New* to *Rejected*, often with a clear textual reason.

Symbol or account restrictions.

If an instrument is restricted (for example, because of regulatory reasons) for a specific account, the broker may accept similar orders for other accounts but reject them for this one. Again, the state change is *New* to *Rejected*; on the client's FIX log, you will see a rejection message with codes indicating the cause.

Cancel or replace requests.

If the trader decides to change the order before it is fully filled, they can send:

- a *cancel* request, moving the remaining quantity toward *Canceled*, or
- a *cancel/replace* (often called "amend"), which changes details such as price or quantity.

During this process:

- the order may enter a *pending cancel* or *pending replace* state,
- the broker or venue decides whether to accept the request,
- the resulting state becomes either *Canceled*, *Accepted / Working* with updated terms, or, in some edge cases, *Filled* if the last shares traded before the cancel took effect.

Understanding these subtleties is important when you are reconciling FIX logs with venue records; short-lived pending states can explain seemingly surprising sequences of messages.

How State Changes Appear in FIX Flows

Even though we are not yet diving into exact tag names, you can already see the pattern:

- When the client sends a new order, the next message *should* be either an acceptance or a rejection.
- After acceptance, each interaction with the matching engine that changes filled or remaining quantity produces an execution report.
- When a cancel or replace is requested, there should be a corresponding confirmation of that action, or a rejection.

From a systems design standpoint, it helps to think in terms of *discrete events*:

- **Order created**: client emits a new order message; internal state *Created*.

- **Order accepted**: broker or venue emits an acknowledgement; state transitions to *Accepted / Working*.
- **Trade executed**: broker or venue emits one or more execution reports; cumulative quantity increases; order may move to *Partially Filled* or *Filled*.
- **Order canceled**: broker or venue emits a cancel confirmation; remaining quantity becomes zero; state *Canceled*.
- **Order expired**: venue removes the order at time-in-force boundary; state *Expired* and a final status is reported.
- **Order rejected**: broker or venue emits a rejection; state *Rejected*; no fills ever occur.

Each of these events corresponds to one or more FIX messages on the relevant session (client-to-broker, broker-to-venue, broker-to-clearing, etc.). When your application reads a FIX log, it should be able to reconstruct the state machine step by step, using the messages as evidence.

Parent and Child Orders

So far we have treated an order as a single, indivisible entity. In real trading, especially for large institutional orders, it is often helpful to distinguish:

- **Parent orders**: high-level instructions, such as "buy 500,000 XYZ over the day."
- **Child orders**: the smaller pieces that are actually sent to venues, such as "buy 10,000 XYZ now" many times through the day.

The parent order lives primarily inside the client OMS or broker algorithm engine. It has its own life-cycle:

- Created when the trader defines the overall objective.
- Progressively filled as child orders accumulate executions.

- Completed or canceled when the total target quantity is reached or the trading horizon ends.

Each child order then has the usual state machine we have already described. In FIX flows:

- The client may see only the parent order's state (especially when using broker algorithms).
- The broker sees both parent and child states; venue-facing FIX sessions carry the child orders.

For reconciliation and analytics (such as transaction cost analysis), it is important that you can tie child executions back to their parent order. FIX supports various ways of carrying such identifiers, but at the conceptual level you can simply think of:

- one parent order aggregating the life-cycles of many child orders.

Why This Life-Cycle Model Matters for FIX

By now you should be able to imagine a specific order, track it with your mind's eye as it moves from state to state, and associate each transition with an event and a message.

This mental model pays off in several ways:

- **Designing FIX-handling code.** When you implement a FIX engine or a trading adapter, you can align your internal order states with the conceptual model. Each incoming message becomes a clear state transition, not an isolated piece of text.
- **Debugging production issues.** When something goes wrong—for example, an order appears filled in your system but not at the broker—you can reconstruct where in the state machine the disagreement started.
- **Interpreting logs and drop copies.** Drop copy feeds show you the "ground truth" of what the broker or venue believes happened. Comparing those feeds to your own order state machine helps detect missed messages or incorrect assumptions.

- **Extending to complex order types.** More advanced types (pegged orders, conditional orders, complex options strategies) still boil down to the same basic idea: they start in a new state, they are accepted or rejected, they may be partially filled, and they eventually reach a terminal state.

In later chapters, when we talk about specific FIX messages such as *New Order Single*, *Execution Report*, *Order Cancel Request*, and so on, we will refer back to this life-cycle. Each message type will be easier to remember and reason about if you always ask:

> "Which state is this order moving from, and which state is it moving to?"

Once you can answer that, FIX stops looking like a random collection of tags and starts to look like a structured, predictable language for describing the evolution of orders over time.

1.3 Networking & Transport for Low-Latency Trading

Up to this point we have focused on *what* flows through FIX sessions: orders, state changes, and executions between buy-side, sell-side, and venues. We now turn to *how* those messages actually travel across the network.

If you are building or operating FIX connectivity, you cannot treat the network as a black box. FIX sessions ride on top of TCP, sometimes wrapped in encryption via TLS or mutual TLS (mTLS). Choices made at this transport layer—socket options, buffering, encryption, routing—directly affect:

- how quickly a new order reaches the broker or venue,
- how predictably execution reports come back, and
- how robustly sessions survive network blips or failures.

This section gives you a realistic feel for what is happening *on the wire* when a FIX message is sent, and how to reason about performance and reliability without needing to be a networking specialist.

FIX Over TCP: Streams, Not Packets

The first conceptual hurdle is understanding the relationship between FIX messages and TCP.

TCP as a byte stream

TCP (Transmission Control Protocol) provides a *reliable, ordered byte stream* between two endpoints. That phrase is dense, so let us unpack it:

- **Stream**: from the programmer's point of view, TCP is like a pipe. You write bytes in, the other side reads bytes out, in the same order. TCP does not inherently know where one message ends and the next begins.
- **Reliable**: TCP ensures that bytes are eventually delivered exactly once, or it tells you that the connection has failed. If network packets are dropped or arrive out of order, TCP retransmits and reorders them.
- **Ordered**: bytes arrive in the same sequence in which they were sent, as long as the connection remains established.

In contrast, FIX is a *message-oriented* protocol at the application layer. We care about discrete messages like "New Order Single" or "Execution Report", each with its own fields and checksums.

To reconcile these views, every FIX engine performs two jobs:

- It treats TCP as an undifferentiated stream of bytes.
- It parses those bytes into individual FIX messages using delimiters and length fields defined by the FIX standard.

From your perspective, when you "send a FIX message" you are in fact:

- serializing a message into a sequence of bytes,
- writing that sequence into a TCP socket,
- trusting TCP to deliver those bytes in order to the peer.

The key implication is that any delay, buffering, or retransmission at the TCP layer applies to whole chunks of your FIX messages, not neatly one message at a time.

Connection establishment and teardown

Before any FIX logon can occur, a TCP connection must be established between the two hosts. This is the familiar three-way handshake:

- Client sends a "SYN" (synchronize) packet to the server.
- Server replies with a "SYN-ACK" (synchronize-acknowledge).
- Client sends an "ACK" to complete the handshake.

This process takes at least one round-trip time (RTT) on the network, sometimes more. Only once this handshake is complete can application-level FIX messages flow.

When a TCP connection closes (cleanly or due to error), the FIX session riding on top must react. In low-latency trading setups, you will often see:

- **Primary and backup** TCP connections, each with its own FIX session, so that a failure on one path does not completely stop trading.
- **Automatic reconnection logic** in the FIX engine that attempts to re-establish TCP and re-synchronize sequence numbers.

The important point is that when you see a FIX session drop, the root cause is often a TCP-level event: socket closed, timeout reached, or too many retransmissions.

Buffering and Latency: Where Time Is Spent

Latency in electronic trading is often discussed as a single number, but it is really the sum of several components:

- time spent in the sender's application,
- time spent in operating system (OS) buffers and TCP stacks,
- time spent in the network (propagation, queuing, routing),
- time spent in the receiver's OS and application.

Understanding where buffering happens helps you reason about both the *average* latency and the *jitter* (variability).

Send-side buffering

When your FIX engine sends a message, it typically:

- serializes the message into a byte array,
- writes that array to the socket,
- returns control to your application.

At this point, several things can be true simultaneously:

- The bytes may be sitting in a user-space buffer inside your application.
- Some or all of them may be queued in the OS's TCP send buffer, waiting to be packaged into network packets.
- Some may already have been put on the wire and be in flight toward the counterparty.

If the OS thinks it can achieve better efficiency by combining several small writes into a single packet, it may hold your data for a short time. This coalescing can reduce network overhead but increase latency for small, urgent messages.

Nagle's algorithm and small messages

One important mechanism here is **Nagle's algorithm**. Its goal is to avoid sending too many small packets by waiting until either:

- enough data has accumulated to fill a larger packet, or
- the previous packet has been acknowledged.

In interactive or batch applications, this is often harmless or even beneficial. In low-latency trading, Nagle's algorithm can introduce small but significant delays when:

- your application sends many small FIX messages,
- the OS decides to wait to combine them rather than sending immediately.

As a result, production trading deployments frequently configure sockets to disable Nagle, instructing the OS to send data as soon as possible rather than waiting to combine writes. This is an example of a deliberate trade-off: you accept slightly more network overhead to gain lower and more predictable latency.

Receive-side buffering and packet boundaries

On the receiving side, the OS also buffers incoming data. Your FIX engine typically calls a "read" function, which returns:

- any bytes already available in the buffer up to some maximum size,
- or blocks until data arrives (depending on configuration).

Crucially, there is no guarantee that each read operation returns exactly one FIX message. You may read:

- half of a FIX message (the rest will arrive in a later read),
- one and a half messages,

- many messages at once.

Your FIX parser must therefore handle arbitrary chunking of data, reassembling complete messages using FIX's own length and delimiter fields. This is a direct consequence of TCP being a byte stream rather than a message protocol.

From a latency perspective, this means that:

- a message can be delayed not only in transit, but also in OS buffers if your application is not reading aggressively enough,
- tuning read loops and buffer sizes can make a noticeable difference to end-to-end response times.

Network Jitter, Congestion, and Retransmissions

Even if you configure your sockets perfectly, the network itself can introduce variability.

Propagation and routing

Physical distance matters. Signals travel through fiber at roughly two-thirds the speed of light in vacuum. For long distances (for example, cross-continent or transatlantic links) there is a minimum possible round-trip time set by physics.

Routing paths through intermediate routers and switches add a small amount of additional latency, and sometimes suboptimal routing decisions can add more.

In practice:

- If you colocate your trading servers in the same data center as a venue or broker, you minimize propagation delay.
- If you connect over the public internet or long private lines, you must accept higher base latency and more variability.

Jitter and queuing

Jitter is the variation in latency from one message to the next. It often arises when:

- network devices (routers, switches) experience bursts of traffic and temporarily queue packets,
- shared links become congested, increasing queuing times,
- operating systems are busy and delay processing of network interrupts.

In FIX trading, jitter can be as harmful as high average latency, because:

- algorithms tuned to microsecond or millisecond timescales may misinterpret delayed updates as stale or missing data,
- session-level heartbeats and timeouts may be triggered unnecessarily if messages occasionally arrive late.

Careful capacity planning and the use of dedicated or high-quality network paths are common strategies to reduce jitter.

Packet loss and TCP retransmissions

Despite best efforts, packets can be dropped due to hardware errors, overload, or transient faults. TCP detects this using sequence numbers and acknowledgements. When it notices that data has not been acknowledged within an expected time window, it:

- retransmits the missing data,
- may also reduce its sending rate to avoid overwhelming the network.

From a FIX perspective, you should be aware that:

- retransmissions can cause *outlier latencies*, where a particular message arrives much later than usual,
- if enough packets are lost or delayed, the TCP connection may time out or reset, forcing the FIX session to log out, then log back in and resynchronize.

Sometimes these events appear at the FIX layer as sequence gaps or as sudden disconnects, but their true origin lies in packet loss and retransmission at the TCP layer.

TLS and Mutual TLS: Security vs. Latency

In many production environments, FIX sessions are not sent in the clear. They are wrapped in TLS (Transport Layer Security), which provides:

- **Confidentiality**: messages are encrypted so that intermediaries cannot read the contents.
- **Integrity**: modifications or tampering can be detected.
- **Authentication**: the client can verify the server's identity (and, with mutual TLS, the server can verify the client's).

TLS handshakes

Before encrypted data can flow, a TLS *handshake* must occur over the established TCP connection. During this handshake:

- the client and server agree on cryptographic algorithms,
- the server presents its certificate, and the client verifies it,
- keys are exchanged or derived for the session.

This handshake adds extra round trips and computation at connection start-up. In low-latency trading this overhead is usually acceptable because:

- FIX sessions are designed to be long-lived rather than constantly torn down and recreated,
- the per-message overhead after the handshake is generally small relative to matching-engine and routing times, especially for human or algorithmic trading that is not at the ultra-high-frequency extreme.

However, if your environment opens and closes many FIX sessions frequently, or if you are extremely latency sensitive, you must account for handshake time in your design.

Mutual TLS (mTLS)

In mutual TLS, both client and server present certificates during the handshake. This provides strong, cryptographic proof of identity in both directions, which is attractive for:

- financial institutions with strict identity and access control requirements,
- setups crossing administrative boundaries (for example, client-to-broker over the public internet or shared networks).

The trade-offs include:

- **Operational complexity**: you must manage certificates, expiry dates, renewals, and revocations for both sides.
- **Failure modes**: if a certificate expires or is misconfigured, FIX sessions will fail to establish even though the network is up, which can be confusing if you do not monitor certificate health.

From a pure latency standpoint, mTLS is similar to regular TLS, but the security posture is stronger.

Encryption overhead in practice

Encrypting and decrypting data consumes CPU cycles, but modern hardware and cryptographic libraries are efficient. In most institutional trading scenarios:

- the incremental per-message latency from encryption is small compared with network and matching-engine delays,
- the main concern is *jitter* if CPU usage spikes and temporarily slows encryption operations.

To manage this, production systems typically:

- allocate sufficient CPU resources to FIX gateways,
- avoid sharing TLS-terminating processes with unrelated workloads,

- monitor CPU and latency distributions to catch performance regressions.

Typical Production Connectivity Patterns

With these building blocks in mind, let us look at how real-world FIX transport setups are arranged.

Cross-connects vs. internet VPN

Two common ways to reach a broker or venue are:

- **Data center cross-connect**: Both parties place their servers in the same data center or exchange colocation facility. A private "cross-connect" (a short, dedicated fiber or copper link) connects their racks.
- **Internet or MPLS VPN**: Each party hosts servers in their own facilities and connects over a virtual private network across the public internet or a managed MPLS backbone.

Cross-connects typically offer:

- lower base latency (short physical distance, minimal routing),
- less jitter (dedicated path, fewer competing flows),
- simpler failure domains (fewer intermediaries).

VPN-based connections are:

- more flexible geographically,
- sometimes cheaper or easier to deploy initially,
- more exposed to internet routing changes and congestion if not fully private.

In both cases, the FIX session logic is the same; what changes is the transport path's latency and stability profile.

Primary and backup connections

To avoid single points of failure, institutions often set up:

- a **primary** TCP path and FIX session over a preferred, low-latency link,
- a **secondary** or backup path and session, possibly through a different data center, carrier, or physical route.

Failover strategies vary, but common patterns include:

- *Hot standby*: both sessions are up, but only one is actively used at any time. If the primary fails, the system switches to the backup.
- *Active-active*: both sessions are used in parallel for different flows, with logic to re-route if one path degrades.

At the FIX level, each session has its own sequence numbers and logon/logout cycles. During failover, your application must be prepared to:

- recognize which session is currently authoritative for a given flow,
- manage any sequence resynchronization requested by the counterparty,
- handle in-flight orders and responses that may be mid-stream when the switch occurs.

Network design and session management are therefore closely intertwined.

Heartbeats, Timeouts, and Transport Health

FIX sessions incorporate heartbeats and test requests to monitor the health of the connection between two endpoints. These mechanisms sit *above* TCP but are deeply affected by transport behaviour.

Heartbeats as an application-level pulse

A typical FIX session is configured with a heartbeat interval (for example, 30 seconds). If neither side has sent any application messages during that interval, they send a heartbeat message to show that:

- the TCP connection is still alive,
- the FIX engine is still responsive.

If one side does not receive a heartbeat or any other message within a specified timeframe, it may:

- send a test request to probe the other side,
- assume the session is dead and initiate logout procedures.

Impact of network delays and pauses

Network jitter, congestion, or short outages can cause heartbeats or test requests to:

- arrive late,
- be delivered in bursts after a pause,
- be lost along with other packets.

If heartbeat intervals are set too aggressively relative to the underlying network's variability, FIX sessions may flap: repeatedly disconnecting and reconnecting even though the TCP layer is only experiencing brief or mild disruption.

Conversely, if heartbeat intervals are too long, genuine failures (for example, a broken link) may only be detected with undesirable delay.

Selecting and tuning heartbeat and timeout values is therefore a joint exercise between:

- application-level FIX designers, and
- network engineers who understand the characteristics of the underlying transport paths.

Putting It All Together: A Mental Model for "Stable" Sessions

When practitioners talk about a "stable" FIX session, they mean more than just "the FIX engine did not crash." They implicitly assume that:

- the underlying TCP connections are healthy (no frequent resets, reasonable retransmission rates),
- buffering behaviour is tuned for low and predictable latency (appropriate socket options, adequate CPU),
- TLS or mTLS is configured and maintained correctly (certificates valid, no surprise handshake failures),
- the network paths provide consistent latency and low jitter (good routing, sufficient capacity),
- heartbeat and timeout settings reflect the realities of the transport layer.

In other words, FIX is only as reliable and low-latency as the transport stack underneath it.

As you design or operate FIX connectivity, keep asking:

> "If I see this behaviour in my FIX logs, what might be happening one layer down, at TCP or TLS or on the network path?"

Cultivating that habit will help you:

- distinguish between application-level bugs and transport issues,
- have more productive conversations with network and security teams,
- build FIX infrastructures that deliver both correctness and the performance that modern electronic trading demands.

In the next sections, we will build on this foundation when we discuss time synchronization and symbology, both of which also rely on a clear appreciation of what is truly happening in the underlying systems each time a FIX message is sent or received.

1.4 Time Synchronization & Clock Hygiene

In the previous sections we treated FIX as messages riding over TCP, sometimes wrapped in TLS, moving orders between clearly defined market roles. We talked about latency and jitter as properties of the transport path. In this section we add another, less visible but equally critical ingredient: *time*.

Every FIX message you send or receive can carry timestamps. Every log line your system writes has a time attached to it. When you later try to reconstruct what happened—for example, why an order appeared to receive a poor price, or whether a risk limit was hit before or after a trade—you will rely on these timestamps.

Those timestamps are only as good as the clocks that generated them. If different machines disagree about the current time, your neatly ordered sequence of events can become scrambled. The result is confusion at best, and regulatory trouble at worst.

This section explains why disciplined clock management is a first-class production concern in FIX trading, and how technologies like NTP and PTP fit into that discipline.

Why Time Matters So Much in FIX Trading

It is tempting to think of timestamps as "nice to have" metadata. In modern electronic markets they are anything but optional.

Sequencing and causality

When you investigate a trading issue, you are often trying to answer questions like:

- Did we send the cancel request before or after the last fill?
- Did the broker reject the order before it reached the venue, or did the venue reject it and then the broker relayed that to us?
- Did two trading algorithms interfere with each other, or was one clearly acting after the other?

These are questions about *causality*. To answer them, you compare timestamps from multiple systems:

- your own trading engine and OMS/EMS,
- the broker's FIX gateway and order router,
- the venue's matching engine and trade reporting system.

If those systems disagree on the time by a few hundred milliseconds or more, the apparent order of events may be reversed. You could be misled into thinking that a venue filled an order before you sent it, or that a cancel was late when it was actually timely.

Latency measurement and performance tuning

Earlier we decomposed latency into:

- application processing time,
- OS and TCP buffering time,
- network propagation and queuing time.

To optimize this, you need to measure delays accurately. A common pattern is:

- The client timestamps an outgoing order as it leaves the system.
- The broker timestamps the order as it arrives and as it leaves for the venue.
- The venue timestamps the order upon arrival, and the resulting execution report upon creation.

- The client timestamps the execution report upon receipt.

By comparing these times, you can break down:

- client-to-broker latency,
- broker internal latency,
- broker-to-venue latency,
- matching-engine turnaround,
- venue-to-client report latency.

This analysis is only meaningful if each clock involved has reasonably small error and drift. Otherwise, a slow broker might appear fast, or vice versa, simply because its clock is behind or ahead.

Regulatory reporting and surveillance

In many jurisdictions, trading regulations require:

- timestamping of orders and trades to millisecond or microsecond precision,
- consistent reporting of event sequences for market surveillance,
- reconstruction of order books and trade flows after the fact.

Regulators often cross-check:

- reported times from different firms,
- market data feeds,
- exchange audit trails.

If your clocks are badly skewed, your reports may show events occurring out of sync with the broader market, raising questions about whether you have adequate controls. In extreme cases, inaccurate timestamps can be treated as a compliance failure, even if your trading decisions themselves were reasonable.

Clock Drift: The Quiet Enemy

Computer clocks do not stay accurate by themselves. Each server has a hardware oscillator that keeps time by counting ticks. These oscillators are not perfect:

- Their frequency can differ slightly from the ideal, leading to *drift* (gradual gain or loss of time).
- Temperature changes and hardware aging can alter their behaviour.
- Operating system load and power-saving features can affect timing.

Over minutes or hours, even a small drift rate accumulates into a noticeable offset from true time.

Offset vs. drift

It helps to distinguish two related concepts:

- **Offset**: how far a clock is from a chosen reference at a specific moment (for example, "this server is 50 ms ahead of UTC").
- **Drift**: how fast a clock's offset is changing over time (for example, "this clock gains 2 ms every minute").

A one-time offset can be corrected by stepping or slewing the clock. Ongoing drift requires continuous correction; otherwise the offset will quickly become large again.

Consequences of unmanaged drift

Imagine that:

- your trading engine is 200 ms ahead of true time,
- your broker's system is roughly correct, within a few milliseconds,
- the venue is also disciplined and close to UTC.

Now consider an order that:

- leaves your system at what *you* think is 10:00:00.000,
- arrives at the broker at 09:59:59.850 true time (but you will log it as later),
- gets filled at the venue at 10:00:00.050 true time.

In your own logs, it might look like:

- order sent at 10:00:00.000,
- broker acknowledgement timestamped (by broker) at 09:59:59.900,
- execution report timestamped at 10:00:00.050 (from the venue).

Comparing your clock with the broker's, it appears that:

- the broker acknowledged the order *before* you sent it (since their 09:59:59.900 is 100 ms earlier than your 10:00:00.000),
- execution happened suspiciously fast or out of sequence.

This is not just confusing in investigations; it can derail systematic latency analysis and raise red flags in surveillance.

NTP and PTP: Two Approaches to Time Synchronization

To keep clocks disciplined, trading systems typically rely on time synchronization protocols. The two most widely used are NTP and PTP. They serve related but distinct purposes.

Network Time Protocol (NTP)

NTP is the long-standing workhorse of internet time synchronization. At a high level:

- Servers designated as time sources (NTP servers) maintain accurate clocks, often synced to GPS or other high-quality references.
- Client machines periodically exchange timestamped messages with these servers.
- By comparing send and receive times, clients estimate the network delay and the offset between their own clock and the server's clock.
- Clients adjust their clocks gradually (slewing) to reduce the offset.

Key properties:

- **Typical accuracy**: on well-managed LANs, NTP can usually keep clocks within a few hundred microseconds to a millisecond of their time source; on the broader internet, tens of milliseconds are more common.
- **Complexity**: relatively easy to deploy and maintain; most operating systems have built-in NTP clients.
- **Use cases**: adequate for many trading firms whose regulatory obligations are at millisecond granularity, and whose strategies are not extremely latency sensitive.

NTP is not perfect—it is sensitive to asymmetric network delays and jitter—but it is far better than leaving clocks to drift freely.

Precision Time Protocol (PTP)

PTP (often referenced as IEEE 1588) aims for much tighter synchronization. Instead of treating the network as an opaque, possibly jittery path, PTP often assumes:

- specialized network hardware (switches, NICs) that understand PTP and can timestamp packets very precisely,
- a hierarchy of time sources, with one *grandmaster* clock distributing time to others.

Key properties:

- **Typical accuracy**: with proper hardware and configuration, PTP can achieve synchronization down to the microsecond or even sub-microsecond range.
- **Complexity**: significantly higher operational complexity. You need compatible switches, NICs, and disciplined configuration; you also need to monitor PTP behaviour carefully.
- **Use cases**: colocation environments, high-frequency trading, and any context where regulations or internal policies require microsecond-level timestamp precision.

Where NTP might be used across a whole enterprise, PTP is more commonly deployed in tightly controlled environments like colocation racks and exchange networks.

Practical Clock Hygiene in a Trading Shop

Whether you use NTP, PTP, or both, having a protocol in place is only half of the story. You also need good *clock hygiene*: operational practices that keep your time infrastructure healthy and observable.

Multiple time sources and redundancy

Relying on a single time source is risky. If that source goes bad (for example, due to hardware failure or misconfiguration), all your clients will follow it off a cliff.

Practical setups therefore include:

- multiple independent time sources (for example, two GPS-backed time servers plus an upstream provider),
- clear rules (stratum, priorities) about which sources to trust and how to fail over between them,
- isolation between environments (for example, production and test might use different time trees to avoid cross-contamination).

For PTP, this translates into multiple potential grandmasters, with election mechanisms to ensure that if one fails or drifts, another takes over.

Monitoring drift and offset

Time synchronization should be monitored like any other production dependency. This involves:

- tracking each server's offset from its reference over time,
- setting alert thresholds for excessive offset (for example, more than a few hundred microseconds or a millisecond, depending on your tolerance),
- watching for sudden jumps, which may indicate hardware issues, NTP/PTP misconfiguration, or operating system bugs.

Visualizing offset as a time series makes it easy to spot:

- healthy behaviour: small offset oscillating within a narrow band,
- unhealthy behaviour: offset steadily increasing (drift not being corrected), or oscillating wildly (unstable synchronization).

Without this visibility, your first sign of time trouble may be inconsistent logs or a regulatory query, which is far too late.

Handling clock adjustments safely

When a clock correction is needed, the operating system can:

- **Slew** the clock: gradually adjust the rate so that the clock runs slightly faster or slower until it converges on the correct time.
- **Step** the clock: immediately jump forward or backward by the required amount.

Slewing is usually preferred in trading systems because it preserves monotonicity: time moves forward without sudden jumps. Stepping backward (for example, setting the clock from 10:00:00.500 to

10:00:00.100) can create log entries and timestamps that appear to go backwards, which is disastrous for sequencing.

However, if a clock has drifted far away from reality (for example, seconds or minutes), a step correction may be unavoidable. In such cases, you should:

- understand how your operating system and time services are configured to perform steps,
- consider temporarily pausing time-critical services or FIX sessions during a large correction,
- document and communicate the event so that later forensic analysis can interpret odd timestamps correctly.

Daylight saving time and leap seconds

Two additional real-world nuisances are:

- **Daylight saving time (DST)** shifts: local wall-clock time jumps forward or backward by an hour.
- **Leap seconds**: occasional extra seconds added to keep Coordinated Universal Time (UTC) aligned with Earth's rotation.

Good practice in trading systems is to:

- run server clocks and logs in UTC, avoiding local time where possible,
- ensure that all time calculations are based on UTC, with any conversion to local time done only at presentation layers,
- understand how your time sync stack handles leap seconds (smoothed vs. stepped), and test that behaviour.

This avoids mistakes where an apparent one-hour jump in time is misinterpreted as a system failure, or where order timestamps around a leap second become ambiguous.

Connecting Clock Quality to FIX Data Quality

How does all of this show up in FIX sessions and trading logs? Let us look at a few concrete examples.

Out-of-order-looking event streams

Suppose your trading engine's clock is 150 ms ahead of your broker's. You send an order at your local time 12:00:00.000. The broker receives it at true time 11:59:59.900 and logs that as 11:59:59.900. It then forwards the order to the venue, and the trade occurs at 12:00:00.050 true time.

In your logs:

- order send time: 12:00:00.000,
- execution report receive time: 12:00:00.060.

In the broker's logs:

- order receive time: 11:59:59.900,
- order send to venue: 11:59:59.920,
- execution receive: 12:00:00.050,
- report to client: 12:00:00.055.

When you overlay logs without adjusting for clock skew, it appears the broker received and even forwarded the order *before* you sent it. This complicates incident analysis and can lead to incorrect conclusions about who was slow or fast.

Latency calculations that lie

If you compute "round-trip time" as:

execution report receive time minus order send time,

a skewed clock will distort the result. If your clock is ahead, you may understate latency; if it is behind, you may overstate latency. Over a large dataset, this bias can mislead optimization efforts and make one venue or broker appear preferable purely due to timekeeping differences.

Regulatory audit trails and drop copy reconciliation

Drop copy feeds are meant to provide an authoritative record of executed trades. When you:

- match your internal order IDs and timestamps to the broker's drop copy,
- reconcile end-of-day positions,
- respond to regulator or client inquiries,

any material clock skew can cause:

- missed matches (events appear outside expected time windows),
- false positives in surveillance (apparent violations of limit or throttling rules),
- difficulty proving that you complied with best-execution standards.

In jurisdictions where you must be able to replay your order and execution history accurately, disciplined clocks become a documented control, not just a technical detail.

Treating Time as a First-Class Production Dependency

The common thread in all of this is that time is infrastructure.

It is tempting to think of time synchronization as a one-off configuration task: "We pointed our servers at an NTP server; we are done." In a serious trading environment, that attitude is dangerous. Robust practice includes:

- **Architecture**: deciding where you need PTP and where NTP suffices, placing time servers near critical systems, and avoiding single points of failure.

- **Operations**: monitoring offsets and drift, alerting on anomalies, managing leap seconds and DST transitions, rotating hardware when its timing quality degrades.
- **Documentation**: knowing, and being able to explain, what level of timestamp accuracy you can claim and how you achieve it.
- **Testing**: periodically validating that your timestamps line up with external references, such as exchange-provided clock signals or independent GPS-based monitors.

When you look at a FIX message's timestamp in a log, you should be confident that:

- it reflects real time within a known and small error margin,
- that error margin is stable and monitored,
- analysts and regulators can safely use that timestamp to reason about the sequence and timing of events.

In short, disciplined clocks and good clock hygiene turn the timestamps in your FIX flows from approximate hints into trustworthy data. Without that foundation, even the most carefully designed order-state models and low-latency networks cannot deliver the clarity and accountability that modern electronic trading requires.

1.5 Financial Instrument Identifiers & Symbology

In the previous sections we focused on *who* is talking (ecosystem roles), *what* they talk about (orders and their states), and *how* messages travel (TCP and disciplined clocks). We now turn to a deceptively simple question:

> When a FIX message says "Buy 10,000 of X", what exactly is *X*?

In casual conversation, traders say things like "buy Apple" or "sell the S&P future". For a human on a particular desk, that may be enough to guess the intended instrument. For a FIX engine—and for legal, accounting, and risk systems behind it—this informality is dangerous.

This section explains how symbols, security identifiers, and venue identifiers work together to unambiguously specify what is being traded. We will also see how getting this wrong leads to rejected orders, misbooked trades, and long nights in operations.

Why "Just the Symbol" Is Not Enough

It is tempting to believe that the symbol field (for example, "AAPL" or "IBM") is a unique key for an instrument. In reality, several complications arise.

Symbol collisions across venues

The simplest issue is that different venues can use the same symbol for different instruments:

- An equity with symbol "ABC" on one exchange may be a completely different company from "ABC" on another exchange in a different country.
- Some regional venues prepend or append letters (for example, "ABC.L" in London, "ABC.N" in New York), but this is not globally standardized.

If you send an order with only a bare symbol, the receiving broker or venue must infer which listing you meant. In local, single-exchange contexts this can work; in global, multi-venue trading it quickly becomes ambiguous.

Corporate actions and symbol changes

Companies change symbols over time due to:

- mergers and acquisitions,
- rebrandings,

- moving between listing venues.

Historical data or long-lived orders may span such changes. If you only store the symbol string, you may later struggle to reconcile trades that occurred before and after a symbol change.

Multiple instruments on the same underlying

A single company or underlying asset can give rise to many tradable instruments:

- common stock, preferred shares, rights, and warrants,
- many option contracts with different strikes and expiries,
- futures contracts on an index with different delivery months.

Symbols alone are rarely sufficient to distinguish among all of these. For example, "ES" might colloquially refer to the S&P 500 futures complex, but you still need:

- which month,
- which year,
- which exchange listing.

In FIX, the solution is to use combinations of identifiers, not just one field in isolation.

Layers of Identification: What, Where, and How

To describe an instrument cleanly, it helps to separate three dimensions:

- **What** economic thing is this? (The security itself.)
- **Where** does it trade? (The venue or market segment.)
- **How** is it represented in a particular domain? (Local symbol conventions, derivatives encoding, etc.)

FIX provides fields for each of these:

- *Security identifiers* (for example, ISIN, CUSIP, SEDOL) to answer "what exactly is this security?"
- *Venue identifiers* (for example, MIC codes) and exchange codes to answer "where does this trade?"
- *Symbol and derivatives fields* (strike, expiry, put/call) to match local trading conventions and symbology.

Let us look at each layer in turn.

Security Identifiers: Pinning Down the Instrument

Security identifiers are designed to uniquely identify a specific financial instrument, independent of where it trades or what nickname traders use.

ISIN: International Securities Identification Number

The **ISIN** is a widely used global identifier. Conceptually, an ISIN represents a particular security issued by a particular entity. For example:

- the common stock of a company listed on a given exchange,
- a specific bond issuance with defined coupon and maturity,
- a fund share class with its own rights and terms.

In FIX, you typically see:

- a field carrying the security identifier value (the ISIN string),
- another field indicating the identification scheme (for example, that this value is an ISIN rather than some other code).

ISINs are especially helpful when:

- trading the same security across multiple venues (for example, cross-listings),
- reconciling positions and trades with custodians and back offices,
- working with bonds and other fixed income instruments, where local ticker symbols can be messy.

CUSIP, SEDOL, and other local identifiers

Different regions have their own identifier schemes:

- **CUSIP** in North America,
- **SEDOL** in the United Kingdom and some other markets,
- exchange-specific local codes for various instruments.

These can be used directly in FIX when both parties understand them, or they can be mapped to a more neutral identifier like ISIN. In practice, many firms maintain an internal *security master* database that:

- stores all known identifiers for each instrument,
- ensures that FIX messages always specify enough information for the broker or venue to recognize the instrument.

Venue Identifiers: Where It Trades

Even with a solid security identifier, the *trading venue* matters. The same ISIN can trade:

- on multiple exchanges in the same country,
- across different trading platforms (lit exchanges, dark pools, systematic internalisers),
- in multiple currencies or settlement regimes.

MIC codes: Market Identifier Codes

MIC (Market Identifier Code) is a standard way to label trading venues and their market segments. A MIC typically represents:

- an exchange or trading facility (for example, a primary stock exchange),
- or a specific segment or platform operated by that exchange (for example, a dark book or auction segment).

In a FIX order, including a MIC (or its equivalent field) tells the broker or venue:

> "I want to trade this security on this specific market."

This is vital in multi-venue environments, where:

- liquidity and fees differ across venues,
- regulations may treat internalizers differently from exchanges,
- you may have explicit instructions to avoid or prefer certain venues.

Exchange codes and routing logic

Sometimes a simpler exchange code is used, especially when:

- there is a clear primary listing,
- you delegate venue selection to the broker's routing logic.

In that case, your order might specify:

- the security identifier,
- the primary exchange or a region,
- an execution instruction such as "smart route" or "primary only".

Brokers then decide which actual venues (and MICs) to use while ensuring they respect the instrument definition and your constraints.

Symbology by Asset Class

Different asset classes use different symbology conventions. Understanding them helps you see what extra fields you must fill in, beyond a simple symbol string.

Equities: Symbols plus identifiers

For common stocks, the combination often looks like:

- *Symbol*: a human-friendly code like "AAPL",
- *Security identifier*: ISIN or CUSIP pinning down the exact share class,
- *Venue identifier*: MIC or exchange code indicating where you want to trade.

In many purely domestic setups, people rely mainly on symbol plus exchange, but in cross-border and multi-broker trading, including a security ID is a best practice.

Futures: Underlying, expiry, and contract size

A futures contract is defined by more than a symbol. You need to know:

- the underlying (for example, an index or commodity),
- the contract month and year (expiry),
- the venue or exchange (since different exchanges may have similar contracts),
- contract size and other contract-specific details, typically encoded in reference data rather than in the order itself.

Symbology systems often encode month and year in the symbol (for example, a root code plus a month letter and year digit). FIX usually supports:

- a *maturity month/year* or full maturity date field,
- a symbol or local code for the futures root,

- a security identifier (sometimes an exchange-specific contract code).

This lets your order say, in effect:

> "Buy 5 contracts of the March S&P 500 index future on exchange X."

Options: Underlying, expiry, strike, and put/call

Options symbology is richer still. A single options chain on one underlying can contain:

- many strikes (different exercise prices),
- many expiries (different dates),
- calls and puts for each strike and expiry.

Thus, an option instrument is defined by:

- the underlying symbol or identifier,
- the option type (call or put),
- the expiry date,
- the strike price,
- the venue and sometimes style (American vs. European).

In FIX, these elements are represented in separate fields rather than buried in a single dense code. That is deliberate: it makes parsing and validation easier and avoids confusion when different markets use different compact coding schemes.

FX and fixed income

For FX spot and forwards:

- the pair (for example, "EUR/USD") is the core identifier,

- the settlement date (spot, next, forward) matters,
- venues may use specific codes for trading platforms.

For bonds:

- a security identifier like ISIN or CUSIP is often primary,
- coupon, maturity, and issuer are defined in reference data,
- venues and trading platforms can be specified with MIC or local identifiers.

In both cases, the FIX message references a combination of identifier and venue, while detailed terms live in security master data.

Combining Identifiers in FIX Messages

In practice, a robust FIX order will include a *tuple* of fields that together remove ambiguity. While exact field names depend on FIX version and local conventions, conceptually you will often see a combination such as:

- a human-readable *symbol* (for trader convenience),
- a formal *security identifier* and source (for unambiguous definition),
- a *venue or exchange code* (for routing or listing specificity),
- additional fields needed for the asset class (expiry, strike, put/-call, etc.).

From the system design point of view, you should think in terms of:

> "What minimal set of fields, when taken together, uniquely identifies this instrument for this counterparty?"

You can then enforce this rule at your FIX gateway or OMS/EMS boundary:

- reject or flag orders that do not specify enough information,
- normalize symbology before sending orders out,
- maintain a mapping between internal identifiers and external FIX fields.

Operational Failure Modes from Bad Symbology

When identifiers are incomplete, inconsistent, or misaligned, several classes of problem arise.

Order rejections

The simplest and, in some sense, safest failure is an outright rejection. A broker or venue might reject your order because:

- the symbol is not recognized on the specified venue,
- the security identifier does not match the symbol,
- required fields (for example, expiry for a future) are missing.

While rejections cause lost opportunities and delay, they at least prevent trading in the wrong instrument. A well-configured broker gateway will validate symbology early and fail fast.

Misbooked and misallocated trades

More dangerous are silent mismatches where the order is accepted but interpreted differently than intended. For example:

- You think you bought a stock on its primary exchange, but the order actually trades on a different market with subtly different settlement or currency.
- An option is mapped to the wrong strike or expiry when imported into back-office systems, leading to incorrect risk and P&L.

These problems often surface later, during reconciliation:

- your position in a security does not match the broker's or custodian's records,
- cash and collateral do not line up with expectations,
- risk systems show exposures to instruments you do not believe you traded.

Tracing the root cause can be painful if logs and reference data are not aligned.

Corporate action and lifecycle confusion

In instruments subject to corporate actions (splits, rights issues, calls on bonds), inadequate identifiers can cause confusion when:

- old symbols and new symbols coexist,
- instruments are replaced or merged,
- cash and share entitlements change.

If your FIX messages and internal databases do not track stable identifiers through these changes, you may double-count or miss positions, or misinterpret which trades refer to pre- or post-action securities.

Best Practices for Symbology in FIX Environments

To reduce these risks, trading organizations typically adopt a set of symbology practices that tie together FIX flows and internal systems.

Maintain a security master

A **security master** is a central repository of instrument definitions. It should:

- assign each instrument an internal ID,
- store all external identifiers (ISIN, CUSIP, local tickers, exchange symbols),
- record venue listings and MICs,

- capture key attributes (asset class, expiry, strike, currency, contract size).

Your FIX gateways and trading systems then:

- look up instruments in the security master when building orders,
- populate the appropriate FIX fields based on that data,
- update the security master as new instruments appear or old ones change.

This reduces the chance that free-form entry or hard-coded symbol strings leak directly into outbound FIX messages.

Normalize across brokers and venues

Different brokers and venues may expect slightly different field combinations or coding conventions. Rather than pushing that complexity into every trading strategy, it is common to:

- define a normalized internal representation of instruments,
- implement translation layers at the FIX gateway that adapt to each counterparty's expectations,
- keep mapping rules under configuration management and change control.

For example, one broker might require an ISIN and MIC, while another prefers a local symbol and exchange code. Your gateway can generate the right combination from your security master, while presenting a consistent internal view to the rest of your systems.

Validate early and often

Symbology validation should not be left solely to counterparties. Within your own environment you can:

- validate that a requested symbol or instrument code exists in the security master before building a FIX message,

- check that all required attributes for the asset class (expiry, strike, put/call) are present,
- enforce that the combination of instrument and venue is legal and intended.

If validation fails, you can surface errors to traders or strategy developers immediately, rather than waiting for a broker rejection.

Log identifiers comprehensively

When you log orders and executions, include:

- both internal instrument IDs and external identifiers,
- venue or MIC information,
- all relevant symbology fields for derivatives (expiry, strike, put/-call).

This makes it much easier to:

- reconstruct exactly which instruments were traded,
- correlate your records with broker and venue drop copies,
- investigate misbookings or reconciliation breaks.

From Names to Unambiguous Definitions

At a human level, it is convenient to say "Apple", "the March S&P future", or "EUR/USD". At the FIX level, that convenience must be translated into precise, machine-readable specification.

You can now see the progression:

- A trader's intent starts as a natural-language description.
- The OMS/EMS translates that into a chosen instrument from the security master.

- The FIX gateway encodes that choice into a set of coordinated identifiers: symbol, security ID, venue ID, plus asset-class-specific fields.
- The broker and venue interpret those fields to act on exactly the intended instrument.

This symbology discipline is as important as well-designed order state machines and stable network transport. Without it, you may be sending fast, well-timestamped FIX messages—about the wrong thing.

As you build or evaluate FIX connectivity, always ask:

> "If I look at this order's fields, can I say, without ambiguity, exactly what instrument this refers to and where it is meant to trade?"

If the answer is anything less than a confident "yes", your symbology layer needs work.

Chapter 2

FIX Architecture and Message Modeling

FIX messages may look like cryptic tag-value soup, but under the surface they're built from a small, disciplined set of ideas: a versioned transport, a rigid message skeleton, a finite alphabet of fields, and reusable building blocks. In this chapter, we peel that structure back layer by layer so that, by the end, you can look at a raw FIX log and understand not just what it says, but why it was designed that way-and how to extend it safely in your own trading stack.

2.1 Version Lineage and FIXT Transport

Up to this point, we have been looking at FIX messages as if there were just "one" FIX: a stream of tag–value pairs, framed into messages, flowing over a session between two trading systems. In practice, there is not just one FIX version, and the way versions are used on the wire has changed in a fundamental way over time.

This section explains that change.

We will start by looking at the original FIX 4.x world, where a single version label controlled everything about the session and the messages.

Then we will see how the FIX community split this into two layers: a stable *transport* (the session protocol) called FIXT, and a separate, more flexible *application* version for the business content. By the end, when you see a BeginString like FIX.4.2 or FIXT.1.1 and an ApplVerID like FIX.5.0SP2, you will be able to infer what is really happening on the wire and what can (and cannot) evolve without breaking the session.

The Monolithic 4.x Model: One Version for Everything

In the early FIX versions (4.0, 4.1, 4.2, 4.3, 4.4), the protocol was *monolithic*. That is, the same version number was used to refer to both:

- The **session layer**: logon/logout, heartbeats, sequence numbers, resends, and so on.
- The **application layer**: the actual trading messages such as *NewOrderSingle*, *ExecutionReport*, *OrderCancelRequest*, and their fields.

You saw this in the BeginString field (tag 8) in the message header. For example:

- 8=FIX.4.1
- 8=FIX.4.2
- 8=FIX.4.4

This one tag carried a lot of responsibility. When the counterparty saw 8=FIX.4.2, it implicitly meant:

- "Use the FIX 4.2 *session* rules" (how to log on, how to manage sequence numbers, what administrative messages exist).
- "Expect FIX 4.2 *application* messages" (which business messages and fields are allowed, which tags are defined, how those messages are structured).

Conceptually, you can think of the 4.x model as a single "FIX stack" with one label stamped on it:

- **FIX 4.2 stack**:
  - Session: 4.2 rules for logon, heartbeats, test requests, resends, logout, sequence numbers.
  - Application: 4.2 message types and field definitions for orders, cancels, trades, allocations, etc.

Operationally, this had some straightforward consequences:

- When you certified with a venue as "FIX 4.2", you certified both your session behaviour and your message set together.
- If either side wanted to use a new application message (say, a new trade capture workflow that arrived with FIX 4.4), the *whole* session had to be upgraded to 4.4.
- Logs were simple to read: every message on that connection carried 8=FIX.4.2, and that alone told you how both layers behaved.

This simplicity was attractive at first, but as FIX adoption grew, the tight coupling started to hurt.

Why Tight Coupling Became a Problem

From the perspective of a trading firm or venue, production FIX sessions are long-lived assets. A buy-side might have hundreds of certified connections with brokers. A large exchange might have thousands of member sessions. Re-certifying all of them every time a new feature appeared in the spec was simply not realistic.

Some of the specific pain points were:

Different evolution speeds.

Session behaviour tends to be *stable*. Once the industry agrees on how to do heartbeats, sequence numbers, and logon, they do not want that to change every year. In contrast, application workflows — new order types, richer execution reporting, complex instruments — keep evolving quickly as markets innovate.

By tying session and application to the same version, any new set of business messages would formally require a new FIX major/minor version. That in turn implied renegotiating and re-certifying all sessions that wanted to use those messages, even if the underlying session framing had not changed at all.

Multiple workflows on a single connection.

Counterparties increasingly wanted to run multiple workflows over one physical TCP connection: for example, classic single-leg order entry and newer block-trade negotiation messages, or a combination of equities and derivatives flows. Some of these workflows might logically align with different application versions.

With 4.x, the BeginString fixed the version for *all* messages on the connection. If you wanted to use a different version for a new service, the usual answer was "open another session," with all the additional operational complexity that brings (more ports, more configurations, more monitoring).

Heterogeneous environments.

Large institutions often run front ends and back ends with different life cycles. You might have:

- A gateway that is comfortable with the latest application-level extensions.
- Downstream systems that are still certified and tested only up to an older FIX version.

With a monolithic version, it was hard to express "I will talk modern application messages to you on top of a session that still looks like the old one," or vice versa.

As the protocol matured, it became clear that FIX needed an architectural split: a stable transport/session protocol that could outlive any particular application dictionary, and a flexible application layer that encoded trading workflows.

The FIXT Idea: Separate Transport from Application

The solution the FIX community adopted was to explicitly separate:

- The **transport** or session layer: how messages are framed, sequenced, and managed over the connection.
- The **application** layer: the business semantics, message types, and fields that represent orders, executions, and so on.

The transport protocol was named **FIXT** (FIX Transport). The first published version you will see on the wire is **FIXT 1.1**. From a wire perspective, this separation shows up in two key ways:

- The **BeginString** (tag 8) now carries the transport version, for example: 8=FIXT.1.1.
- A new header field **ApplVerID** (tag 1128) carries the application version used for the business message, for example:
  - 1128=9 for FIX 5.0SP2 (in the standardized enumeration scheme), or
  - A string like FIX.5.0SP2 in environments that use the human-readable literal.

This immediately decouples the two concerns:

- All the messages on a given connection are framed and sequenced using the *same* FIXT transport rules.
- Within that session, individual application messages can be expressed according to one or more *application* versions, as negotiated between counterparties.

Architecturally, you can now picture your FIX stack as two stacked layers instead of one blended block:

- Bottom: FIXT 1.1 session engine, handling logon, heartbeats, test requests, resends, and logout in a stable way.

- Top: one or more application dictionaries, such as FIX 5.0SP2 or "FIX Latest" for business messages.

Right after we introduce this separation, it is a good moment to visualize the evolution from monolithic 4.x to the layered FIXT model.

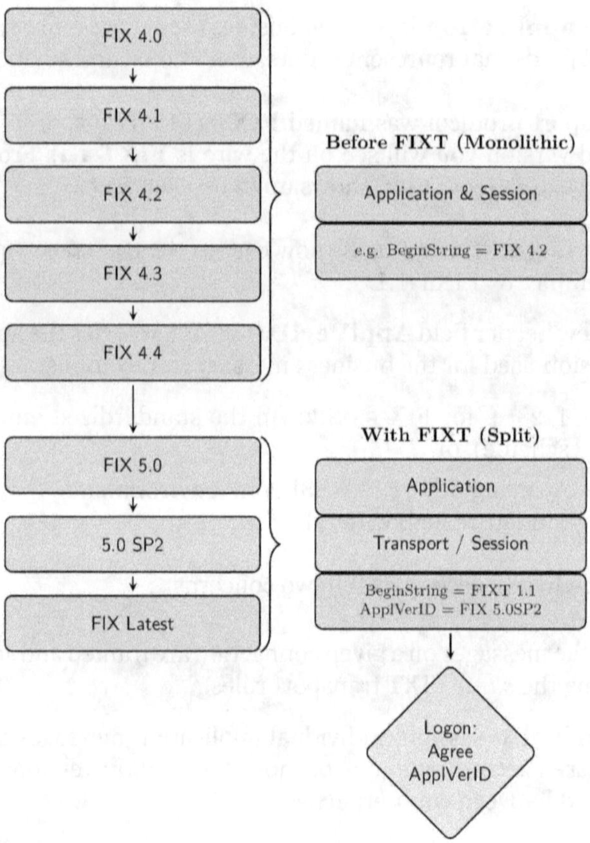

This diagram shows the key shift: from a single, monolithic stack labelled "FIX 4.2" to a layered model where "FIXT 1.1" defines the session, and the application version is advertised separately.

Reading the Header: BeginString vs. ApplVerID

Once you are aware of this split, the fixed header fields become much more informative. In the 4.x world, BeginString fully determined the protocol. In the FIXT world:

- BeginString (tag 8) tells you the **transport** version. For a FIXT session this will look like FIXT.1.1. It says: "This connection uses FIXT 1.1 rules for session establishment, heartbeats, and retransmission."
- ApplVerID (tag 1128) tells you the **application** version for the message. It says: "This particular message uses the FIX 5.0SP2 (or other) dictionary for its business content."

In a FIXT-based log line, you will often see both together in the header. In practice, gateways may combine these with another field:

- DefaultApplVerID (tag 1137) appears in the Logon message to say: "Unless otherwise specified, we will use this application version for business messages on this session."

So, when you are scanning logs:

- If you see 8=FIX.4.4 and no 1128 at all, you are looking at a traditional 4.x session where transport and application are both 4.4.
- If you see 8=FIXT.1.1 together with 1128=FIX.5.0SP2 (or its numeric code), you are looking at a FIXT session carrying FIX 5.0SP2 application messages.

This alone lets you quickly categorize a session and understand which parts of the spec to consult when troubleshooting.

How Counterparties Negotiate Versions

In a FIXT-based environment, version agreement becomes a two-part story:

- **Transport agreement:** both sides must implement the same FIXT version, commonly FIXT 1.1, and must be configured to expect that BeginString on this port.
- **Application agreement:** both sides must support at least one common application version (for example, FIX 5.0SP2) and know which message types, fields, and workflows that version implies.

Operationally, venues and brokers usually handle this through documentation and configuration rather than dynamic, on-the-fly negotiation. A typical arrangement looks like this:

- The venue publishes a specification saying: "All order-entry sessions use FIXT 1.1 as transport and FIX 5.0SP2 as the application dictionary."
- During certification, you configure your gateway such that:
  - It sends 8=FIXT.1.1 in all messages on that port.
  - Its Logon message includes DefaultApplVerID=FIX.5.0SP2.
- The venue validates that your messages conform to the advertised application version, and that your session behaviour obeys FIXT 1.1.

Behind the scenes, a FIX engine that supports multiple venues may be configured with several pairs of transport/application versions. But the key point is that this is no longer a single, global setting. It is part of the per-session agreement, and it is expressed explicitly in the header.

Carrying Multiple Application Versions on One Transport

One of the major advantages of FIXT is that you can, in principle, carry multiple application versions on the same transport.

In the simplest setups, venues stick to a single application version per session type, to keep things straightforward. However, in more advanced infrastructures, you might see patterns like:

- A gateway speaks FIXT 1.1 to clients and can accept both:
  - Clients that send FIX 4.4-style application messages encoded within FIXT 1.1, and
  - Clients that send newer FIX 5.0SP2 application messages.
- The gateway then normalises or routes these flows internally, perhaps publishing downstream using its own preferred application version.

On the wire, this shows up as:

- All messages share the same BeginString=FIXT.1.1.
- Different clients (or even different flows on the same connection) might use different ApplVerID values, as allowed by the session configuration.

From a design perspective, this lets you separate concerns inside your system:

- The **session handler** only cares about the FIXT rules: maintaining sequence numbers, detecting gaps, handling test requests and heartbeats, requesting resends, and so on.
- The **application handler** or router looks at ApplVerID and MsgType, then hands the message to the correct business workflow implementation for that version.

As a reader of log files, this also gives you more context. When investigating an issue, you can immediately see which application dictionary was in force for a problem message, without guessing from the port or environment name.

Operational Implications for Gateways and Certification

The move to a FIXT transport model has several practical consequences that show up in day-to-day operations.

Long-lived sessions, evolving workflows.

Because the session layer is now more stable, you can keep using the same FIXT 1.1 session implementation even as you introduce new application-level workflows. For example:

- Today, you might certify an order-entry session using FIXT 1.1 + FIX 5.0SP2 application messages.
- Next year, the venue may add a new type of negotiation or block-trading workflow, still defined within the FIX 5.0SP2 or "FIX Latest" dictionary.
- Your session engine does not need to change at all; you simply extend your application message handling as per the updated spec.

This reduces the operational risk of version changes. Session drop-handling, resend logic, heartbeats — the parts that are most likely to cause outages if mis-implemented — remain untouched.

Clearer separation of responsibilities in system design.

Internally, many firms reflect the FIXT split in their architecture:

- A **session gateway** component that:
  - Implements FIXT 1.1 once, robustly.
  - Handles connectivity, TLS, recovery from network breaks.
  - Delivers fully framed, sequence-checked messages to downstream components.
- One or more **application adaptors** that:
  - Know particular application versions and venue-specific extensions.
  - Map messages into internal trading models (orders, executions, allocations).
  - Can be upgraded or swapped without disturbing the session gateway.

When reading this book, you can think of FIXT as something you want to implement correctly once and then forget about, while the application layer will stay the area of active change and customization.

Certification and test environments.

In a 4.x world, a certification document might say simply: "This interface is FIX 4.2." Now, you are more likely to see something like:

> Transport: FIXT 1.1.
> Application: FIX 5.0SP2 with venue-specific extension pack XYZ.

Your certification test cases will deliberately exercise both dimensions:

- Tests for correct FIXT session behaviour (logon sequence, heartbeats, sequence resets, gap fills).
- Tests for correct application semantics (valid combinations of tags, required fields for each OrdType, etc.) under the agreed application version.

The investment of separating your code into session and application modules pays off here: you can often reuse the same session conformance tests across multiple interfaces and focus your change-testing on the business workflows.

Implications for Log Analysis and Debugging

Finally, as someone troubleshooting issues, understanding FIXT will change how you read logs.

When you open a log file:

- First, look at BeginString:
  - If it is FIX.4.x, you are in the monolithic world; you now know both session and application version from that one tag.
  - If it is FIXT.1.1, you are in the layered world; you know the session rules, but not yet the application dictionary.

- Next, look for ApplVerID (and possibly DefaultApplVerID in the Logon). That tells you which application version to consult when interpreting business tags and message types.

This two-step reading process becomes second nature after a while. It is particularly important when you are comparing logs from different environments (for example, a UAT environment using one application version and production using another) or when a venue changes its application dictionary but keeps the same transport.

In later sections, when we dissect full messages and trace order lifecycles, we will always make this distinction explicit. The *session* layer explains how messages get from A to B reliably; the *application* layer explains what those messages *mean*. FIXT is the architectural bridge that keeps those concerns cleanly separated while still allowing both to evolve.

2.2 Anatomy of a FIX Message

In the previous section we treated FIX largely at the architectural level: versions, the FIXT transport, and how session and application layers are separated. We will now zoom in from that big-picture view to the finest level of detail: a *single FIX message on the wire.*

If you work with FIX in production, the raw log files stop being mysterious only when you can look at one long line of tags and mentally see its structure. That is the goal of this section. We will:

- Explain the basic wire format: tag–value pairs and the delimiter that separates them.
- Break a message into its three parts: **standard header**, **message body**, and **standard trailer**.
- Show how the ordering of fields is constrained rather than arbitrary.
- Walk through how BodyLength and CheckSum are computed and used for basic validation.

- Highlight common real-world pitfalls that break these assumptions.

By the end, a raw FIX message will feel less like random noise and more like a structured sentence written in a very compact alphabet.

Wire Format: Tag–Value Pairs and the SOH Delimiter

At its core, FIX uses a very simple encoding for all messages:

- Each piece of information is a **field**.
- Each field consists of a **numeric tag**, an equals sign, and a **value**.
- Fields are separated by a special delimiter character.

Conceptually, a field looks like:

```
Tag=Value
```

When you look at log files, you will see fields written one after another, for example:

```
8=FIX.4.4|9=176|35=D|49=BUY_SIDE|56=SELL_-
SIDE|34=7|...
```

Here, the | symbol is just a human-friendly stand-in for the *real* delimiter that appears on the network: the ASCII "Start of Heading" control character, often referred to as **SOH**. Its byte value is 1.

You will commonly see people say "SOH-delimited FIX" to describe this encoding. On the wire:

- After each `Tag=Value` pair comes a single SOH byte.
- There are no commas, no line breaks, and no extra spaces.

This simplicity is intentional. It makes parsing straightforward, but it also means FIX is sensitive to any accidental extra characters. An invisible newline or a stray space can break the structure enough to cause a session to drop, which is why we will repeatedly emphasise the importance of exact byte-level representation.

The Three-Part Structure: Header, Body, Trailer

Although the wire format is just a flat sequence of fields, logically every FIX message is divided into three parts:

- The **standard header** – who is talking, what version and type of message this is, and basic routing.
- The **message body** – the business content (for example, the fields of a new order).
- The **standard trailer** – integrity checks, most notably the checksum.

You can think of this like an email:

- The fixed header of an email (From, To, Subject) plays a role similar to the FIX standard header.
- The message body is like the email text or payload.
- The trailer is like an automatic signature that confirms the message content has not been mangled in transit.

Let us take a stylised example of a FIX New Order Single message, with visual separators. Remember that | stands in for the SOH character:

Header:
8=FIX.4.4|9=176|35=D|49=BUY_SIDE|56=SELL_-SIDE|34=7|52=20240112-09:30:00.123|
Body:
11=ORD12345|55=AAPL|54=1|38=1000|40=2|44=185.50|59=0|60=2024
09:30:00.123|

Trailer:
10=128|

In the log, there is no blank space between these parts; they are just fields in sequence. But conceptually, splitting the message this way makes it much easier to understand what is going on.

Immediately after presenting the example, we will reinforce this visually.

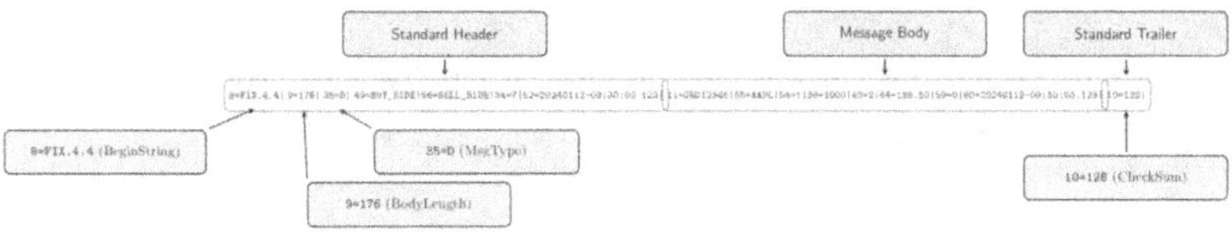

This diagram is not just decorative. When you look at real logs, mentally drawing these brackets and labels is exactly the skill you want to build.

The Standard Header: Fixed Fields in a Fixed Order

The standard header appears at the very beginning of every FIX message. It is not arbitrary; certain fields must appear, and in a specific order. The core header fields you will see again and again include:

- BeginString (tag 8): Identifies the overall protocol family, such as FIX.4.2, FIX.4.4, or FIXT.1.1. This is the first field in *every* FIX message.
- BodyLength (tag 9): Gives the length of the body of the message, in bytes, from immediately after tag 9 up to just before tag 10 (the checksum).
- MsgType (tag 35): Identifies what kind of message this is: New Order Single, Execution Report, Logout, Heartbeat, and so on, typically via a short letter or digit.

Immediately following those three, you will see sender/target information and basic sequencing:

- SenderCompID (tag 49): The logical ID of the firm or system sending the message.
- TargetCompID (tag 56): The logical ID of the intended recipient.
- MsgSeqNum (tag 34): The sequence number of this message in the session.
- SendingTime (tag 52): The timestamp when the message left the sender (typically in UTC).

There are other optional header fields (for example, on-behalf-of routing fields, sub IDs, and so on), but these core fields are enough for you to recognise the header and to understand its role.

Why the Order Matters

In casual data formats (like JSON or CSV files), you might be used to field ordering that does not matter. FIX is more strict, especially at the start and end of the message.

Protocol rules require that:

- BeginString (8) *must* be the very first field.
- BodyLength (9) *must* be the second field.
- MsgType (35) *must* be the third field.
- CheckSum (10) *must* be the last field.

Different vendors and venues may have their own expectations about the exact ordering of some of the later header fields, but these positions for 8, 9, 35, and 10 are effectively universal.

From a practical debugging point of view, if you do not see these tags where you expect them, you should immediately suspect a broken encoder, an incorrectly edited log, or some parsing issue.

The Message Body: Business Content

After the standard header comes the **message body**. This is where the protocol describes what you are actually doing: sending a new order, acknowledging a cancel, reporting a fill, sending a heartbeat, and so on.

The body fields:

- Are defined by the message type (35) and the application version.
- Can be required or optional.
- May include components and repeating groups, which we will cover in detail in a later section.

In our example New Order Single, typical body fields include:

- ClOrdID (tag 11): Your unique identifier for this order.
- Symbol (tag 55): The instrument being traded (for example, a stock ticker).
- Side (tag 54): Buy or sell.
- OrderQty (tag 38): Quantity.
- OrdType (tag 40): Market, limit, and so forth.
- Price (tag 44): Limit price, when applicable.
- TimeInForce (tag 59): Day, Immediate-or-Cancel, etc.
- TransactTime (tag 60): The time the order was initiated.

Unlike the header and trailer, the body has much more flexibility in ordering. Different implementations may emit fields in slightly different sequences, as long as they comply with:

- Any ordering constraints defined in the official spec or in the venue's implementation guide.

- The requirement that the body fields, together with the header (excluding 8 and 9) and any trailer fields before 10, are correctly counted into BodyLength and CheckSum.

For now, the key thing is simply to recognise that everything after the header and before CheckSum is body content. Later in the chapter we will learn to see structure within that body (components and repeating groups), but you do not need that extra complexity to start reading logs effectively.

The Standard Trailer: CheckSum and Integrity

At the end of every FIX message is a **standard trailer**. The most important field here is:

- CheckSum (tag 10): A simple integrity check over the message contents.

The checksum is one of the basic defences against corruption in transit or buggy encoders. The idea is straightforward:

- Take all bytes in the message from the very beginning (the "8" of 8=...) up to and including the delimiter after the BodyLength field, through all header and body fields *except* the checksum field itself.
- Add up their byte values.
- Take the sum modulo 256.
- Represent the result as a three-digit number (padding with leading zeros if necessary).

That three-digit number is then placed as the value of CheckSum (tag 10), followed by the final delimiter.

Why CheckSum Catches Real Problems

Although this sounds primitive compared to modern cryptographic hashes, it is surprisingly effective for this context. It will catch:

- A missing or extra character anywhere in the message.
- A changed character (for example, if a digit was altered).
- Any miscounting of bytes that would throw off BodyLength, because the same miscount will usually also corrupt the checksum.

In a well-behaved FIX engine:

- Every incoming message is first subjected to a checksum validation.
- If the checksum fails, the message is rejected as invalid (often with a session-level *Reject* message) and the session may be considered compromised.

For you as a human reader, being able to recompute the checksum by hand for a message in a log is a powerful diagnostic tool. If your engine insists that a message is corrupt, you can verify whether the log line truly matches what was received, or whether some intermediate transformation (for example, replacing SOH with | characters in an unsafe way) has damaged the message.

BodyLength: The Other Critical Sanity Check

Alongside the checksum, BodyLength is the other crucial integrity field. It serves two purposes:

- It lets the receiver know exactly where the message ends.
- It provides a coarse consistency check: if the announced length does not match the actual byte count, something is wrong.

Formally, BodyLength is defined as the number of *bytes* starting immediately after the delimiter that terminates the BodyLength field itself, up to (but not including) the delimiter that follows the CheckSum field.

In our conceptual example:

- The body length covers:

- The rest of the header (from 35=D onwards),
- All message body fields,
- And the 10=xxx field *value and tag* itself, excluding the final delimiter.

When a FIX engine reads a stream from the network, it typically works like this:

- Read until it finds the first delimiter; parse 8=....
- Read until it finds the second delimiter; parse 9=... and convert the value to an integer.
- Knowing the body length, read exactly that many bytes after the second delimiter.
- Expect the last field in that block to be 10=..., followed by a delimiter.

If the engine cannot find the checksum field at the expected position, or the delimiter appears too early or too late, it knows something has gone wrong, and it will usually drop or reject the message.

From a debugging perspective, if you are given a raw message and asked “why did the engine complain about invalid body length?”, your first move should be:

- Count the bytes between the correct start and end points, using the same encoding as the engine.
- Compare your count with the declared BodyLength.

Discrepancies point directly to where invisible characters, wrong encodings, or manual edits may have sneaked in.

Subtle Real-World Pitfalls

The rules we have outlined so far are conceptually simple, but many real-world problems arise from subtle violations of these assumptions. Some of the most common include:

Newline contamination.

Sometimes loggers or middleware insert newline characters, carriage returns, or extra spaces into FIX messages. These characters are not allowed inside fields unless explicitly part of a value, and they will:

- Change the byte count used in BodyLength.
- Change the overall byte sum used in CheckSum.

The result is a message that looks mostly fine to the eye but fails both length and checksum validation.

Mismatched encodings.

FIX is defined over bytes; the spec expects ASCII-compatible encodings. If a system accidentally treats messages as multi-byte encoded strings (for example, UTF-8 with transformations), you can end up with:

- Character sequences that expand into multiple bytes, altering the body length.
- Non-ASCII bytes that the receiver's parser does not expect.

Again, length and checksum calculations will disagree, and the message will be rejected even though it displays correctly in a modern editor.

Manual editing of logs.

It is tempting during debugging to manually tweak a recorded message (for example, to anonymise an ID or to experiment with a different field value) and then replay it. Unless you also:

- Recompute the BodyLength, and

- Recompute the CheckSum,

the modified message will be invalid. Even replacing a single digit in a price field changes the checksum.

Fields out of place.

Developers sometimes produce messages with header fields in the wrong order or checksum not placed at the end, especially when hand-coding instead of using a mature FIX engine. Many counterparties' parsers are strict on both ordering and field position and will reject such messages even if the body content is correct.

Understanding these pitfalls is not just academic; it stops you wasting time looking at business-level explanations ("did we set the wrong order type?") when the real issue is that the message never passed basic frame validation.

Learning to Read FIX Messages as Structured Sentences

Putting all of this together, you can now approach any FIX message in a methodical way:

- **Locate the header.** Starting from the beginning of the line, confirm 8, 9, and 35 are the first three tags. Note the version and message type.
- **Identify the trailer.** Scan to the end and locate 10=.... This is the final field; everything after it should just be the delimiter or line termination.
- **Bracket the body.** Everything between the header and the checksum is the message body — the business content.
- **Check framing.** If you suspect a problem, verify that the byte count implied by 9 and the checksum implied by 10 are consistent with the raw bytes.
- **Interpret the fields.** Only after you are satisfied that the message is structurally sound is it worth reasoning about the business

logic: what order was sent, what execution state is being reported, and so on.

This process turns an intimidating block of characters into something more like a well-formed sentence: a standard opening (header), a meaningful middle (body), and a standard closing (trailer). The more messages you read this way, the more natural it will feel.

In the next sections, we will deepen this understanding by looking inside the message body: field types, enumerations, reusable components, and repeating groups. But everything we do later assumes the foundation you have just seen: a precise mental model of how a single FIX message is laid out and validated on the wire.

2.3 Field Data Types, Tags & Enumerations

In the previous section we treated a FIX message as a structured container: a standard header, a body, and a trailer, all expressed as a flat list of tag=value pairs. We focused on *where* fields appear and how they are used for framing and validation.

In this section we turn to the *vocabulary* itself: what the tags mean, what kinds of values they can carry, and how to read common one-character codes as plain trading intent. Once you are comfortable with this vocabulary, you can look at a field list and quickly infer:

- Whether a value "looks right" for its type.
- How much precision and range to expect.
- What a short code like 40=2 or 54=1 actually says about the order.

The goal is not to memorise the entire FIX dictionary, but to build an intuition for the core data types and the most important enumerations you will see in everyday order flow and drop copy.

Tags: Numeric IDs for Business Concepts

Every FIX field is identified by a **tag**, which is just a positive integer. Over time, the FIX community has assigned specific tags to specific business concepts:

- Tag 11 is **ClOrdID** (Client Order ID).
- Tag 55 is **Symbol**.
- Tag 54 is **Side**.
- Tag 40 is **OrdType**.
- Tag 44 is **Price**.

You will see two parallel naming systems in practice:

- The *numeric* IDs (11, 55, 54, 40, 44) which are what actually appear on the wire.
- The *semantic* names (ClOrdID, Symbol, Side, OrdType, Price) which are what human-readable documentation and code usually prefer.

A crucial design choice in FIX is that *tags are stable across versions*. Once the community decides that tag 54 means *Side*, that mapping does not change in later versions, even if:

- New side values are introduced (for example, "Sell Short" vs. "Sell Short Exempt"), or
- The allowed combinations of fields around Side become more sophisticated.

This stability is what lets a FIX engine or log analysis tool written long ago still make basic sense of fields in newer application versions. When you see 54=1, your brain can immediately match it to "Side = Buy".

For you as a practitioner, it is worth learning the numeric tags of the top couple of dozen common fields. You will then be able to skim log lines and understand them, even if the logger prints only numbers.

Primitive Data Types: The Building Blocks

Behind every field is a **primitive data type**. The FIX specification defines a small set of such types, each with clear rules about how values are encoded as text on the wire. The major ones you will encounter are:

- Boolean-like types (true/false).
- Integer-like types (whole numbers).
- Decimal-like types (prices, quantities, percentages).
- Textual types (strings, characters).
- Temporal types (dates and timestamps).

Understanding these primitives is the first step towards sanity-checking values before you even look at business rules.

Integers and Quantities

Many FIX fields are of some integer type:

- **int**: A whole number, optionally signed, with no decimal point. Used for counts, sequence numbers, and some identifiers.
- **Qty** / **Qty-type**: Conceptually a quantity, but on the wire still represented as a number without thousands separators or currency symbols.

Examples include:

- 34=12345 for **MsgSeqNum**.
- 38=1000 for **OrderQty**.

Practical points:

- A minus sign is allowed for signed integers, but most trading quantities and counts should be non-negative.

- There are no commas or spaces: 1000 is valid, 1,000 is not.
- Extremely large values might be technically allowed but practically suspicious. For example, an order quantity of 1000000000000 may signal a bug.

If you are scanning logs and see an integer field with a decimal point or stray spaces, that is immediately suspect.

Prices and Decimals

Prices, yields, and some quantities in FIX are represented using decimal-like types such as **Price**, **Amt**, or other specific numeric primitives. On the wire they appear as:

- A sequence of digits.
- An optional decimal point.
- Optional digits after the decimal point.

For example:

- 44=185.50 for a limit price of 185.50.
- 99=0.005 for a stop price.

Key considerations:

- FIX itself does not prescribe a specific number of decimal places. That is left to the asset class and the venue. Equities might use two or four decimals; FX and rates products can go much finer.
- Leading zeros before the decimal point (0.005) are valid and common.
- Trailing zeros (185.50) are also valid; they carry no special meaning in FIX but often reflect human formatting conventions.

From a risk or analytics perspective, knowing the allowed tick size on a venue will tell you what decimal precision to expect in prices. When a log shows a price that does not align with the tick size, it could be a bug or a rounding issue.

Characters and Short Codes

Some of the most important fields in FIX are of type **char**: a single printable character. Rather than printing full words like "Buy" or "Market", the protocol uses compact codes:

- 54=1 means **Side** = Buy.
- 54=2 means **Side** = Sell.
- 40=1 means **OrdType** = Market.
- 40=2 means **OrdType** = Limit.

We will explore the most common char-based enumerations later in this section. For now, the key idea is that:

- A char field is a *single* character, not an arbitrary string.
- That character often stands for a small, fixed set of allowed values, each with a precise meaning.

If you see a field defined as char but carrying multiple characters (for example, 54=BUY), that is a violation of the spec and a red flag for parser errors down the line.

Strings and Text

FIX uses string-like types for fields that hold free-form or semi-structured text. These include:

- **String**: Generic text or identifiers. For example:
  - 49=BUY_SIDE for **SenderCompID**.

  - 11=ORD12345 for **ClOrdID**.

- **LocalMktDate**: A date without time, formatted as YYYYMMDD.
- **MonthYear**: A year and month, sometimes with a day or week code for futures expiries.
- **data**-like types: Opaque binary blobs (for example, compressed data or digital signatures), which are handled with additional length fields.

While String fields are flexible, they are not arbitrary:

- They should not contain the SOH delimiter; otherwise they would break the message structure.
- Venues often impose length limits and character-set restrictions even for strings, to keep logs readable and robust.

As a rule, treat string fields defined by the spec as meaningful business identifiers or labels, even if they are free-form. Do not assume they behave like unbounded comments.

Dates and Times

Time is critical in trading, and FIX defines several temporal types, all encoded as text without time zones unless stated:

- **UTCTimestamp**: A combined date and time, typically YYYYMMDD-HH:MM:SS with optional fractions of a second.
- **UTCDateOnly**: A date in UTC, YYYYMMDD.
- **UTCTimeOnly**: A time of day in UTC, HH:MM:SS with optional fractional seconds.

In practice you will see values like:

- 52=20240112-09:30:00.123 for **SendingTime**.

- 60=20240112-09:30:00.123 for **TransactTime**.

Important points for production systems:

- Times are typically in UTC. If a venue deviates from this, it must be clearly documented, because mixing up time zones leads to painful errors in compliance and analytics.
- Fractional seconds are increasingly used, with three digits (milliseconds) or six digits (microseconds). Your FIX engine and downstream systems need to agree on how many digits they support.
- Clock skew matters. If your SendingTime is consistently behind the venue's clock by several seconds, that can complicate sequencing and latency measurement.

When sanity-checking a log, obvious anomalies in dates and times (such as timestamps in the future, or wildly inconsistent time-of-day) can help you quickly spot misconfigured clocks or test systems accidentally talking to production.

From Types to Meaning: Enumerated Fields

Primitive types tell you what values are *syntactically* allowed. But for many fields, only a small subset of those values make sense in trading. FIX captures these business-meaning constraints through **enumerations**.

An enumerated field is one where the spec defines:

- A fixed set of allowed literal values (often single characters).
- A human-readable interpretation of each value.

Learning the most common enumerations pays off enormously, because they appear in almost every message you will work with.

Key Enumerations in Everyday Trading

Let us look at four of the most important enumerated fields you will see in order flow and drop copy: Side, OrdType, TimeInForce, and ExecType.

Side (tag 54)

Side tells you whether an order or execution is a buy or a sell, and in some products, more nuanced variations. Some core values you will often see are:

- 54=1: Buy.
- 54=2: Sell.
- 54=5: Sell Short (in many equity implementations).
- 54=6: Sell Short Exempt (where supported).

These are defined as char values. Even with just 1 and 2, you can already interpret half of the trading direction in your FIX logs. Values like Sell Short become important in markets with short-sale constraints and locate requirements.

OrdType (tag 40)

OrdType describes how the order should be executed, given market prices. Some fundamental values include:

- 40=1: Market order – execute immediately at the best available prices.
- 40=2: Limit order – execute at a specified price or better.
- 40=3: Stop order.
- 40=4: Stop Limit order.
- 40=F: Market-on-Close (depending on venue).

OrdType is crucial because it heavily conditions which other fields must be present or meaningful. For example:

- For 40=2 (Limit), you expect a valid Price (tag 44).
- For 40=1 (Market), a price might be absent or ignored.

Understanding this enumeration helps you interpret order behaviour and spot invalid or incomplete messages (for instance, a limit order missing a price).

TimeInForce (tag 59)

TimeInForce tells the venue how long an order should remain active. Typical values include:

- 59=0: Day — valid until the end of the trading day.
- 59=3: Immediate-or-Cancel (IOC).
- 59=4: Fill-or-Kill (FOK).
- 59=6: Good-till-Cancel (GTC), subject to venue rules.

Reading this correctly is essential for understanding why orders disappear from the book:

- An IOC order that partially fills will have the remainder cancelled immediately.
- A Day order might rest all day and be cancelled automatically at market close.

From a drop copy or surveillance perspective, TimeInForce gives important context to execution patterns and cancellations.

ExecType (tag 150)

In execution reports, **ExecType** describes what kind of event the report represents. Common values include:

- 150=0: New – order accepted.
- 150=1: Partial fill.
- 150=2: Fill (complete fill).
- 150=4: Canceled.
- 150=8: Rejected.
- 150=I: Order status update not directly tied to a trade (for example, restatement).

ExecType is one of the key fields for reconstructing the lifecycle of an order from drop copy or execution feeds. Combining ExecType with fields like OrderQty, CumQty, and LeavesQty lets you draw a clear picture of how an order moved from new to fully filled or cancelled.

Using Types and Enumerations to Validate Intuitively

Once you know the primitive type and enumeration of a field, you can often validate a message "by feel" before consulting any formal rules. For example:

- Seeing 54=3 in an equities flow where only 1 (Buy) and 2 (Sell) are documented might be a sign of a configuration mismatch.
- Seeing 40=2 (Limit) but no 44 (Price) suggests an incomplete or malformed order.
- Seeing 59=3 (IOC) combined with an execution report showing no fills but final ExecType=4 (Canceled) is expected; the order had no liquidity to hit.

Similarly, type knowledge helps you catch accidental format errors quickly:

- An integer field like 38 (OrderQty) containing 1000.0 is suspicious: quantities are typically integers in many cash equity markets.
- A UTCTimestamp without the date portion (for example, only 09:30:00) may not meet the spec for SendingTime.

In a well-designed trading system, your FIX library and message models will enforce many of these constraints programmatically. But as someone reading logs, being able to reason about them yourself is invaluable for debugging and audit work.

How Venue Extensions Fit In

Most venues and brokers extend the base FIX dictionary with custom fields. These are usually:

- Tags in a range reserved for user-defined use (for example, tags above a certain threshold).
- Documented in an "implementation guide" or a venue-specific FIX specification.

Crucially:

- Each custom tag still has a primitive type (int, Price, String, etc.).
- Many custom tags also define their own enumerations, following the same pattern as standard FIX fields.

Once you are comfortable with the standard types and enumeration concepts, reading venue extensions becomes much easier. You simply:

- Identify the primitive type.

- Check whether the field is enumerated (often the docs will list allowed values).
- Interpret the codes in the same style as you do for Side, OrdType, and so on.

In other words, you are learning a small number of grammatical rules that apply across both core FIX and venue-specific dialects.

Building a Mental Cheat Sheet

As you continue through the book and into practice, it is useful to have a mental (or literal) cheat sheet of:

- The primitive types and how they are written on the wire.
- The numeric tags and meanings of perhaps 20–30 core fields.
- The key enumerations for order direction, type, time-in-force, and execution status.

With that alone, you can often:

- Read a New Order Single and summarise its trading intent in plain language.
- Read a sequence of Execution Reports and understand the lifecycle of an order.
- Notice when a field looks out of place or invalid, long before you dig into documentation.

In the next section, we will use this vocabulary to recognise more complex structure inside messages: components and repeating groups. Those patterns allow FIX to represent arrays and nested objects (such as multiple parties or legs) within the flat tag stream you see on the wire. The primitive types and enumerations you have just learned are the atoms from which those larger structures are built.

2.4 Components & Repeating Group Patterns

So far we have treated a FIX message as a flat list of fields. We know where the header, body, and trailer sit; we understand the core field types and key enumerations. In real trading, however, messages often need to represent more than just single values:

- An order may have *multiple* parties attached (client, executing broker, clearing firm).
- A trade may allocate to *several* accounts.
- A strategy order may have *many* legs or underlying instruments.

In programming languages, you would naturally reach for arrays, lists, and nested objects. On the FIX wire, you still only see a flat sequence of tag=value pairs. The question is: how does FIX express these richer structures without changing that simple wire format?

The answer is in two powerful patterns:

1. **Components**: reusable bundles of fields that behave like named sub-objects.
2. **Repeating groups**: sequences of similar sub-objects, announced by a count field and laid out in a predictable pattern.

Once you can recognise these patterns, a long FIX message becomes easier to read. You stop seeing one undifferentiated stream of tags and start seeing nested structure: a header, body, and trailer, and inside the body, blocks of related fields and arrays of repeated items.

Why FIX Needs Components and Groups

Imagine trying to define all the messages you need for a modern exchange or broker:

- Order entry messages.
- Execution reports.
- Order cancel and replace.
- Position reports.
- Allocation instructions and confirmations.

Many of these messages share common concepts:

- **Instrument** information: symbol, security ID, security type, maturity, etc.
- **Parties**: identifiers and roles of firms and individuals involved.
- **Legs** of a multi-leg strategy or spread.

If every message type independently listed all of these fields, the specification would become huge and repetitive, and the risk of inconsistency would be high. Moreover, dealing with repeated structures (for example, multiple allocations) would be awkward and error-prone.

Components and repeating groups solve this in different but complementary ways:

- **Components** provide *reusable bundles*. They reduce duplication in the spec and help your internal models stay consistent.
- **Repeating groups** provide a way to express *lists* and *arrays* of such bundles within the flat tag stream.

Understanding the difference between the two is important:

- Components are a *specification* convenience; on the wire, you just see their fields in sequence.
- Repeating groups are a *wire-level* pattern; they have a precise encoding that you must parse correctly.

We will tackle them in that order.

Components: Reusable Bundles of Fields

In FIX documentation, a **component** is a named block of fields that can appear in multiple message types. Some well-known examples include:

- **Instrument**: all the fields needed to describe the traded instrument (symbol, security ID, security type, maturity, coupon, etc.).
- **Parties**: information about parties involved in the transaction (firm IDs, roles, sub-IDs).
- **YieldData**, **SpreadOrBenchmarkCurveData**, and others.

When you read the spec for a message like *NewOrderSingle*, you will often see something like:

> **Component**: Instrument

Instead of listing all the instrument-related tags inline, the spec references this component. Similarly, an Execution Report might also reference the *Instrument* component, guaranteeing that the same set of fields is used consistently across messages.

How Components Appear on the Wire

On the wire, a component is *not* marked with special begin/end tags. Its fields simply appear in the tag stream in the order defined for that component. For example, a simplified Instrument component might include:

- 55 (Symbol)
- 48 (SecurityID)
- 22 (SecurityIDSource)
- 167 (SecurityType)

In a New Order Single, you might then see:

```
11=ORD12345|55=ESZ3|48=ESZ3_-
ID|22=8|167=FUT|54=1|38=10|40=2|44=4500.00|...|
```

Nothing here says "begin Instrument component" or "end Instrument component." However, because you know from the spec that the Instrument component is included at that point in the message definition, you can mentally group these fields:

```
ClOrdID (11)
Instrument:
Symbol (55)
SecurityID (48)
SecurityIDSource (22)
SecurityType (167)
Side (54), OrderQty (38), OrdType (40), Price (44), ...
```

From an implementation point of view, components drive how you design your internal data models:

- A NewOrderSingle object might have an `instrument` field of type `Instrument`, which groups 55, 48, 22, 167, etc.
- An ExecutionReport object might also have an `instrument` field of the same type, ensuring consistent handling across workflows.

But again, this is *your* modeling choice; the FIX wire format is oblivious to components as such.

Repeating Groups: Lists Inside the Tag Stream

Components help with reuse, but they do not solve the problem of multiplicity: what if you need multiple instruments, multiple parties, or multiple allocations in a single message?

For that, FIX uses **repeating groups**. A repeating group is a compact way to represent a list of similar items. The pattern always looks like this:

1. A **count field** that says how many group entries follow. Its name typically starts with No (for example, NoPartyIDs).
2. One or more **group fields** that define each entry. The first field in the group acts as an *anchor*; the rest follow until the next occurrence of the anchor or the end of the group.

Conceptually, this is very much like:

```
NoItems = N
Item[1] = { ... fields ... }
Item[2] = { ... fields ... }
...
Item[N] = { ... fields ... }
```

But on the wire, it is encoded as a flat sequence of fields.

A First Example: NoPartyIDs

The Parties component is one of the best examples of a repeating group in action. At its core, it uses:

- 453 = **NoPartyIDs** — the count of party entries.
- 448 = **PartyID**.
- 447 = **PartyIDSource**.
- 452 = **PartyRole**.

Suppose you want to express that an order involves two parties:

1. A client firm.
2. An executing broker.

A simplified FIX snippet using the Parties repeating group might look like:

453=2|448=CLIENT_A|447=D|452=1|448=BROKER_-X|447=D|452=3|

Read with some spacing and labels, this becomes:

- 453=2 (two party entries follow)
- Entry 1:
  - 448=CLIENT_A (PartyID)
  - 447=D (PartyIDSource)
  - 452=1 (PartyRole = Executing Firm, for example)
- Entry 2:
  - 448=BROKER_X (PartyID)
  - 447=D (PartyIDSource)
  - 452=3 (PartyRole = Client ID, depending on the enumeration)

Notice how:

- The count field 453 comes first.
- Then the **first** group entry starts with **448**, the group's leading tag.
- The second entry also starts with **448**.

The leading tag (448 in this case) acts like a marker for each new entry. A FIX parser, knowing the group definition, reads:

1. The count (453=2).
2. For each of the two entries:
   - Start at the leading tag 448.
   - Read all other group fields that follow (447, 452, and possibly optional extras) until:

- The next occurrence of the leading tag (indicating a new entry), or
- A field that is not part of the group definition (indicating the end of the group).

This is the essence of how a flat tag stream encodes a list.

Visualising a Repeating Group as a Tree

Seeing the group in text is useful, but it really helps to picture how that flat stream maps to something more tree-shaped: a message that contains a Parties component, which itself contains a list of Party entries, each with its own fields.

Right after our NoPartyIDs example is a good place to include a visual.

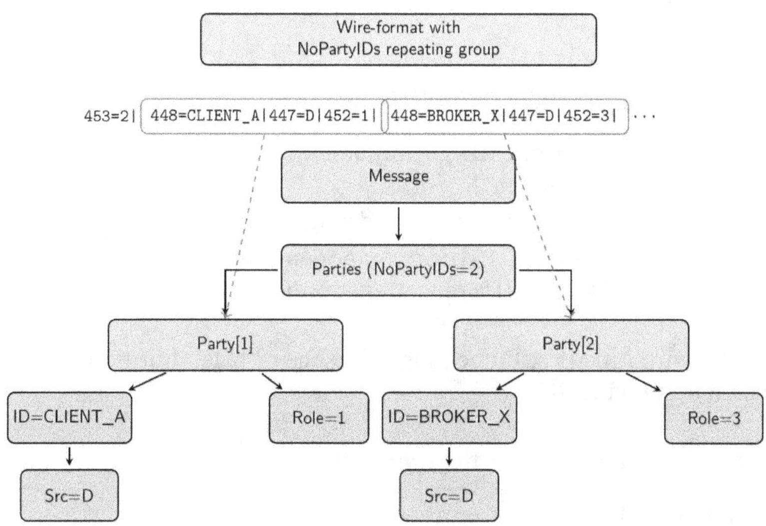

On the left, you see the raw FIX snippet, with brackets around each Party entry. On the right, you see the corresponding logical structure: a *Parties* node containing two Party children, each with its own fields.

When you read logs, your job is to mentally perform this transformation. The more often you do it, the more naturally you will see the tree hiding inside the stream.

Nested Groups: Groups Inside Groups

Repeating groups can themselves contain components and even other repeating groups. This is how FIX represents complicated structures such as:

- An order with multiple legs, where each leg has its own Parties block.
- A trade allocation, where each allocation group has sub-groups for individual accounts and sub-allocations.

For example, a high-level pattern for a multi-leg order might look like:

- NoLegs (count of legs)
  - For each leg:
    * InstrumentLeg component (fields describing that leg's instrument).
    * LegQty, LegPrice, and similar fields.
    * Optional Parties component, which itself includes a NoPartyIDs repeating group.

On the wire, this is still one long sequence of tags. But now you can read it systematically:

1. Encounter a NoLegs field with value 2.
2. For leg 1:
   - Read InstrumentLeg fields.
   - Read optional Leg-specific fields.
   - If present, read the Parties group for that leg (using NoPartyIDs and its associated fields).

3. For leg 2:

    - Repeat the same pattern.

In practice, your FIX engine will do this for you. But for troubleshooting and design, being able to recognise that groups are nested is essential. It stops you from mis-assigning fields to the wrong level (for example, interpreting a leg-level price as if it were an order-level price).

Common Implementation Mistakes with Repeating Groups

Because repeating groups rely on correct counts and ordering, several implementation traps crop up again and again:

Mismatched counts.

The value of the count field (for example, 453=2) must match the number of entries that actually appear. If:

- 453=2 but only one Party entry follows, or
- 453=1 but two Party entries appear,

the receiver's parser will become confused:

- It might treat some subsequent non-group fields as part of a missing group entry.
- It might conclude that the message is malformed and generate a Reject.

In logs, this often manifests as "incorrect NumInGroup count" or similar error messages.

Unexpected ordering inside groups.

The leading tag of the group (for example, 448 for Parties) is especially important. Some engines expect it to appear first within each entry; fields arriving in a different order may break group parsing.

While FIX allows some flexibility in field ordering, many implementations assume that group entries follow the dictionary order. Deviating from this can trigger subtle bugs, especially with optional fields.

Optional fields inside groups.

Within a group, some fields are optional. This is where parsers need to be careful:

- The absence of an optional field is allowed.
- But parsers must still know when to stop reading the current entry and start the next.

This is typically handled by using the repeating group's leading field as the marker of a new entry. If a sender puts fields in surprising positions, a naive parser may misinterpret where one entry ends and the next begins.

Nested groups mis-implemented.

When groups are nested, sender and receiver must agree exactly on:

- Which groups are inside which others.
- The order in which nested groups appear.

Getting this wrong can lead to deeply confusing errors where inner-group fields are misaligned with their parent entries, and the message appears structurally sound at first glance but fails parsing at runtime.

Learning to See Arrays and Objects in the Stream

Putting everything together, you can now look at a non-trivial message and mentally reconstruct its structure in several passes:

1. **First pass:** Identify the main message type and core body fields (as in previous sections).
2. **Second pass:** Spot any NoXXX fields; each one announces a repeating group.

3. **Third pass:** For each count field, bracket off that many entries, marking where each group entry starts (at the leading tag) and ends.
4. **Fourth pass:** Within each group entry, mentally regroup fields into components (Instrument, Parties, etc.) based on your knowledge of the spec.

For example, a simplified New Order Single with Parties might look like this, when "spoken aloud":

> New Order Single,
> with this instrument,
> for this side, quantity, and price,
> involving two parties: a client and a broker.

On the wire, it is just:

```
35=D|11=ORD12345|55=ESZ3|48=ESZ3_-
ID|22=8|54=1|38=10|40=2|44=4500.00|453=2|448=CLIENT_-
A|447=D|452=1|448=BROKER_X|447=D|452=3|...|
```

But you now know how to see:

- The **Instrument** component fields grouped around 55/48/22.
- The **Parties** group announced by 453, with its two entries.
- Each Party entry as its own little sub-object with PartyID, source, and role.

This mental model is not just useful for human understanding. It mirrors how modern FIX engines and data models represent messages:

- A message is an object.
- Components are nested objects.
- Repeating groups are lists of such objects.

In later parts of the book, when we talk about FIX Orchestra and machine-readable dictionaries, you will see how these same concepts are captured and enforced in tooling. For now, you have the essential skill: reading arrays and nested structures inside a flat stream of tags, and reconstructing the intended business object with confidence.

2.5 Machine-Readable Dictionaries with FIX Orchestra

By this point in the chapter, you have a mental model of FIX at several levels:

- Architecturally, you know how FIXT separates the session layer from the application layer.
- At the message level, you can see the header, body, and trailer inside a raw message, and you understand the role of key structural fields.
- At the field level, you recognise core data types, tags, enumerations, components, and repeating groups, and you can mentally rebuild nested structures from a flat tag stream.

In other words, you now understand *what* FIX messages look like and *how* they are structured.

The remaining question is: how do we manage all this knowledge at scale in real trading systems? In many organisations, the answer historically has been a messy mixture of:

- PDF specification documents from venues.
- Internal wiki pages and spreadsheets describing "how this venue really behaves."
- Handwritten code in FIX engines and adaptors encoding field lists and conditional rules.

- Tribal knowledge in the heads of the people who did the last certification.

This is fragile. It is too easy for the documentation, the code, and the actual behaviour of systems to drift apart. Every new version of a venue's spec becomes a mini-project of manual reading, comparison, coding, and re-testing.

FIX Orchestra was designed to fix this. It is a way of representing the FIX dictionary and related behaviour in a *machine-readable* form so that you can move from "reading specs and hand-coding rules" to "compiling specs and generating code and tests".

In this section, we will:

- Explain what a FIX Orchestra file contains in terms you now know: fields, components, repeating groups, and message layouts.
- Show how Orchestra captures conditional rules and workflows, not just static lists of tags.
- Connect Orchestra to practical payoffs: code generation, validation, certification, and change management.

You do not need to know the low-level syntax of Orchestra to benefit from it. What matters is understanding what it represents and how that changes the way you think about FIX in a production stack.

From PDFs to Machine-Readable Specs

Historically, a venue would publish a "FIX Specification" as a static document. It would:

- List supported message types (NewOrderSingle, ExecutionReport, etc.).
- For each message type, describe which fields are required, which are optional, and in what contexts.

- Define any venue-specific tags and values.

To implement an interface, your team would:

1. Read the PDF.
2. Manually transcribe the field lists into code, configuration, or both.
3. Write tests based on examples in the document (if any).
4. Iterate with the venue's certification team until your interpretation matched theirs.

The bottleneck here is not the FIX protocol itself; it is the way the spec is transmitted: human-readable only. Every machine that needs to "understand" the spec has to go through a human brain first.

FIX Orchestra changes the medium. An Orchestra file is a structured, machine-readable representation of:

- The **dictionary**: fields, their tags, data types, and enumerations.
- The **components** and **repeating groups**: how fields are bundled and repeated.
- The **messages**: which fields and components appear in each message type and under what conditions.
- The **workflows**: sequences of messages and state transitions that implement common scenarios (order lifecycles, cancel flows, etc.).

You can think of Orchestra as "FIX's schema and behaviour, described in a form a compiler could read."

What an Orchestra Dictionary Describes

At the simplest level, an Orchestra dictionary repeats some of the information we have already discussed, but in a structured way that a program can use directly.

Fields. For each field, Orchestra records:

- Its numeric tag (for example, 54).
- Its name (for example, Side).
- Its primitive data type (for example, char).
- Any enumerated values (for example, 1 = Buy, 2 = Sell, etc.).

This is essentially the same information you saw in the "Field Data Types, Tags & Enumerations" section, but now expressed in a way that a tool can parse. From this, a code generator could safely:

- Create strongly-typed fields in a language of your choice.
- Validate that only allowed values are used for enumerated fields.

Components and groups. For each component and repeating group, Orchestra describes:

- The list of fields and/or sub-components it contains.
- For repeating groups, the count field and the leading tag of each group entry.

This mirrors the "Components & Repeating Group Patterns" section you just read. Instead of you mentally remembering that NoPartyIDs (453) introduces a group of PartyID, PartyIDSource, and PartyRole fields, Orchestra encodes it explicitly. A parser generator can then automatically:

- Recognise groups in the tag stream.
- Map them into arrays or lists of objects in your internal model.

Messages. For each message type (identified by MsgType, tag 35), Orchestra records:

- The message name (for example, NewOrderSingle, ExecutionReport).

- Which fields and components belong to the header, body, and trailer for that message.
- For each field, whether it is required or optional.

Up to this point, you can think of Orchestra as a very detailed, structured version of the tables you typically see in a FIX spec PDF.

The real power, however, appears when Orchestra captures not just "what fields can appear", but also *when* and *under what conditions* they must or must not appear.

Conditional Presence Rules: Encoding "If-Then" Constraints

In realistic interfaces, the presence of a field often depends on the value of another field. For example:

- If OrdType (40) is 2 (Limit), then Price (44) is required.
- If Side (54) is 5 (Sell Short), then some short-sale reason or locate tag must be set.
- If a message is an Execution Report with ExecType (150) equal to New (0), certain quantities must be zero; if it is a Fill (2), they must be strictly positive.

Traditional FIX dictionaries express these sorts of rules in English paragraphs. For example: "When OrdType = 2 (Limit), Price is required." Humans can read that; computers cannot, unless you write extra code.

Orchestra is designed to encode these rules in a formal way. Inside the Orchestra file, you can attach conditional logic to fields and messages, saying, in effect:

> Field Price is required when OrdType equals Limit, and forbidden otherwise.

A validation engine that reads Orchestra can then:

- Automatically check incoming and outgoing messages against these conditions.
- Provide precise error messages like "Price is required when OrdType = Limit."

For you, this means:

- Less custom validation code mangled into each adaptor.
- Clear, testable specification of behaviour that lives in one place: the Orchestra file.

As interfaces evolve, updating the Orchestra specification and regenerating validation logic becomes much safer than scattered, manual code edits.

Capturing Workflows: States and Message Sequences

Beyond individual messages, trading workflows are about *sequences* of messages and how they change the state of an order or trade. For example, a simple order lifecycle might be:

1. Client sends New Order Single.
2. Venue acknowledges with an Execution Report (ExecType = New).
3. Venue sends one or more Execution Reports with ExecType = Partial Fill.
4. Venue sends an Execution Report with ExecType = Fill, closing the order.

In everyday practice, you internalise these flows, and risk systems and OMSs are built around them. But they are rarely written down in a machine-readable way.

Orchestra extends its scope here by allowing the definition of:

- **States**: conceptual stages such as "New," "PartiallyFilled," "Filled," "Canceled," etc.
- **Transitions**: allowed moves from one state to another, triggered by specific messages (for example, an Execution Report with certain ExecType).

This gives you a kind of "state machine" for an order, encoded directly in the Orchestra file. With that in place, tools can:

- Validate that a particular sequence of messages represents a legal progression of states.
- Generate test cases that walk through specific workflows (for example, New → Partial Fill → Fill, or New → Canceled).
- Highlight unexpected transitions, such as a Fill being reported without an initial New.

This is especially valuable for drop copy and surveillance: instead of manually reverse-engineering what "normal" looks like, you can refer to the explicitly encoded workflow in Orchestra.

Practical Payoffs: From Spec to Code, Validation, and Tests

It is helpful to connect these ideas back to concrete tasks that trading teams perform.

Code generation.

Given a complete Orchestra file for a venue's FIX interface, a tool can generate:

- Data structures representing messages, components, and repeating groups.
- Parsing and serialization logic that knows how to map between flat tag streams and internal objects.

- Enumerations and constants for fields like Side, OrdType, ExecType, etc.

Instead of hand-writing these models and parsers (which is error-prone and tedious), your developers can:

- Focus on mapping between these generated models and the rest of the trading system.
- Rely on the generator to keep the wire-level details in sync with the spec.

When the venue issues a new version of its Orchestra spec, you regenerate, recompile, and run your tests, much as you would with a new version of an API definition in other domains.

Validation engines.

Because Orchestra encodes both the dictionary and conditional rules, you can build (or buy) a validation engine that:

- Takes an Orchestra file as input.
- Subscribes to a stream of FIX messages (for example, your drop copy feed, or messages at your gateway).
- Flags any message that violates the spec: missing required fields, disallowed combinations, out-of-sequence workflows.

This is invaluable in several contexts:

- During development, to catch mistakes early.
- During certification, to make sure your behaviour matches the venue's expectations.
- In production monitoring, as an extra line of defence against configuration drift and unexpected changes.

Because the rules come from Orchestra, you avoid hard-coding them in multiple places, and you can update them consistently when the spec changes.

Certification and regression tests.

Certification with venues is essentially a structured conversation: they send you test cases; you send messages; they verify that what you did matches their specification.

If the venue and participants both work from the same Orchestra definition, much of this can be automated:

- Test harnesses can be generated from the workflows encoded in Orchestra.
- Expected message sequences and field values can be derived automatically from state transition rules.
- Regression tests can be rerun every time you change your FIX engine or upgrade your models.

This does not eliminate human interaction in certification, but it turns a large part of the process into a repeatable, tool-driven exercise.

Aligning Multiple Venues and Strategies

Most serious trading operations connect to many venues, each with its own quirks and versions. Without a unifying approach, you end up with:

- Slightly different hand-coded models for each venue.
- Duplicated logic for common patterns (for example, reading Parties or Instrument components).
- Divergence over time, as some connections are updated and others lag behind.

Using Orchestra consistently, you can impose more structure:

- For each venue, keep an Orchestra file that reflects the superset of what you actually use.
- Use generators and validators derived from these files to standardise how messages are represented internally.
- Where possible, harmonise your internal models so that common components (Instrument, Parties, etc.) map cleanly across venues, even if wire-level details differ slightly.

This makes it easier to:

- Add a new venue by starting from a familiar modelling pattern.
- Audit your FIX connectivity estate: you can inspect Orchestra versions and see exactly which flows are using which message types and fields.
- Plan upgrades: for example, moving multiple venues from one application version to another in a coordinated way.

From Documentation Problem to Engineering Problem

Perhaps the most important conceptual shift with FIX Orchestra is this:

> FIX connectivity is no longer primarily a documentation problem; it becomes an engineering problem.

Instead of:

- Reading static documents.
- Re-implementing rules in code.
- Hoping your implementation stays in sync with the latest PDF.

You move to:

- Treating the Orchestra spec as a source of truth, version-controlled like code.
- Generating a significant portion of your FIX handling logic from that source.
- Using automated validation and tests derived from Orchestra to enforce conformance.

Organisationally, this changes the role of the "FIX specialist":

- Less manual mapping of tags from documents into code.
- More design of internal models and workflows, and more stewardship of the Orchestra artifacts themselves.
- Closer collaboration with both developers and business users to ensure that what is encoded in Orchestra matches real-world trading needs.

For you as a reader of this book, the immediate takeaway is that all the structures you have learned-fields, types, components, groups, and workflows-are not just concepts; they can be *expressed and enforced* in a formal language. FIX Orchestra is that language.

As you work on real systems, you will still need to understand the raw messages and the architecture of FIX sessions. But with Orchestra in place, much of the tedious and error-prone translation from human-readable specs to machine behaviour can be automated, freeing you to focus on more interesting problems: designing robust trading workflows, managing risk, and building systems that can evolve as markets and specs change.

Chapter 3

Session Protocol & Reliability Mechanics

Trading systems don't fail in the obvious places. It's rarely the order type that kills you; it's the silent sequence gap, the unacknowledged heartbeat, the duplicated fill that sneaks in during recovery. This chapter peels back the FIX session layer-the part most people treat as "plumbing"-and shows how it actually guarantees business integrity. You'll see how logons define the rules of engagement, how liveness is continuously tested, how sequence numbers act as the ledger of truth, and how resend logic stitches broken conversations back together without double-trading. By the end, you'll be able to read a FIX session transcript the way a mechanic reads an engine diagnostic: quickly spotting what's healthy, what's risky, and what absolutely must be fixed before the next open.

3.1 Session Establishment and Parameter Negotiation

At this point in the book you have seen individual FIX messages and the basic idea of a FIX transport session. We now zoom in on the moment when that session comes to life and how two peers agree on the rules that will govern everything that follows. A FIX *session* is not just a TCP socket; it is a long-lived, stateful conversation with a shared identity on each side, agreed timing rules, and a carefully managed history in the form of sequence numbers. Sessions begin with a Logon exchange and end with Logout. In between, all order flow, drop copy, and recovery traffic is wrapped inside this session "envelope". In this section we will treat Logon and Logout as first-class protocol events: how they create the session, how they negotiate the key parameters, and how they decide whether to carry forward the existing sequence state or wipe the slate clean.

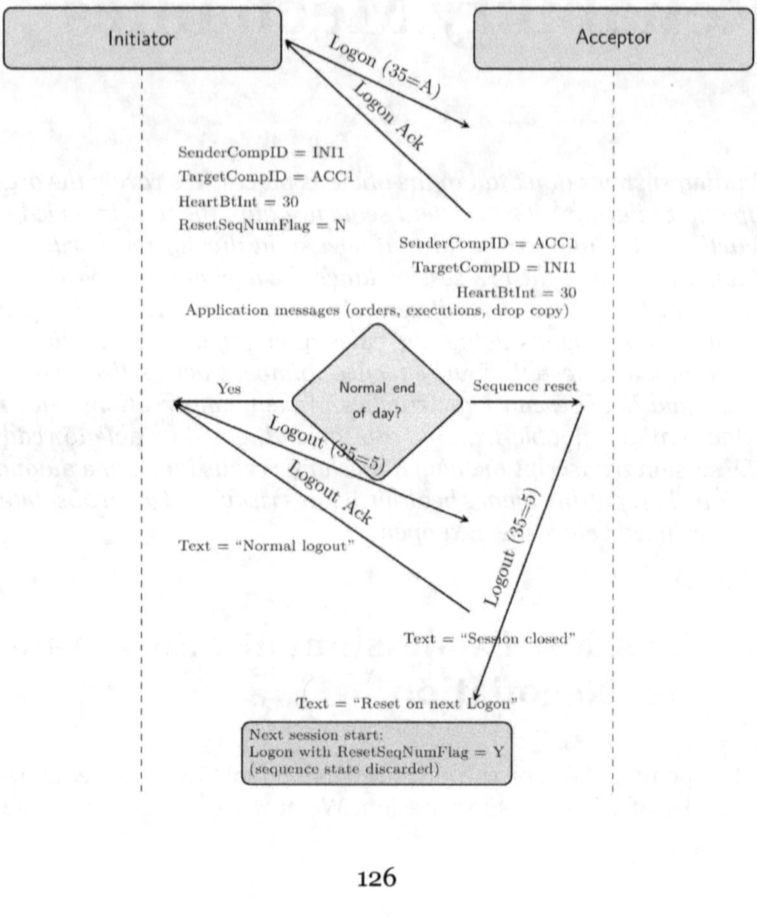

What a FIX Session Really Is

It is tempting to think of a FIX session as simply "a connection to the exchange" or "a pipe for orders". From the protocol's point of view, it is more precise to say:

- A session is identified by the pair of identities on each side (for example, your firm as SenderCompID and the broker or venue as TargetCompID), sometimes plus a qualifier such as environment or trading segment.
- The session maintains two running sequence counters: one for messages you send and one for messages you expect to receive. These numbers give you a strict order of events.
- The session enforces timing rules: how often heartbeats are expected, how long you can stay silent before being probed, and how quickly you should respond.
- The session has a life cycle: it begins with a Logon handshake, moves through active trading, then ends with Logout and a closed connection.

Once this envelope is in place, every business message—a new order, a cancel, an execution report, or a drop copy—is just a payload carried inside the session, always tagged with the session's identities and its sequence numbers.

Roles: Initiator and Acceptor

Most trading relationships distinguish two roles:

- The *initiator* is the party that dials out: it opens the TCP connection and sends the first Logon. Typically this is the buy-side firm, a client gateway, or an order management system.
- The *acceptor* listens on a known address and port, accepts incoming connections, and waits for the client to Logon. This is usually the broker, exchange, or service bureau.

Functionally, both sides run a FIX engine and both implement the same protocol rules. The role matters mainly for who starts the conversation and who enforces some of the parameters. For example, the acceptor often dictates which identities are allowed, what range of heartbeat intervals is acceptable, and whether sequence resets are permitted at arbitrary times.

The Logon Message: Opening the Conversation

The FIX Logon message (message type 35=A) is the first application-level message sent once the TCP connection is up. It serves several purposes at once:

1. Introduces the two parties to each other using their identities.
2. Proposes or confirms timing parameters such as the heartbeat interval.
3. Optionally signals that previous sequence history should be discarded.
4. Confirms the protocol version to be used for application messages.

Let us walk through the most important fields that appear in a Logon and understand what they mean in plain language.

Identities: SenderCompID and TargetCompID

Every FIX message, including Logon, carries SenderCompID and TargetCompID. Conceptually:

- SenderCompID tells the world "who is speaking".
- TargetCompID tells the world "who this message is intended for".

During Logon, this is more than decoration: it defines *which* session you are trying to establish. The acceptor may serve many clients, each with their own identity and own sequence state. When it sees a Logon with SenderCompID = ALPHA_FUND and TargetCompID = BROKER_NY, it can locate the right configuration and the last stored sequence numbers for that pair.

This is similar to walking up to a staffed trading desk and saying: "I am Alpha Fund. I'm here to speak with the New York Broker desk." The desk checks their records: "Yes, we know you, we have your previous orders and our shared history, and here's where we last left off."

If the acceptor does not recognize the identity pair, or the identity is not allowed to connect on this line, it will generally refuse the Logon and close the connection.

HeartBtInt: Negotiating the Session's Pulse

The field HeartBtInt (heartbeat interval) tells the counterparty how many seconds you expect between heartbeat messages during idle periods. It is one of the core timing parameters of a session.

In practice:

- The initiator proposes a heartbeat interval in its Logon, often something like 30 seconds.
- The acceptor either accepts that value (echoing it back in its own Logon response) or rejects the session if the value is out of policy.

Once both sides agree, this number becomes the session's "pulse rate". If there are no order messages to send, each side must send a Heartbeat at least as often as HeartBtInt specifies. This is how each engine proves it is still alive even in quiet markets.

The exact number is part technical and part business decision:

- A shorter interval (for example 5 seconds) detects broken connections quickly but creates more traffic and log volume.
- A longer interval (for example 60 seconds) reduces overhead but slows down detection of problems.

Trading venues typically publish their required or recommended heartbeat interval in their FIX rules of engagement, and your engine should be configured to match.

EncryptMethod and Security-Related Fields

EncryptMethod indicates what, if any, message-level encryption is in use. In modern deployments, channel security is almost always handled at the transport layer using TLS, VPNs, or private lines, so EncryptMethod is frequently set to "none" at the FIX level.

The important lesson for operators is not the specific number codes, but the idea that security assumptions must be agreed as part of the session contract. If the venue requires a particular security set-up and your Logon does not comply, the session should not be established.

Default Application Version

In FIXT-based environments (for example using FIXT 1.1 as the transport and FIX 5.0 SP2 as the application layer), Logon also carries tags that declare the default application message version for the session.

This prevents confusion such as one side sending a NewOrderSingle in an older format while the other expects a newer layout. The Logon handshake makes sure both peers have the same picture of how business messages will be encoded.

Sequence Numbers at Logon: Continue or Reset?

The most delicate decision during Logon is how to handle sequence numbers. Remember that each side maintains:

- An outgoing message sequence number for messages it sends.
- An expected incoming sequence number for messages it receives.

When a session drops and is re-established—which happens frequently in real trading due to network issues, restarts, or planned maintenance—the two sides must decide:

> Should we continue counting from where we left off, or should we reset our counters and start again from 1?

FIX provides two mechanisms for this, which you will see in practice as two distinct styles of Logon.

Normal Logon: Continuing Existing State

In a *normal* Logon, both peers intend to preserve the existing history. The goal is to reconnect and carry on as if the connection had never dropped.

Operationally:

- The initiator's engine loads its last persistent sequence state for this session (based on the identity pair) and prepares to send the next sequence number.
- It sends a Logon with ResetSeqNumFlag either omitted or explicitly set to "No".
- The acceptor checks its own stored state. If the numbers look compatible, it accepts the Logon and replies with its own Logon message.

Immediately after Logon, each side compares what it expects with what it actually receives. If there is a gap or mismatch, they use the gap recovery mechanisms (ResendRequest, SequenceReset) described later in the chapter to repair it.

The advantage of a normal Logon is continuity: you retain an unbroken, numbered history of all messages across temporary disconnects. For audit and reconciliation, this is valuable because it gives you a single ordered "ledger" of all traffic.

Reset Logon: Starting From a Clean Slate

Sometimes, it is safer or operationally simpler to deliberately throw away the old sequence history and start fresh. This is called a *reset* Logon and is signaled using ResetSeqNumFlag = Y.

Common situations include:

- Start of day, when both sides agree that the previous day's sequence history is complete and will be archived.
- After a major recovery event, where the sequence state is believed to be badly out of sync and trying to repair it would be messy or error-prone.
- Environment switches, for example moving from a test environment to production, where the sequence history is not shared.

In a reset Logon:

- The initiator sends ResetSeqNumFlag = Y in its Logon. This is a clear request: "Let us both forget our sequences and restart from 1."
- If the acceptor agrees and its own operational policy allows it, it resets its stored sequence numbers for this session and responds in kind.
- Both sides then begin sending messages with sequence number 1, 2, 3, and so on, as if it were a brand-new relationship.

A reset is powerful but must be used with care. Any unresolved gaps or mismatches from the previous sequence history are effectively buried. This is acceptable only when both firms are confident that the business state is reconciled and that no further FIX-level recovery is needed for that period.

Authentication, Authorization, and Session Qualifiers

Beyond the core tags, Logon is the natural place to attach additional information that helps the acceptor decide whether to allow the session and how to route its traffic.

Examples include:

- User or sub-account identifiers, if the same SenderCompID can represent multiple trading desks or funds.
- Session qualifiers indicating which environment this is (for example "UAT", "CERT", "PROD") or which market segment (for example "EQUITY", "OPTIONS").
- Passwords or tokens, where allowed by the venue's security policies.

Practically, you can think of the acceptor as doing three checks when it receives a Logon:

1. *Who are you?* (Check SenderCompID and any credentials.)
2. *Which conversation do you want to resume?* (Look up stored sequence and configuration for this identity pair and qualifier.)
3. *What rules are you proposing?* (Heartbeat interval, reset or continue, protocol version.)

Only after all of these checks pass does the acceptor respond with its own Logon and move the session into an "active" state.

Logout: Closing the Session Deliberately

Just as Logon is a formal way to start a session, Logout (message type 35=5) is the formal way to end it. A clean Logout is a courtesy to both sides: it tells the engines and the human operators that the session end was intentional, not a network accident.

There are three broad categories of Logout:

Normal Clean Shutdown

In a normal end-of-day or maintenance scenario:

- One side, often the initiator, decides it is time to close the session.

- It sends a Logout message, typically including a human-readable reason in the Text field such as "End of trading day" or "Planned maintenance".
- The other side responds with its own Logout, optionally echoing a reason, and then both sides close the TCP connection.

Engines often log the reason string prominently so that operations staff can quickly see whether a disconnect was planned or unexpected when scanning overnight logs.

Error-Triggered Logout

Sometimes a severe error forces a session to be shut down immediately. Examples include:

- Repeated, serious sequence number violations.
- Authentication failures or unauthorized use of an identity.
- Protocol violations where the counterparty sends invalid or unsupported messages.

In these cases, the impacted side will send a Logout with a Text reason describing the error and then close the session. The clarity of this reason is crucial for post-mortem analysis. Good engines surface it prominently, and good operators insist on meaningful, specific wording rather than generic "Error" messages.

Logout as a Precursor to Reset

Logout also plays a role in planned sequence resets. As the earlier diagram hinted, a common pattern is:

1. During the current session, one side sends a normal Logout including a Text message such as "Closing session; will reset sequence on next Logon".

2. Both sides close the connection and archive their current session logs.

3. At the next planned session start (for example next trading day), the initiator performs a reset Logon with ResetSeqNumFlag = Y, and both sides begin from sequence 1.

Using Logout to announce the plan helps human operators distinguish between an ordinary end-of-day and an end-of-day that will be followed by a sequence reset. This matters because reconciliation tools and monitoring systems will interpret the first sequence-1 messages differently depending on whether a reset was expected.

Designing Clear Operational Semantics

From an engine designer's or operations team's point of view, good session management is not just about conforming to the FIX specification; it is about making behavior predictable and observable.

A few practical guidelines tie together what we have discussed:

- **Document your session rules of engagement.** For each counterparty, agree and document the allowed heartbeat intervals, when sequence resets may happen, and the daily session schedule.

- **Be explicit at Logon.** Always set ResetSeqNumFlag deliberately rather than relying on defaults, and ensure any implied behavior (such as a daily reset) is written down and communicated.

- **Use human-readable reasons in Logout.** Treat the Text field as a message to your future self, who will be debugging a problem at 3 a.m. months from now.

- **Separate planned from unplanned events.** When shutting down for maintenance or end-of-day, use Logout. When a network failure occurs without Logout, treat it as unplanned and be ready for recovery logic on the next Logon.

In the next sections, we will examine how the parameters agreed at Logon—especially the heartbeat interval and sequence handling choices—drive the day-to-day mechanics of liveness monitoring, sequence number management, and gap recovery. For now, keep in mind that a carefully designed Logon/Logout handshake is the foundation on which all other session reliability features rest.

3.2 Keepalive, Heartbeats, and Liveness Probes

In the previous section we treated Logon and Logout as the opening and closing handshake of a FIX session and saw how they establish the core parameters: who is talking to whom, which sequence numbers to use, and what heartbeat interval to expect. We now turn to what happens in the long middle of a session: how each side continuously verifies that the other side is still alive, reachable, and processing messages.

In human terms, Logon is like joining a conference call and agreeing on the agenda. Heartbeats and liveness probes are the occasional "can you still hear me?" check-ins that make sure the call has not silently dropped. In FIX, this continuous health check is not optional decoration; it is a core reliability mechanism that determines when you keep trading, when you stop, and when you fail over to a backup path.

Why Liveness Matters So Much

Electronic trading is unforgiving of ambiguity. If your FIX engine keeps sending orders into a session that is dead, you risk:

- Assuming an order is working when it never reached the venue.
- Missing critical execution reports or cancel acknowledgments.
- Building a business state (in your OMS or risk system) that diverges from the true state at the broker or exchange.

On the other hand, if you declare the session dead too aggressively, you can:

- Disconnect during brief network jitter that would have recovered on its own.
- Trigger unnecessary failovers or trading halts.
- Flood operations teams with false alarms.

The design of heartbeat and liveness logic is therefore a balancing act. FIX gives you the building blocks—heartbeats, TestRequest messages, and explicit timeouts—but each firm must configure them carefully to match its risk appetite and infrastructure.

The Role of HeartBtInt Revisited

At Logon, the two peers agreed on a heartbeat interval, typically called HeartBtInt. This field is best thought of as the *maximum allowed silence* on the session during normal operation.

Importantly, HeartBtInt is not only about sending heartbeat messages. It defines:

- How frequently each side must at least send *something* (either business messages or heartbeats).
- How long each side will wait for any sign of life from the other side before becoming suspicious.

In a typical configuration:

- If there is ongoing business traffic (orders, executions, cancels), heartbeats may not be needed because those messages themselves demonstrate that the session is active.
- If the line is idle—no application messages for some fraction of HeartBtInt—the engine schedules a heartbeat to reassure the counterparty.

This dual role prevents the session from chattering with heartbeats when the line is already busy, but still ensures regular "keepalive" messages when markets are quiet.

Heartbeat Messages: The Basic Keepalive

A FIX Heartbeat is a simple administrative message whose main purpose is to say: "I am still here, and my sequence numbering is still consistent."

Key points about heartbeats:

- They are sent by each side independently. You do not "reply" to a heartbeat with another heartbeat; your own heartbeat schedule is driven by your local timers and the absence of other outgoing traffic.
- They increment sequence numbers just like any other message. Each heartbeat has its own MsgSeqNum, and missing heartbeats will trigger gap detection just as missing business messages do.
- They may carry a small amount of optional information (for example TestRequest identifiers, as we will see later), but they are not meant to carry business data.

To understand how heartbeats work in practice, imagine the following scenario:

1. The session has HeartBtInt set to 30 seconds.
2. For several minutes, the client is sending orders and receiving execution reports. No explicit heartbeats are sent, because the stream of business messages itself proves the session is alive.
3. Activity slows down. The client's engine notices that it has not *sent* anything for, say, 25 seconds. It schedules a heartbeat so that, by the 30-second mark, the counterparty will have received some message.
4. The heartbeat goes out, the timer is reset, and the cycle begins again.

From the receiver's perspective, all incoming messages—business or heartbeat—are signs of life. The receiver measures the interval since it last saw any message. If that interval grows longer than some multiple of HeartBtInt, suspicion rises.

Under-Sending and Over-Sending Heartbeats

An engine that never sends heartbeats is obviously broken. But there are more subtle failure modes:

Under-sending heartbeats. If your implementation waits *longer* than HeartBtInt before sending a heartbeat in idle periods, your counterparty will interpret the silence as a possible problem. They might:

- Fire TestRequests (explicit pings) that you then have to answer.
- Declare the session dead and disconnect you.

From their point of view, you have broken the contract you both agreed to at Logon.

Over-sending heartbeats. At the other extreme, some naive implementations send heartbeats at fixed intervals regardless of traffic. If the market is busy and you send a heartbeat every few seconds *in addition* to hundreds of business messages, you:

- Consume bandwidth and CPU that could be used for business flow.
- Generate excessive log volume, making it harder for operators to sift through logs during an incident.

Good engines implement heartbeat timing in a traffic-aware way: they only send explicit heartbeats when they have otherwise been silent and need to satisfy the agreed maximum silence period.

Detecting a Stalled or Silent Counterparty

Heartbeat logic on the *sending* side is only half of the story. The receiving side must continuously monitor whether the other party is still talking to it.

Operationally, an engine typically tracks:

- The time of the last message received on the session (any message type).
- The current time.
- A configurable threshold, often tied to HeartBtInt, that defines how long is too long to wait without receiving anything.

If the elapsed time since the last incoming message exceeds this threshold, the receiver does not immediately tear down the session. Instead, FIX provides a more polite mechanism: the TestRequest.

TestRequest: When You Suspect the Line Is Stuck

A TestRequest is a control message that effectively says: "I have not heard from you in a while. If you can see this message, please prove it."

The process works as follows:

1. The receiver (say, the acceptor) notices that no message has arrived for longer than allowed.
2. It sends a TestRequest to the initiator. This message includes a small identifier so that any response can be tied back to this specific probe.
3. Upon receiving a TestRequest, the initiator must respond as quickly as possible by sending a Heartbeat that echoes the identifier from the TestRequest.
4. When the acceptor sees that heartbeat and checks the identifier, it knows that:
    - Its outbound path is working (because the TestRequest got there).

- Its inbound path is working (because the Heartbeat came back).
- The remote engine's FIX logic is still running and responsive.

This pattern is similar to sending a ping in a network context, but with an added guarantee: not only is the TCP connection alive, but the remote FIX application code is alive enough to receive, interpret, and respond according to the protocol.

Escalation: From Suspicion to Disconnect

What if the TestRequest goes unanswered? FIX does not prescribe concrete time values, but operationally firms adopt a clear escalation path:

1. **First timeout: suspicion.** When the receiver sends a TestRequest, it starts a timer. If no corresponding heartbeat is received within a short window (for example, one or two heartbeat intervals), suspicion escalates.
2. **Repeated TestRequests.** Some engines will send one or more additional TestRequests, possibly with different identifiers, to rule out a one-off glitch.
3. **Session disconnect.** If multiple TestRequests are unanswered and no other messages arrive, the receiver concludes that the session is effectively dead. It may:
    - Log a clear error describing the timeouts and missed probes.
    - Optionally send a Logout (if the connection is not already broken at the TCP level).
    - Close the TCP connection.
4. **Failover or trading halt.** On top of the FIX-level disconnect, the trading application or smart order router might:
    - Route flow to a backup link or alternative broker.
    - Halt trading in specific instruments or markets until connectivity is restored.

The key design point is that the move from "this is a bit quiet" to "we must disconnect and possibly fail over" should be driven by explicit, observable events: missed heartbeats and unanswered TestRequests, recorded in logs with precise timestamps.

Concrete Timeout Patterns for Different Market Conditions

Although the FIX standard leaves exact timings up to you, it is useful to think in terms of *relative* tolerances rather than absolute seconds.

For example, suppose two peers agree on HeartBtInt $=$ 30 seconds. Reasonable policies might be:

- If no message is received for 1 $\times$ HeartBtInt (30 seconds), send a TestRequest.
- If no suitable heartbeat response is received within another 1 $\times$ HeartBtInt (another 30 seconds), consider sending a second TestRequest and raise an operator alert.
- If still nothing arrives by 3 $\times$ HeartBtInt (90 seconds total silence), declare the session down, disconnect, and trigger any automated failover.

In volatile market conditions, firms may choose shorter intervals or lower multiples to detect issues faster. In quieter markets, or across high-latency networks, they may tolerate longer silences. The important thing is that these policies are:

- Symmetrical enough that both sides have compatible expectations.
- Documented in the session's rules of engagement.
- Supported by monitoring systems that can alert human operators when thresholds are crossed.

Anti-Pattern: Relying on TCP Keepalive Alone

Network stacks and firewalls often provide their own notion of "keepalive", using low-level TCP probes. While these are useful at the infrastructure level, they are *not* a substitute for FIX-level liveness checks.

TCP keepalives can tell you:

- Whether the underlying socket is still open and routes are not completely broken.

They cannot tell you:

- Whether the remote FIX engine is running, not hung, and processing messages correctly.
- Whether sequence numbers are still consistent and gaps are being handled.
- Whether your TestRequests, heartbeats, and business messages are being interpreted and logged as expected.

A classic failure mode is a remote FIX engine that is stuck (for example due to a software bug) but whose TCP connection remains technically up. Without FIX-level heartbeats and TestRequests, you might not notice that your orders are not truly being processed until you see missing fills or reconciliation breaks much later.

Therefore, TCP keepalive should be seen as a lower-level safeguard, complementing but never replacing FIX heartbeats and TestRequests.

Heartbeat and Liveness Design: Practical Guidelines

Putting the pieces together, we can summarize a set of practical design and operational guidelines:

- **Drive heartbeat sending from local silence.** Your engine should watch how long it has been since it last sent *any* message.

If that duration approaches HeartBtInt, it should send a heartbeat even if it has not yet reached the exact threshold. This ensures that, from the other side's point of view, you never exceed the agreed maximum silence.

- **Drive TestRequests from remote silence.** Your engine should separately track how long it has been since it last *received* any message. If this duration exceeds a configured multiple of HeartBtInt, it should send a TestRequest and start a short response timer.
- **Respond to TestRequests promptly and correctly.** When you receive a TestRequest, you should send a heartbeat as soon as possible and echo whatever identifier was included. This is not optional; it is part of being a good counterparty.
- **Separate suspicion from certainty.** Do not drop the session the moment a single heartbeat is late. Use explicit TestRequests as an intermediate step between "all is well" and "disconnect now".
- **Tie liveness to trading decisions.** Make it clear in your trading system what conditions must hold to consider a session "healthy enough to trade". For example, you may require that no TestRequests are outstanding and the last message was received less than one heartbeat interval ago.
- **Log everything clearly.** Every TestRequest sent, every missed response, and every disconnect triggered by liveness failures should produce concise, human-readable log entries. This is invaluable for post-incident analysis and for demonstrating to regulators that your connectivity controls are robust.

Liveness in the Context of Drop Copy and Multiple Sessions

Many modern architectures use multiple FIX sessions for different purposes: one for order entry, one for drop copy, perhaps another for post-trade allocations. Liveness monitoring must be considered in this broader context.

Some considerations:

- **Independent health.** Each session has its own heartbeat interval, TestRequest logic, and sequence numbers. A healthy order-entry session does not guarantee that a parallel drop copy session is also healthy.

- **Cross-checking flows.** In some designs, the absence of expected drop copy messages, combined with silence on the session, may be interpreted as a more serious problem than silence alone. Your monitoring can cross-check: "We just sent a burst of orders but have seen no drop copy traffic for a while; is the drop copy session alive?"

- **Failover behavior.** It may be appropriate to fail over order flow when the order-entry session is unhealthy, even if the drop copy session is still technically up. Defining these rules explicitly avoids surprises during outages.

Treat each session's liveness as a separate signal, but interpret them together when deciding whether your overall connectivity to a venue is trustworthy enough to keep trading.

From Mechanics to Policy

At a mechanical level, heartbeats and TestRequests are simple: send periodic keepalives when idle, probe when silent too long, and disconnect after unanswered probes. The real nuance lies in the *policy* you build around these mechanics:

- What heartbeat interval do you choose at Logon, given your latency requirements and network quality?

- How many heartbeat intervals of silence do you tolerate before sending a TestRequest?

- How many unanswered TestRequests do you allow before disconnecting?

- When you disconnect, what do your trading systems do: fail over automatically, go into a safe mode, or pause all activity pending human review?

These are business-risk decisions as much as technical ones. As you design and tune them, always keep in mind the core goal: to avoid both "zombie" sessions that are silently dead and hyper-sensitive sessions that cry wolf at the slightest hiccup.

In the next section we will connect this liveness layer to the backbone of FIX reliability: sequence numbers. There we will see how every heartbeat, TestRequest, and recovery message contributes to a single ordered history that both sides can rely on for audits, reconciliations, and real-time risk control.

3.3 Persistent Sequence Number Management

In the previous sections we established how a FIX session is born (Logon), how its timing parameters are negotiated (HeartBtInt, reset or continue), and how the two peers prove to each other that they are still alive (heartbeats and TestRequests). We now turn to something more subtle but absolutely central to FIX reliability: sequence numbers.

Every FIX message carries a *message sequence number*, commonly referred to as MsgSeqNum. At first glance this may look like just another integer field, but in reality it is the backbone of the protocol's reliability model. If heartbeats are the session's pulse, sequence numbers are its memory. They provide a strict ordering of all events, allow both sides to spot missing or out-of-order messages, and make recovery possible after disconnections or failures.

This section explains how FIX engines track, persist, and advance MsgSeqNum so that both sides share a consistent view of message order and history. We will build from simple mental models to more realistic operational patterns.

Two Counters Per Side: Sender and Target

A common source of confusion for beginners is that each side of a FIX session maintains *two* sequence counters at any given time:

- A **Sender** sequence number: the next MsgSeqNum that this side will use when it sends a new message.
- A **Target** sequence number: the next MsgSeqNum that this side *expects* to receive from its counterparty.

To keep the language concrete, imagine a buy-side client (initiator) connected to a broker (acceptor):

- On the client:
  - The client's *Sender* counter increases as it sends orders, cancels, and heartbeats.
  - Its *Target* counter increases as it receives execution reports, broker heartbeats, and administrative messages.
- On the broker:
  - The broker's *Sender* counter increases when it sends execution reports, acknowledgments, and heartbeats back to the client.
  - Its *Target* counter tracks the messages coming in from the client.

The symmetry is important. What one side calls its *Sender* sequence is, from the other side's viewpoint, its *Target* sequence. In a healthy session:

- Every outgoing message uses a MsgSeqNum equal to the sender's current Sender counter.
- Each successful receive increments the receiver's Target counter by one, assuming there are no gaps.

Conceptually, the counters move in lockstep as messages flow: senders increment forward, receivers advance their expectations.

Monotonic Advancement: One Step at a Time

A core design principle in FIX is that sequence numbers are *monotonic and gap-free* within a given direction of a session, unless gaps are explicitly managed via recovery mechanisms.

At a basic level:

- When your engine sends any message on a session, it must:
  - Attach the current Sender sequence number as the MsgSeqNum.
  - Then advance the Sender counter by one for the next send.
- When your engine receives a message:
  - It compares the message's MsgSeqNum with its expected Target counter.
  - If they match, it processes the message and increments its Target counter by one.
  - If not, it treats this as either a gap, a duplicate, or an out-of-order arrival and invokes special handling.

This rule is deliberately simple: always move forward by exactly one for every successfully sent or received message (ignoring special administrative resets, which we will discuss later in the chapter). The power comes from the fact that both peers are independently applying the same rule. That is how they can both infer the state of the conversation from the numbers alone.

Sequence Numbers and Session Identity

Sequence numbers are not global; they are *per session*. A session is defined by the identity pair we discussed earlier: SenderCompID, TargetCompID, plus any session qualifier in use.

From your engine's perspective, this means:

- It must maintain separate Sender and Target counters for each distinct FIX session.

- When a Logon is received, the engine uses the identity pair to look up the correct sequence state.
- When a Logout occurs or a sequence reset is agreed, the engine may choose to archive and possibly reset that state, but only for that particular session.

This isolation is crucial. You do not want a problem on one client's session to spill over into another client's sequence state, nor do you want test-environment sequences to contaminate production.

Persistence: Making Sequence State Durable

So far we have talked as if the engine is running forever. In reality, processes crash, servers reboot, and software is upgraded. When that happens, sequence state cannot simply vanish; otherwise, the next time you connect your peer would have no consistent history to compare against.

This is where *persistence* comes in. Persistence is the practice of writing the in-memory Sender and Target counters to some durable store, such as a file or database, so that they can be restored after a restart.

At a minimum, a robust FIX engine should:

- Persist the current Sender and Target sequence numbers whenever:
  - It sends a message (after incrementing the Sender counter), or
  - It successfully processes an incoming message (after incrementing the Target counter),

  or at least at regular checkpoints in a way that guarantees no ambiguity after a crash.
- On startup, load the last persisted numbers for each session and resume from there, unless a reset Logon is explicitly requested and agreed.

Persistence ensures that temporary outages do not cause the two sides to lose their shared notion of history. Without it, an engine might restart with counters back at 1 when its peer is expecting, say, 10,001, causing chaos and forcing emergency resets.

The Dual State: In-Memory vs. Persisted

It is helpful to imagine two layers of sequence state:

- **In-memory state:** The counters that the engine is actively using in the current process.
- **Persisted state:** The last known-good snapshot written to durable storage.

Most of the time, these two layers move together. However, around process crashes and restarts there is a risk of them diverging. The classic problem is the *off-by-one* error:

1. The engine sends a message using Sender sequence N and increments its in-memory counter to $N + 1$.
2. The message is successfully written to the TCP socket and leaves the machine.
3. Before the engine persists the fact that it has advanced to $N + 1$, the process crashes.
4. On restart, the engine loads the last persisted Sender state, which still says N.
5. It sends its next message with sequence N again, creating an unintentional duplicate from the peer's point of view.

The reverse scenario—persisting $N + 1$ but crashing before actually sending the message—creates an apparent *gap* in the history. The broker sees that your next message jumps from N to $N + 2$ and assumes $N + 1$ is missing, prompting unnecessary recovery.

Avoiding these race conditions is one of the central design challenges in sequence number management.

Visual Model: How Sequence Numbers Evolve

Before we dive into persistence strategies for avoiding off-by-one errors, it is useful to have a visual mental model of how Sender and Target counters evolve as the session runs.

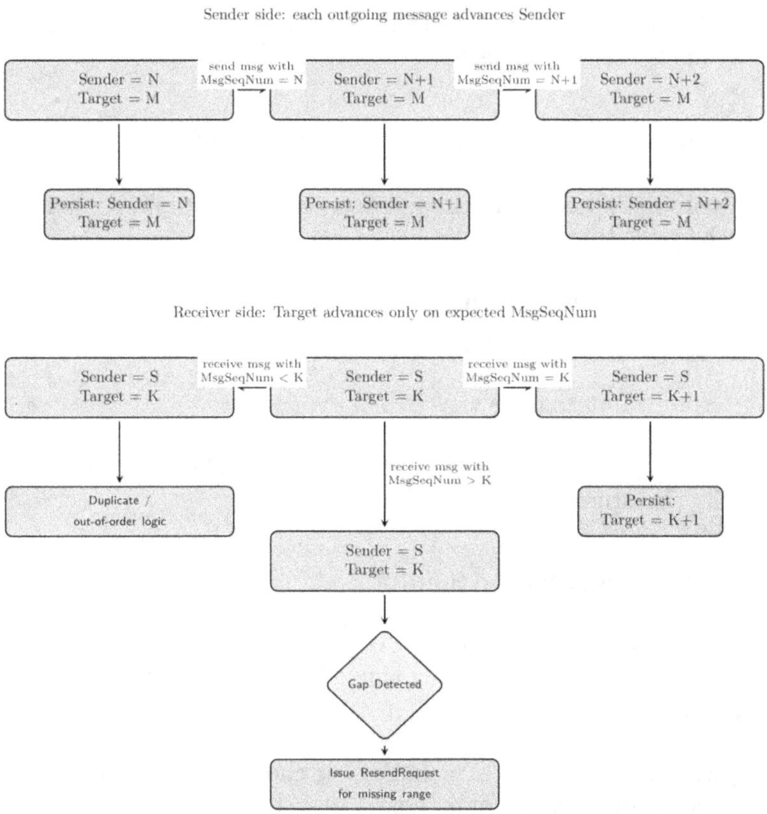

This diagram captures three fundamental ideas:

- Normal sending: Sender advances from N to $N+1$ to $N+2$ with each message, with persistence checkpoints keeping the durable state in step.

- Normal receiving: Target advances from K to $K + 1$ when the expected sequence arrives, again with persistence checkpoints.
- Exceptional branches: when the receiver sees a future sequence (gap) or a past sequence (duplicate or out-of-order), it diverges into special handling paths without advancing Target.

With this mental picture in place, we can now discuss how to persist these states in a robust way.

Persistence Strategies and Trade-Offs

The main design challenge in persistence is to maintain a consistent story between three actors:

1. Your in-memory counters.
2. Your durable store.
3. Your counterparty's view of history.

We will not prescribe specific implementation techniques, but we can identify robustness patterns.

Atomic Update Around Send

One safe pattern is to treat the act of sending a message and updating the persistent Sender state as a single logical unit. In practice, this might mean:

- Writing the message (including the chosen MsgSeqNum) to a local log or journal that is fsynced to disk.
- Only after the journal write is secure, handing the message off to the network layer for transmission and updating the in-memory Sender counter.
- Ensuring that, upon recovery, the engine can reconstruct the last used MsgSeqNum by reading the journal, even if the process died immediately after sending.

This approach minimizes both duplicates and phantom gaps, because the persisted state always reflects what was actually sent, not just what the in-memory counters believed they were about to send.

Checkpointing With Idempotent Recovery

In some systems, persisting on every single message may be too expensive. An alternative is to persist sequence state at regular checkpoints (for example, every N_{iter} messages), but this increases the window in which a crash can cause ambiguity.

To make this workable, the rest of the system must be designed to tolerate possible duplicates and gaps without business harm. This is where idempotent application-level logic becomes important (we address this more deeply in the duplicate-handling section). The sequence store might be slightly behind reality, but if re-sent messages are safely ignored at the business layer, the system can still behave correctly.

The trade-off is clear:

- Frequent persistence: more I/O overhead, less ambiguity after a crash.
- Infrequent persistence: less overhead, more ambiguity, requiring stronger duplicate-handling at higher layers.

Per-Session vs. Shared Stores

Another design choice concerns how you organize persistent storage:

- **Per-session stores:** each FIX session has its own separate file or database record holding its Sender and Target state.
- **Shared store:** all sessions share a central store, perhaps keyed by identity pair and qualifier.

Per-session stores make it easier to inspect and manipulate the state of a single session without worrying about others. Shared stores can simplify backup and allow bulk operations, but require careful indexing and consistency across sessions.

Operational teams often prefer per-session visibility: when debugging a single client or venue, they can look at that session's specific sequence numbers and history in isolation.

Handling Out-of-Order, Missing, and Future Messages

With persistence in place, we can return to the runtime behavior illustrated in the diagram and unpack what happens when messages arrive in unexpected ways. Even though detailed recovery flows are covered in the next section, you need a solid intuition here to appreciate why sequence numbers are tracked so carefully.

Missing Messages (Future MsgSeqNum)

If your engine expects Target = K but receives a message with MsgSeqNum = $K + 10$, it infers:

- Messages K through $K + 9$ are missing (from your perspective).
- Either they were never sent, got lost in transit, or arrived but were processed incorrectly.

Your engine must not simply advance Target to $K + 11$ and carry on; that would paper over real data loss. Instead, it:

- Leaves Target at K (the next expected sequence).
- Triggers a gap recovery procedure (typically by issuing a ResendRequest for that numeric range).
- May temporarily buffer or reject the future message, depending on configuration.

The precise mechanics of ResendRequest and SequenceReset are covered in the next section, but the key concept here is that the Target counter is the engine's assertion about what history it believes it has fully processed. It does not move forward until that assertion is actually true.

Duplicates or Out-of-Order (Past MsgSeqNum)

Conversely, suppose your engine expects Target = K but receives a message with MsgSeqNum = $K - 1$. This can happen during recovery flows where old messages are resent, or due to network reordering.

In this case:

- The message's sequence is older than what you consider fully processed.
- You must *not* decrement Target; that would break the monotonically-increasing invariant.

Instead, your engine applies duplicate/out-of-order logic:

- It rescans logs or internal state to see whether that sequence number has been seen before.
- It may treat the message as a harmless duplicate (for example, a resent execution report) and either discard it or process it idempotently.
- It keeps Target unchanged at K.

Again, the key is that the Target counter represents a firm boundary: everything below it has already been accounted for; everything at or above it is still under consideration.

Operational Tooling: Inspecting and Adjusting State Safely

In real trading operations, there are times when humans must look at or even manually adjust sequence state. For example:

- A client's session gets into a persistent gap-recovery loop due to a misconfigured reset.
- An exchange instructs you to advance a session's sequence to a new baseline after a major outage.

To do this safely, you need tooling and processes that respect the invariants we have discussed.

Good operational tools provide:

- A read-only view of current Sender and Target counters for each session.
- A history of changes to these counters, including when resets were performed and by whom.
- A controlled mechanism to adjust counters, typically:
  - Only when the session is disconnected.
  - Only to values agreed with the counterparty.
  - With mandatory operator comments that explain the reason for the change.

Blindly editing sequence numbers while a session is active is almost guaranteed to cause confusion and possible data loss. All manual interventions should be coordinated with the other side and followed by a clearly signaled Logon (often with ResetSeqNumFlag = Y) so that both peers converge on the same new story.

Sequence Numbers as the Authoritative Ledger

By now you should see that MsgSeqNum is far more than a counter tacked onto messages for convenience. Within a FIX session, it effectively plays the role of an authoritative ledger of communication:

- It gives each side a compact representation of everything that has been said and heard.
- It allows both sides to spot discrepancies and recover missing pieces.
- It guides persistence strategies and supports post-mortem reconstruction of events.

When disputes arise—for example, about whether an order was truly sent or a cancel request was received in time—the session's sequence history becomes crucial evidence. Carefully managed counters and logs allow firms to replay what happened, message by message, in order.

In the next section, we build directly on this foundation. Once you understand how sequence numbers are tracked and persisted, you are ready to see how FIX uses them for active gap recovery via ResendRequest and SequenceReset, and how those mechanisms interact with the business reality of orders, cancels, and fills.

3.4 Gap Recovery with ResendRequest & SequenceReset

In the previous section we treated MsgSeqNum as the backbone of FIX reliability and saw how each peer maintains two monotonic counters: one for what it sends and one for what it expects to receive. That framework works perfectly as long as messages arrive in strict order with no losses. Real networks, however, are not that kind. Packets get dropped, routes flap, engines restart halfway through a burst of traffic, and messages can arrive late or in a different order than they were sent.

FIX anticipates this messy reality. Rather than pretending the network is perfect, it provides explicit *gap recovery* mechanisms so that both sides can repair their session history and re-align their sequence numbers. The two main tools for this are:

- **ResendRequest**: a ranged request for missing messages.
- **SequenceReset**: an administrative message that can either declare that a range of messages will never be resent (gap fill) or jump the sequence number to a new value in exceptional cases.

In this section we will see how these tools work together to heal gaps, when you should resend business messages versus sending gap fills, and why pacing and careful design are vital to avoid overwhelming the session during recovery.

Detecting a Gap: When Future Numbers Arrive

Recall that each side maintains a Target counter: the next MsgSeqNum it expects to receive. Suppose your Target is currently 101, meaning you believe you have processed all messages up to 100. Now you receive a message with:

- MsgSeqNum = 120

Immediately you know something is wrong: messages 101–119 have not been seen. You have detected a *gap*. At this moment, several things must happen on your side:

1. **Do not** advance your Target counter beyond 101. It still represents the highest fully-processed sequence.
2. Flag the session as being in gap recovery.
3. Trigger the sending of a ResendRequest message, asking the peer to resend the missing range.
4. Decide how to treat the future message (120) in the meantime: buffer it, reject it, or temporarily park it until the gap is healed.

The main idea is simple: as soon as you see a future MsgSeqNum, you ask for what you missed and refuse to pretend the gap does not exist.

ResendRequest: Asking for a Numbered Range

ResendRequest is the engine's way of saying: "From my point of view, we are missing message numbers in this numeric range. Please resend anything you still have for that span, in sequence."

A ResendRequest includes two key numeric fields:

- **BeginSeqNo**: the first sequence number you are missing (or want replayed).
- **EndSeqNo**: the last sequence number you are asking for, or a special value meaning "up to the latest you have".

Returning to the example above, where you expect 101 but see 120, you would typically send:

- BeginSeqNo = 101
- EndSeqNo = 119

This tells the counterparty: "I am missing everything from 101 through 119. Please help me fill in that hole."

Several design points are worth emphasizing:

- **The range is about numbers, not times.** You are not asking for "messages sent in the last 5 minutes", but for literal sequence numbers.
- **The request is directional.** You can only ask for replays of messages the other side previously sent (your Target side).
- **The range can be large.** In big outages, the missing span may cover thousands or millions of messages; this is where pacing and gap-fill strategies become critical.

What the Sender Does When It Receives a ResendRequest

On the other side of the session, the engine receiving a ResendRequest has to inspect its own history and act on the numeric range. Conceptually, it asks:

> For every sequence number in this range, do I still have the original message, and should I resend it, or should I send an administrative "gap" instead?

There are three broad categories of messages to consider:

1. **Application messages that are still valid to replay.** For example, an earlier ExecutionReport or OrderCancelReject that is still meaningful and safe to re-send.

2. **Application messages that would be dangerous or pointless to replay.** For example, old new-order messages that were fully superseded, or time-sensitive instructions that would confuse downstream systems if replayed.
3. **Administrative messages** such as heartbeats or earlier ResendRequests, which often do not add much value on replay.

For each sequence in the requested range, the sender must choose between:

- *Business resend*: actually resend an application message.
- *Gap fill*: send a SequenceReset with "gap fill" semantics to jump over a block of numbers without resending business payloads.

This is where the SequenceReset message enters the picture.

SequenceReset (Gap Fill): Declaring What You Will Not Replay

The SequenceReset message can be used in two different ways in FIX, but in the context of recovery we are most interested in the *gap fill* variant:

- With the GapFill flag set, a SequenceReset effectively says: "For the next span of sequence numbers, please do not expect any business messages; treat them as logically skipped. The next message you see from me will have sequence number X."

From a receiver's perspective, a gap-fill SequenceReset tells you that:

- Certain missing sequence numbers will never be replayed as application messages.
- You can safely advance your Target counter over that skipped range.

This mechanism is powerful and potentially dangerous. Used well, it prevents unnecessary replay of outdated or irrelevant business messages. Used poorly, it can hide real data loss.

Putting It Together: A Typical Recovery Flow

To see how ResendRequest and SequenceReset collaborate, let us walk through a full example.

Step 1: Gap Detection and Request

1. You (the client) expect Target = 101.
2. You receive an ExecutionReport with MsgSeqNum = 120.
3. You flag a gap [101–119] and send a ResendRequest for that range.

Step 2: The Sender Prepares a Response

The broker's engine inspects the requested range 101–119 in its own sent-message store and finds:

- 101–104: execution reports and cancel rejects that are still relevant. These will be re-sent as-is.
- 105–115: a long series of heartbeats and administrative messages that add no value to replay.
- 116–118: a sequence of order acknowledgments that are still semantically valid.
- 119: an expired order-cancel request that has no present meaning.

The broker decides:

- To resend 101–104 and 116–118 as business messages.
- To gap-fill 105–115 and 119.

Step 3: Resends and Gap Fills on the Wire

The broker now sends a sequence of messages back to you, in ascending MsgSeqNum order. The flow might look like:

- Resent messages:
- ExecutionReport #101 (replayed)
- ExecutionReport #102 (replayed)
- OrderCancelReject #103 (replayed)
- ExecutionReport #104 (replayed)
- A gap-fill SequenceReset covering 105–115.
- Resent messages:
- ExecutionReport #116 (replayed)
- ExecutionReport #117 (replayed)
- ExecutionReport #118 (replayed)
- Another gap-fill SequenceReset covering 119.

Every one of these resends and gap fills carries its original or appropriate MsgSeqNum so that your Target counter can advance correctly.

On your side, as you receive them:

1. You process each resent application message, usually in an idempotent way so that you do not double-book orders or executions.
2. For each gap-fill SequenceReset, you advance Target without expecting application messages for the skipped range.
3. When you have processed everything up through 119, your Target is now 120, and you can finally process the original 120 message that triggered the gap detection.

At that point, both sides are back in sync: their view of the sequence ledger matches again.

Full Flow Diagram: Detect, Request, Resend, Fill, Re-Synchronize

To consolidate this understanding, the following diagram shows the full gap-recovery sequence between an Initiator (client) and an Acceptor (broker or venue). Numeric labels on the arrows indicate MsgSeqNum values; different line styles conceptually distinguish normal application messages, ResendRequests, and SequenceReset gap fills.

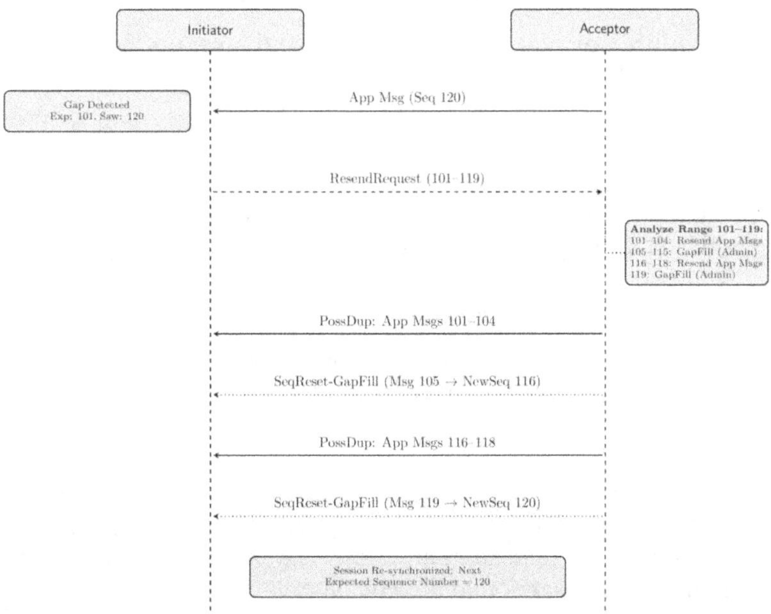

This diagram shows how one out-of-order message (120 arriving early) triggers a cascade of targeted recovery activity, after which both sides converge again on the same Target and Sender sequence numbers.

Business Resends vs. Gap Fills: What Should Be Replayed?

The heart of any robust recovery design is the policy on *what* to replay when a ResendRequest arrives. As a sending engine, you have competing goals:

- **Accuracy and completeness:** The receiver should end up with a coherent, consistent view of all business-relevant events that actually took place.
- **Safety:** Replaying old messages must not cause double-booked trades, duplicate cancels, or invalid state transitions.
- **Scalability:** Recovery must be fast and must not flood the link or destabilize the session during busy periods.

A common pattern is:

- Replay application messages that directly describe trade and order state (ExecutionReport, OrderCancelReject, important administrative confirmations) because they help the receiver reconstruct the reality of the order book and their positions.
- Use gap-fill SequenceResets for purely administrative messages (heartbeats, Logons, Logouts) and for outdated application messages that no longer reflect any live business state.

For example, if an old new-order message led to several subsequent fills and then a cancel, replaying the original new-order might mislead a naive consumer. Instead, it is safer to rely on the execution reports and final state messages that directly describe the order's lifecycle. In practice, firms often define clear rules for which message types are eligible for business resend and which must always be gap-filled.

Pacing Limits: Avoiding a Replay Storm

During a severe disruption, a ResendRequest range can be huge. Consider an active market where thousands of messages per second are flowing, and a drop copy session has been disconnected for several minutes. A naive resend strategy that tries to blast all missing messages across the wire as fast as possible can:

- Saturate the network and cause further packet loss.
- Overload both FIX engines with parsing and disk I/O.
- Starve real-time business traffic, making the live situation even worse.

To prevent this, sensible FIX engines implement resend *pacing*:

- They limit the number of resent messages sent per second or per batch.
- They interleave resends with current live traffic, ensuring that new orders and time-critical messages are not blocked behind a wall of historical replays.
- They may break large requested ranges into smaller chunks and handle them step by step.

On the requesting side, it is also wise not to ask for unnecessarily broad ranges. For instance, if you know from Logon or logs where you last left off, you can narrow your ResendRequest to the minimum span that covers truly missing messages, rather than blindly asking for everything from sequence 1.

Avoiding Deadlocks: Overlapping ResendRequests

Another practical challenge in gap recovery is avoiding "recovery deadlocks" when both peers notice gaps and send ResendRequests to each other at the same time.

Imagine:

- Side A detects a gap in messages from B and sends a ResendRequest.

- Almost simultaneously, Side B detects a gap in messages from A and sends its own ResendRequest.

If both sides then wait for the other to finish resending before they send anything else, the session may stall. To avoid this, well-designed engines adopt rules such as:

- Always be prepared to *both* respond to a peer's ResendRequest and continue sending resends for your own outstanding requests.
- Avoid circular dependencies like "I will not answer your ResendRequest until you answer mine."
- Use clear internal state machines and timeouts so that recovery progresses even when the other side is also in recovery mode.

In practice, recovery is often incremental and interleaved: each side sends some resends or gap fills, processes what it receives, and continues to adjust its own Target and Sender sequences until both directions are clean.

SequenceReset Without Gap Fill: Jumps for Exceptional Situations

So far we have described SequenceReset in its gap-fill mode. There is another, less common usage: *resetting* the sequence number without filling a specific gap, effectively jumping both peers to a new baseline.

This kind of reset is typically reserved for exceptional scenarios, such as:

- After a major system upgrade or disaster recovery event where the previous sequence history is no longer trustworthy.
- Under explicit agreement with the counterparty, often out of band, with meticulous documentation.

Unlike gap-fill SequenceResets, which are part of normal, day-to-day reliability operations, hard resets are blunt instruments. They make the ledger "start over" and can conceal unresolved message loss if used casually. That is why many venues restrict their use and prefer resets to be performed at session boundaries via Logon with ResetSeqNumFlag = Y, discussed earlier in the chapter.

The key lesson is that SequenceReset is powerful enough to realign sequence numbers but should never be used as a quick fix to mask unexplained gaps. If you do not understand why a gap occurred, blowing it away with a reset may keep your engines running but will likely cause trouble for risk, compliance, and clients later.

Designing Robust Recovery Policies

To make gap recovery reliable in practice, you should treat it as a first-class part of your FIX session design, not an obscure edge case. Good policies answer questions like:

- Under what conditions do we automatically send ResendRequests, and for what ranges?
- Which message types are safe to replay as business messages, and which must be gap-filled?
- What pacing limits do we enforce on resends so that live traffic is not starved?
- How do we handle overlapping ResendRequests from both sides without stalling the session?
- When, if ever, are we willing to use hard SequenceResets to jump sequence numbers, and what approvals are required?

These policies should be documented in your FIX rules of engagement with each counterparty and backed by monitoring that makes recovery behavior visible. For example:

- Dashboards showing the volume and ranges of ResendRequests.
- Alerts when unusually large or frequent gap recoveries occur.
- Logging that clearly distinguishes between normal business traffic, resends, and gap fills.

From Session Repair to Business Integrity

Gap recovery is not just about making numbers line up in logs. It directly affects how confident you can be in your business view of the world:

- If you mis-handle gaps, you may miss fills, overstate working orders, or fail to see cancel rejects.
- If you over-replay business messages without idempotent handling, you may double-count trades or erroneously adjust positions.

In later sections we will look at how the session's at-least-once delivery semantics interact with business-level idempotency to achieve effectively "exactly-once" outcomes. For now, keep in mind that ResendRequest and SequenceReset are not just administrative niceties. They are the mechanisms that let FIX confront an imperfect network and still produce a coherent, auditable record of everything that happened on your orders and trades.

3.5 Duplicate Detection and Idempotent Processing

In the previous sections we built up the mechanics of a reliable FIX session: how a session is established, how liveness is monitored, how sequence numbers are tracked, and how gaps are repaired with ResendRequest and SequenceReset. All of those features share a common side effect: they increase the chance that the same business event will be delivered more than once.

Whenever you replay history to fill gaps, or resend messages that might have been lost, you are deliberately choosing *at-least-once delivery* at the session layer. This is the right choice for safety: better to see an execution report twice than to miss it completely. But it shifts responsibility to the application to ensure that extra deliveries do not cause extra trades.

In this section we explain how FIX helps you *identify* possible duplicates and how well-designed trading systems process them *idempotently*—that is, in a way that does not change the final business state if the same event is applied once or multiple times.

Why Duplicates Are Inevitable in Gap Recovery

Let us start with a simple scenario. Your client OMS detects a gap in incoming messages from a broker and sends a ResendRequest for sequences 101–110. The broker, acting cautiously, replies with:

- Fresh copies of several ExecutionReport messages for fills 101–108.
- Gap fills for 109–110.

But what if the original messages 105–108 had in fact arrived the first time, just very late or slightly out of order, and your engine had already processed them? Now you will see the same fills again as part of the resend.

From the broker's point of view, this is acceptable: it is safer to replay than to risk missing something. From your point of view, it is dangerous unless your application can recognize that these resends refer to trades you have already booked and therefore should not be booked again.

This basic pattern repeats in many variations:

- A resend overlaps with the tail of what you have already processed.
- A network issue causes the same message to be delivered twice at the TCP level.
- A partial replay is interrupted and then restarted, creating multiple copies of the same resend.

You cannot avoid these situations entirely. Instead, you must make sure your systems remain economically correct even when duplicates occur.

FIX-Level Signals for Possible Duplicates

To help distinguish original messages from resends, FIX defines several key fields:

- **PossDupFlag** – indicates that the message *might* be a duplicate of one previously sent.
- **PossResend** – a similar flag used particularly in order-entry contexts.
- **OrigSendingTime** – captures when the message was originally sent, before any retransmission.

These fields work together as follows.

PossDupFlag: "Treat Me With Suspicion"

When a sender retransmits a previously sent message—for example, as part of fulfilling a ResendRequest—it is required to set the PossDupFlag to indicate that this is *not* a newly generated event. Instead, it is potentially a duplicate of something you may already have seen.

From the receiver's perspective, the presence of PossDupFlag has two important implications:

- The message must be processed with extra care. You should not blindly apply it as if it were new business.
- The sequence number alone is not enough to determine whether it is new or old; you may have already advanced past that sequence during earlier processing or gap fills.

A robust engine will treat PossDupFlag as a cue to consult local history: "Have I already processed a message with this sequence number or these business identifiers?"

PossResend: "This Instruction May Have Been Sent Before"

PossResend is often used on the order-entry side when a client is unsure whether an earlier message got through and decides to send the same instruction again. For example, if an OMS times out waiting for an acknowledgment, it might resend a NewOrderSingle with PossResend set.

The semantics are similar: the broker is being told, "This order may be one you have already received; please check your records before treating it as a new child order." The broker will typically look at the combination of ClOrdID, account, and instrument to determine whether the order is indeed a repeat of something in its book.

OrigSendingTime: Distinguishing Old From New

When PossDupFlag is set, FIX also expects the sender to include OrigSendingTime: the timestamp from the first time the message was sent. This allows the receiver to distinguish between:

- A message that is truly arriving late for the first time (no PossDupFlag; sending time close to now).
- A replay of an old message (with PossDupFlag and an earlier original timestamp).

This matters operationally. For example, if you receive a cancel request with a very old OrigSendingTime, your application logic might need to decide whether the cancel is still meaningful or whether the related order is already fully filled or expired.

Why Sequence Numbers Alone Are Not Enough

Given that FIX enforces an ordered sequence of messages, you might ask: why not simply trust MsgSeqNum for duplicate detection? If I see a message with a sequence number less than my current Target, I know it is old; why can I not just ignore it?

There are several reasons this is not sufficient:

- **Gap fills can advance Target without business payloads.** When you receive a gap-fill SequenceReset, your Target jumps over a range of sequence numbers that you never saw as actual business messages. Later, a resend in that range may bring you valid business that you must process, even though its sequence is less than your current Target.
- **Some resends are the only copy you will ever see.** If the original transmission was lost on the wire, the resend (with PossDupFlag) is logically the first time you see that business event, even though its sequence number is older.
- **Application-level state is indexed differently.** Your OMS or risk system typically indexes orders and trades by business identifiers such as ClOrdID, OrderID, and ExecID, not by sequence numbers.

In other words, MsgSeqNum and PossDupFlag tell you about the *transport history* of a message, but they do not uniquely identify the business object it refers to. To handle duplicates correctly, you must bridge from session-level identifiers to business-level identifiers.

Business Identifiers as Stable Keys

The core idea of idempotent processing is that you key your application state off identifiers that are:

- Stable across resends and replays.
- Naturally tied to the economic object of interest (an order, a trade, a fill).

In FIX, the most important such identifiers include:

- **ClOrdID** – the client's unique identifier for an order or cancel request.
- **OrderID** – the server's unique identifier for the order in its own system.

- **ExecID** – the broker's unique identifier for an execution or trade.

These fields have the desirable property that:

- A given order (as seen by the client) should have a single ClOrdID across all its related messages.
- Each logical trade or execution should have a single ExecID, even if its associated execution report is replayed many times.

Thus, if your system receives multiple execution reports with the same ExecID, you can infer that they all refer to the same business event and should collectively be treated as one. This is the essence of idempotent processing.

Designing Idempotent Consumers: Conceptual Patterns

An idempotent consumer is one where applying the same event more than once does not change the final outcome. At a high level, such a consumer typically:

1. **Checks** whether it has seen the business identifier before.
2. **If new**, applies the business logic (for example, updating positions, cash, and order state) and records the event as processed.
3. **If seen before**, verifies that the new copy is consistent with the previously seen one, and then either ignores it or uses it to fill in missing details without double-booking.

Let us make this concrete in three common domains: orders, cancels, and fills.

Orders: Avoiding Duplicate Child Orders

Suppose your OMS sends a NewOrderSingle with ClOrdID $=$ X123. Due to a network issue, it is not sure whether the broker received it, so it resends the same order with PossResend $=$ Y.

On the broker side, a robust implementation:

- Looks up whether an existing live or historical order already has ClOrdID = X123, for that client, account, and instrument.
- If none exists, treats this as a new order: creates a fresh order record, assigns an OrderID, and acknowledges it.
- If one exists with the same parameters (side, quantity, symbol, etc.), treats this as a duplicate and refrains from creating a second child order. It may still send an acknowledgment back, confirming the status of the existing order.
- If one exists but with conflicting details, raises an exception or rejects the duplicate, because this situation cannot be safely resolved automatically.

The key is that ClOrdID anchors the decision; MsgSeqNum and PossResend guide the logic but do not determine the business identity by themselves.

Cancels: Late and Duplicate Cancel Requests

Cancel and replace flows introduce similar risks. A late cancel request may be resent several times in an attempt to ensure it is applied. Each cancel request carries its own ClOrdID and refers back to an original order via a field such as OrigClOrdID.

A robust OMS, when receiving a cancel request from an upstream system (or from an internal user interface), should:

- Check whether it has already processed a cancel with this ClOrdID.
- Check the current state of the referenced order (from OrigClOrdID):
- If the order is still working, the cancel is meaningful and should be forwarded to the market.

- If the order is already fully filled or previously canceled, the cancel is economically moot and should either be acknowledged as "too late" or logged as already satisfied.

When the resulting cancel confirmations return as execution reports, they will refer to the same underlying order and may be replayed as part of gap recovery. The consumer should again de-duplicate based on stable order and execution IDs rather than on sequence numbers.

Fills: Exactly-Once Position Updates from At-Least-Once Delivery

Fills are where duplicates hurt the most. If you double-count a trade, you will overstate your positions and P&L. Fortunately, FIX's ExecID is designed exactly to prevent this: each execution report should have a unique ExecID per broker.

An idempotent position-keeping component typically:

- Maintains a table or store of all seen ExecID values, keyed by broker and possibly instrument.

- Each time an execution report arrives:

- If the ExecID is new, it applies the fill to positions and cash, and records the ExecID as processed along with the key economics (quantity, price, side).

- If the ExecID has been seen before, it compares the new report's economics with the stored record. If they match, the message is treated as a harmless duplicate and ignored for position purposes. If they differ, this is a serious inconsistency requiring investigation.

This pattern lets you safely accept resends and replays without creating phantom trades. It is the core of "exactly-once" behavior at the business level, even though the session is delivering data at least once.

De-Duplication Tables and State Tracking

The previous examples hint at a general implementation pattern: *de-duplication tables* keyed by business identifiers. Conceptually, these tables answer yes/no questions:

- Have I already processed an event with this ClOrdID?
- Have I already processed an event with this ExecID?

In practice, a de-duplication design needs to consider:

- **Scope and partitioning.** Keys should usually be scoped by counterparty and possibly by session or market. An ExecID from Broker A has no relation to an ExecID from Broker B.
- **Lifetime of entries.** You do not need to remember every ExecID forever. Once positions and trades are fully settled and reconciled, older IDs can be archived or pruned according to your retention policy.
- **Performance.** De-duplication must be fast; you will be consulting these tables on every inbound execution report and many other message types.
- **Durability.** De-duplication state should be persisted so that replays after a restart do not cause double-booking. Otherwise, you could lose your "memory" of processed executions and apply them again when the venue resends history.

This brings us back to the interplay between session-level persistence (for sequence numbers) and business-level persistence (for IDs and states). Both layers need to survive restarts if you want a consistent, reliable system.

Edge Cases: Late Cancels, Mass Actions, and Drop Copy

Some of the most challenging duplicate-handling scenarios arise in more complex flows.

Late Cancels and "Too Late to Cancel"

A cancel request may be transmitted late and then retried multiple times. On the broker side, this may result in a sequence of execution reports:

- Several partial fills (with distinct ExecIDs).
- A CancelReject indicating the order was already fully filled when the cancel arrived.

During gap recovery, some of these reports may be replayed. An idempotent consumer:

- Recognizes each partial fill by its ExecID and applies it at most once.
- Recognizes the cancel reject (also typically with a stable identifier) and uses it to update order state from "cancel requested" to "filled / too late to cancel", without double-counting any fills.

Mass Cancels and Overlapping Actions

Mass cancel or mass action messages can affect many orders at once. In a stormy market, you might see:

- A client-triggered mass cancel across a portfolio.
- Several individual cancel requests on specific orders.
- Exchange-triggered mass cancels for risk or market-protection reasons.

Some of these actions may overlap, and their acknowledgments may be replayed during recovery. To remain consistent, your system should:

- Represent each order's final state based on the latest applicable event, regardless of how many paths led there.
- Use stable identifiers for mass action messages as well, so that if the same mass-cancel acknowledgment is seen twice, it does not flip the order's state back and forth.

Drop Copy Replays

Drop copy sessions, by design, often replay large swaths of history, either on request (for recovery) or as a daily initialization. This can mean:

- A full day's worth of executions arriving again on a backup drop copy session.
- Incremental replays whenever a gap is detected.

A good architecture treats drop copy as an additional *source of truth*, not a separate trading channel. The de-duplication tables keyed by ExecID and OrderID allow you to merge events from primary and backup sessions without double-booking. When carefully designed, this enables robust failover: you can lose an entire primary feed, resubscribe to a drop copy replay, and reconstitute positions without creating phantom trades.

From Session Semantics to Economic Correctness

Stepping back, it is useful to separate two layers of guarantees:

- The **FIX session layer** ensures ordered, at-least-once delivery of messages, with tools to detect gaps and repair them.
- The **business application layer** is responsible for interpreting those messages in a way that yields the correct economic outcome exactly once.

FIX's duplicate-related fields (PossDupFlag, PossResend, OrigSendingTime) are signposts that tell you, "Be careful; this may be a replay." Sequence numbers give you a ledger of what passed over the wire. But only by combining these with stable business identifiers and idempotent logic do you fully protect yourself from double-booking orders, cancels, and fills.

As you design and review your own systems, ask:

- For every business entity (order, trade, cancel), which identifier is its stable key?
- Do we have a persistent record of which keys we have already processed?
- If the same key appears again, do we know how to safely ignore or reconcile it?
- Are we using FIX's duplicate flags and timestamps to trigger that idempotent logic?

The answers to these questions determine whether your trading infrastructure can turn FIX's raw reliability machinery into something more important: economic correctness, even in the face of network glitches, replays, and the messy realities of production trading.

3.6 Scheduling Windows & Planned Sequence Resets

Up to this point in the chapter we have treated a FIX session as if it were a single, continuous conversation: you Logon, keep the session alive with heartbeats, manage sequence numbers carefully, recover gaps, and detect duplicates. In reality, production trading environments are organized around *time*: exchanges have opening and closing bells, brokers have maintenance windows, and firms schedule batch processes and risk checks. FIX sessions must fit into this temporal structure.

In this section we zoom out from individual messages and even single sessions to the broader *calendar* of connectivity. We will see how firms define trading session windows, how they coordinate planned sequence resets (daily or event-driven), and how they handle scheduling complexities such as holidays and daylight saving time shifts. The goal is to show that reliability is not just about protocol mechanics; it is also about disciplined scheduling and shared expectations.

From "Always-On" Links to Structured Session Windows

Many newcomers imagine that a FIX connection to a broker or exchange is permanently up, 24 hours a day. In practice, most relationships follow a more structured pattern:

- There is a **pre-open** period before the market officially opens, during which you might connect, perform basic checks, and submit certain types of orders.
- There is a **continuous trading** period where the bulk of order flow occurs.
- There is a **post-close** period for late trades, allocations, and post-trade messaging.
- There are **maintenance windows** when connectivity may intentionally be torn down.

A *FIX session window* describes when, within this daily cycle, a given session is expected to be:

- Up and actively trading.
- Up but quiescent (for example, only heartbeats).
- Down for planned reasons (maintenance, resets, holidays).

Both sides should have a shared understanding of these windows, usually documented in a "rules of engagement" document: what times each day the client should connect, when the broker will disconnect idle sessions, and when sequence resets are expected.

Daily Session Rhythms and Sequence Resets

Sequence numbers in FIX are technically unbounded, but in real systems it is common to reset them at logical boundaries, typically once per trading day. There are several reasons for this:

- **Operational clarity.** Having sequence numbers start from 1 (or another agreed baseline) each morning makes logs easier to navigate and align with trading days.
- **Risk containment.** If a day has severe issues, you can archive its entire message history, and the next day starts cleanly, reducing the chance that yesterday's problems bleed into today.
- **Implementation simplicity.** Some legacy systems or log formats handle smaller sequence ranges more easily.

A common daily pattern looks like this:

1. Before the market opens, the client connects and performs Logon.
2. Logon may include ResetSeqNumFlag = Y if a daily sequence reset is part of the agreement.
3. The session stays up throughout the trading day, using normal gap recovery and duplicate handling if needed.
4. After the market closes, one side initiates a clean Logout, including a reason such as "End of day, sequences will reset on next Logon."
5. The session is torn down, logs are rolled, and any end-of-day processing is run.

The key is that the sequence reset is *planned*, not an emergency measure. Both sides know in advance that at the next Logon, they will treat sequence numbers as starting over from 1, and monitoring systems expect this.

Planned Resets vs. Emergency Resets

In earlier sections we saw that SequenceReset messages and Logon with ResetSeqNumFlag = Y can be used to jump sequence numbers in exceptional situations. It is important to distinguish these *emergency* resets from normal, scheduled ones.

- **Planned resets** occur at well-defined times (for example, every trading day at 06:30 UTC) and are pre-announced in documentation. They are usually implemented at the session boundary: you Logout, then Logon with reset.
- **Emergency resets** are ad hoc responses to operational problems (for example, after a severe outage when sequence state is irretrievably confused). They may occur intraday and often require manual coordination and approvals.

Healthy FIX ecosystems minimize emergency resets by:

- Designing robust persistence and gap recovery.
- Allowing daily or periodic planned resets to clear the slate under controlled conditions.

When you do need an emergency reset, treating it as a special event—with change tickets, clear communication, and careful log annotation—prevents it from being mistaken for a normal daily reset.

Coordinating Daily Resets Across Multiple Sessions

Most firms do not have a single FIX session per counterparty; they have many. Examples include:

- Separate sessions for order entry, drop copy, and allocations.
- Separate sessions per asset class, market, or region.
- Redundant sessions for primary and backup connectivity.

This raises an important coordination question: *When and how should all of these sessions reset?* Options include:

- **Synchronized resets.** All related sessions reset at the same planned time, often just before the main trading day begins. This simplifies reasoning about sequence histories: each day corresponds to a neat block of sequences across all channels.

- **Staggered resets.** Some sessions (for example, global drop copy) might remain up across multiple trading days, while others (per-market order entry) reset daily. This can be useful but requires careful documentation so you do not misinterpret a new "day 1" sequence as part of an older day.

From an operational standpoint, the safest approach is usually to:

- Pick a consistent reset schedule per session type.
- Ensure that order-entry and corresponding drop copy sessions have compatible reset plans to avoid confusing recovery logic.
- Document these schedules in a way that operations teams, not just developers, can understand.

Holiday Calendars and Dark Days

Financial markets observe complex holiday calendars. On some days a given venue is completely closed; on others there are early closes or half days. FIX sessions must behave appropriately:

- **Full holidays.** No trading. Sessions may stay down the entire day, or they might be briefly brought up for testing or housekeeping, but no production order flow is expected.
- **Half days.** Trading ends earlier than usual, and sessions may be torn down sooner.
- **Regional holidays.** A global client may be open while a regional market is closed, leading to an asymmetry of expectations.

To avoid surprises, each side should integrate the relevant holiday calendars into their scheduling logic:

- Clients should not keep hammering a session that is down for a published holiday.

- Brokers and venues should not treat holiday-time connection attempts as unauthorized attacks; they should respond with clear log messages or documentation.

Sequence resets around holidays deserve special care. Some firms prefer to treat a long holiday weekend as a single extended "day", resetting only upon the next actual trading day. Others may perform maintenance resets during the holiday. In either case, clear communication is essential so that, when trading resumes, both sides know whether to continue previous sequences or begin fresh ones.

Daylight Saving Time (DST) Shifts: A Subtle Source of Confusion

Daylight saving time transitions are a frequent source of subtle problems in scheduled FIX environments. Consider:

- Twice a year, local clocks jump forward or backward by one hour in many regions.
- Some markets observe DST; others do not, even within the same currency or asset class.
- Different countries may change clocks on different dates.

If your FIX scheduling logic is tied directly to local wall-clock times without a clear reference, you can end up with:

- Sessions coming up or resetting one hour earlier or later than expected relative to the market's open.
- Overlapping or missing time intervals in logs, making it hard to interpret event sequences.

Best practice is to:

- Express session schedules and reset times in a neutral, non-changing timezone, typically UTC.

- Use local time only for human-facing documentation, with explicit mention of how it maps to UTC and how that mapping changes during DST.
- Timestamp FIX messages and logs in UTC (or include both UTC and local time), so that sequence histories remain chronologically consistent even as wall clocks shift.

From a sequence reset perspective, it is often easier to say: "We reset the session at 21:00 UTC each trading day" than to define it as "5 p.m. local time" and then adjust every time the clocks move.

Scheduled Maintenance and Event-Driven Resets

Not all resets are tied to the daily market rhythm. Sometimes you need event-driven resets:

- A broker upgrades its FIX engine and wants all clients to disconnect and reconnect within a maintenance window.
- An exchange performs a weekend cutover and mandates sequence resets on the following Sunday night.

In such cases, the process typically looks like:

1. The venue or broker announces the maintenance window and reset plan in advance, specifying exact dates, times (in UTC), and which sessions are affected.
2. On the day, sessions are either Logged out gracefully before maintenance begins or forcibly disconnected if still active.
3. When maintenance is complete, clients are allowed to Logon again, often with $\text{ResetSeqNumFlag} = \text{Y}$ as pre-agreed.
4. Monitoring systems are primed to expect a wave of fresh sequence-1 Logons and not to treat them as anomalies.

The main challenge is coordination: if some clients reset and others attempt to continue with old sequence numbers, the acceptor will see confusing Logons and may reject connections. This reinforces the importance of robust communication and documentation around planned event-driven resets.

Operational Runbooks: Making Scheduling Visible and Actionable

From the perspective of trading and operations teams, all of the scheduling behavior we have discussed must be more than theory; it must be captured in practical, actionable runbooks. A good runbook for FIX session scheduling and resets includes:

- **Daily timelines** for each major session: expected Logon window, trading hours, typical Logout time, and when sequences reset.
- **Holiday rules**: which markets or sessions are affected by which holidays, and whether sessions will be up for testing or completely down.
- **DST handling**: explicit notes on how scheduled times shift (or do not shift) around clock changes, including example dates.
- **Procedures for missed events**: what to do if a client forgets to Logon before the reset window, or if a scheduled reset is missed and sequences accidentally continue.
- **Escalation paths**: who to contact (at the counterparty and internally) if a scheduling-related issue arises.

Equally important is making sure monitoring and alerting systems know about these schedules. For instance:

- Do not page an on-call engineer at 2 a.m. because a session is down during a known maintenance window.
- Do raise an alert if a session is still up and actively trading after a time when it was supposed to be quiescent and resetting.

Aligning human expectations, monitoring logic, and FIX behavior prevents a large class of false positives and missed issues.

Interpreting "Gaps" at Session Boundaries

One subtle but important benefit of well-defined scheduling and resets is that it helps systems and humans interpret what appears in the logs. Consider:

- A new trading day begins, and you see a Logon with $\text{ResetSeqNumFlag} = \text{Y}$. The first application message has $\text{MsgSeqNum} = 1$.
- If you were not aware of the planned reset, your gap-detection logic might see the jump from yesterday's last sequence (for example, 45,000) to today's 1 as a catastrophic gap.

To avoid this confusion, systems should:

- Treat sequence-reset Logons at the start of planned windows as natural boundaries, not as errors.
- Reset internal historical expectations when a new scheduled session starts, so that sequence numbers are interpreted relative to the current session window.

In runbooks and tools, you can reinforce this by:

- Labeling sessions explicitly with dates (for example, "BrokerX_-EQUITY_2025-11-26") in logs and dashboards.
- Summarizing each day's sequence range and status at the end of the day, so that archival and audit processes have clear day-by-day segments.

Putting It All Together: Reliability as a Scheduling Discipline

Throughout this chapter we have focused on the mechanics of maintaining a healthy FIX session: Logon/Logout, heartbeats and TestRequests, sequence persistence, gap recovery, and duplicate handling. Scheduling windows and planned sequence resets add a final, crucial dimension:

- **Time boxing**: Each session's life is structured into clearly defined windows aligned with the trading day and maintenance needs.
- **Predictability**: Both sides know when to expect Logons, Logouts, and resets, reducing surprise and ambiguity.
- **Clarity at boundaries**: Planned resets, holidays, and DST changes are handled in well-defined ways, preventing spurious gap alarms and misinterpretation of logs.

When FIX scheduling is treated casually, firms often see strange issues: unannounced resets that cause replay storms, markets opening while sessions are still down, or logs that cannot be reconciled across time zones. When scheduling is treated as a disciplined, documented process, many of these issues disappear.

As you design or review your own FIX connectivity, ask not only whether your messages are correctly formatted and your engines are feature-complete, but also:

- Do we have clear, shared schedules for when each session is up, down, and reset?
- Are holidays, DST shifts, and maintenance windows explicitly modeled and communicated?
- Do our monitoring systems and runbooks reflect these schedules, so humans and machines react appropriately?

A positive answer to these questions is a strong indicator that your FIX sessions will be not just technically correct, but *operationally* reliable across the full calendar of real-world trading.

Chapter 4

Order Flow Workflows

Most FIX sessions spew out a blizzard of tags and values-but every trading desk really cares about just one thing: "What's happening to my orders right now?" In this chapter you'll turn individual FIX messages into coherent order journeys, learning how accounts and PartyIDs drive routing, how a NewOrderSingle actually becomes a live order, how to modify and cancel safely under race conditions, how to read the ExecutionReport event stream as an order state machine, and how to pull the emergency brake with mass actions when risk demands it.

4.1 Accounts, Parties, and Routing Context

In the previous chapter we treated FIX messages mostly as abstract envelopes: a header with session information, a body with business fields, and a trailer for integrity. To do real trading, however, the content of the message must mean something concrete inside your firm: whose money is at risk, which strategy or desk is in control, which prime broker is involved, and where the order should actually be routed.

This section connects those dots. We will:

- Distinguish clearly between *clients*, *accounts*, *sub-accounts*, and *intermediaries*.
- Show how FIX represents these concepts using Account, PartyID, PartyIDSource, and PartyRole.
- Explain how this routing context drives downstream decisions: which risk limits to apply, which books and ledgers to update, and where orders are physically sent.
- Propose practical normalization and validation rules so that every subsequent message (NewOrderSingle, cancels, replaces, and mass actions) carries a consistent, unambiguous identity.

Business Entities vs. Routing Entities

Before getting into tags, we need a shared vocabulary. In typical institutional electronic trading flows, you will see at least four distinct types of entities:

- **Client**: The beneficial owner of the assets or the owner of the trading mandate. This could be a pension fund, hedge fund, asset manager, or a retail customer.
- **Account**: The legal and operational container for positions and cash. In practice this is often a brokerage or custody account at a firm or prime broker.
- **Sub-account / Strategy**: A more granular slice inside an account: for example, "Global Equity Long/Short" vs. "Stat Arb" under the same legal fund, or individual managed portfolios under a wrap account.
- **Intermediary**: Any third party involved in the trade flow other than the client and the executing broker: for example, a prime broker, a clearing broker, or an introducing broker.

From a business perspective, you might say:

> Client Alpha Capital, via its Fund A account at PrimeBroker X, is trading in its STAT_ARB sub-account through Broker B as the executing broker.

From a FIX and systems perspective, that sentence must be decomposed into:

- Who is my trading counterparty on this connection?
- On whose behalf is the order ultimately placed?
- Which internal book or strategy should take the risk?
- Which external prime or clearer will receive the allocation?

FIX does not impose a single standard answer. Instead, it gives you a small toolbox of fields that you can combine flexibly. Your job as a designer is to choose a clear scheme and enforce it everywhere.

Core Identification Fields in FIX

The two main building blocks are:

- Account **(tag 1)**: A single string often treated as "the account for this order". Historically this field did a lot of heavy lifting and is still widely used.
- NoPartyIDs / PartyID **repeating group (tags 453, 448, 447, 452)**: A structured way to attach multiple entities to a single message, each with a role and an identifier type.

Conceptually:

- Account is a *primary account identifier* from the point of view of the receiving firm.
- The Party group is a *rich relationship descriptor* saying who is the client, who is the executing broker, who is the clearing agent, and so on.

A typical Party group entry consists of:

- PartyID (448): The actual identifier (for example, ALPHACAP, a BIC, or an internal code).
- PartyIDSource (447): The type of identifier (for example, BIC, proprietary code, LEI).
- PartyRole (452): How this party relates to the transaction (for example, client, executing firm, clearing firm, prime broker).

By combining multiple party entries, you can teach your system exactly which real-world entities are involved in each order.

Relating Client, Account, Sub-Account, and Intermediary

The most common confusion for new practitioners is mixing up account and client. In many environments, the account ID is actually an internal code at the executing broker, not the client's own legal identifier. To make this distinction concrete, it is useful to visualize the relationships before talking about message formats.

Reading this diagram from top to bottom:

- The *client* owns an *account* (for example, a fund or omnibus account).
- The account is divided into one or more *sub-accounts* or strategies that originate orders.
- The account has a relationship with an *intermediary* such as a prime broker or clearer.
- A particular sub-account sends an order to an *executing broker*.
- The *FIX order* carries:

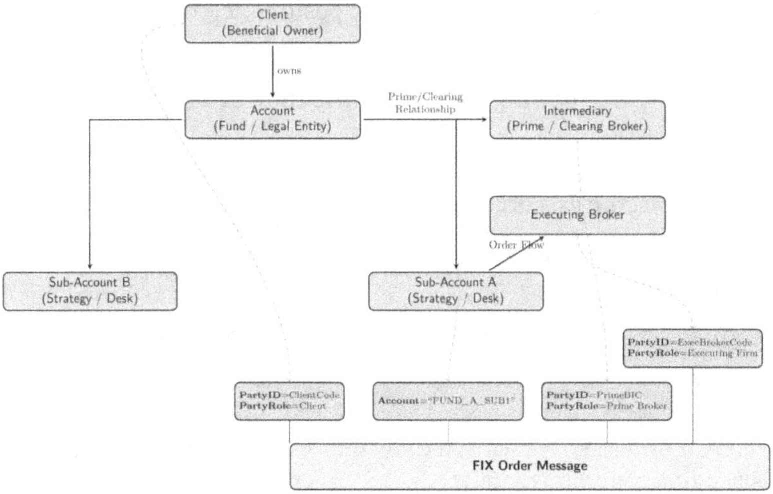

- A primary Account string, often encoding the sub-account or strategy.
- One or more PartyID entries indicating the client, prime broker, and executing firm with appropriate PartyRole values.

This visual structure is what we will now translate into concrete conventions.

Using Account **as the Routing Key**

The simplest and still very common pattern is:

> *Treat* Account *as the primary routing key at the executing broker.*

In this scheme:

- Account is mapped one-to-one to an internal book or sub-book.

- Risk limits (max notional, max position, credit checks) are defined per Account.
- Back-office posting and P&L attribution are performed per Account.

For example, the executing broker might maintain a table:

Account	Internal Book	Description
FUND_A_STAT	BK_1001	Alpha Capital Fund A Stat Arb
FUND_A_LNG	BK_1002	Alpha Capital Fund A Long Only
FUND_B_MAIN	BK_1010	Alpha Capital Fund B Master

When an order arrives with Account = FUND_A_STAT, the OMS or risk engine can immediately:

- Associate it to BK_1001.
- Apply the corresponding risk profile.
- Place fills, commissions, and fees into the correct ledger.

The advantage is simplicity and performance: a single lookup gives you everything you need for routing and risk. The disadvantage is that one field must carry many meanings: sometimes "trader", sometimes "fund", sometimes "strategy". Over time this leads to overloaded and inconsistent use.

Layering PartyID for Richer Semantics

To relieve Account from carrying everything, the modern pattern is:

> *Use* Account *for the primary risk and booking container, and use Party groups to describe the surrounding relationships.*

Concretely, a buy-side order to a broker might specify:

- Account = FUND_A_STAT (sub-account / strategy).
- Party #1: PartyID = ALPHACAP, PartyIDSource = proprietary, PartyRole = Client.
- Party #2: PartyID = PBICUS33, PartyIDSource = BIC, PartyRole = Prime Broker.
- Party #3: PartyID = BROKERB, PartyIDSource = proprietary, PartyRole = Executing Firm.

Inside the broker:

- Account still drives internal routing and risk.
- The Client party links the order to onboarding and KYC data.
- The Prime Broker party drives give-up instructions, margin treatment, and reporting.
- The Executing Firm party is sometimes implicit (the broker itself) but becomes more important in pass-through or routing scenarios.

By explicitly encoding all parties, you make it possible to:

- Share a single execution pipe with multiple funds or managed accounts, yet apply separate risk and reporting.
- Build rich downstream analytics (flows by client, by prime, by introducing broker) without guessing from the account code.
- Route orders to different venues or clearing arrangements based on combinations of roles (for example, specific primes vs. self-clearing).

Prime Brokerage and Give-Up Relationships

Prime brokerage and give-up arrangements introduce an intermediary between the client and the final clearer. From the execution venue's perspective, the important questions are:

- Should this trade clear at the executing broker's house, or be given up to a prime?
- If given up, to which firm and under which account?

A common FIX pattern for a prime give-up is:

- Account: Holds the prime account or sub-account code known to the prime broker.
- Client party: Identifies the underlying client (beneficial owner or fund).
- Prime broker party: Identifies the prime firm with PartyRole set appropriately (such as Prime Broker or Clearing Firm).
- Executing broker party: Identifies the broker or venue where the order is actually executed.

The executing broker may then adopt a simple rule:

> If a Prime Broker party is present, route this trade for give-up to that prime using the Account as the give-up account code; otherwise, clear internally.

Risk logic will typically:

- Apply market risk limits at the client or sub-account level (to prevent runaway strategies).
- Apply credit and margin checks at the prime or clearing relationship level (to ensure the prime is willing to guarantee those trades).

This separation is important. A single client may trade with multiple primes. Conversely, a single prime may support many funds. Encoded properly in Party groups, your system can distinguish these combinations and apply correct risk limits.

DMA vs. Agency Order Flows

Account and Party usage also encode whether an order is *direct market access* (DMA) or *agency*.

- **DMA flow**: The client effectively controls the order parameters sent to the venue, often under the broker's participant ID. The broker still carries regulatory responsibility but performs minimal discretion on the order.
- **Agency flow**: The broker exercises discretion or provides services beyond simply passing orders through (for example, working a large block, slicing and routing, or providing research-driven trading).

In DMA scenarios, the broker often wants clear, machine-readable separation by:

- End-client identity (for regulatory reporting, sponsored access rules).
- Sub-account or strategy (for risk limits).

A straightforward DMA pattern is:

- Account: Unique per DMA sub-account or sponsored access ID.
- Client party: Required, identifying the underlying beneficial owner.
- Executing Firm party: Broker or venue, sometimes implicit.

In agency flows, there can be additional layers:

- The broker may send child orders to venues under its own account while internally tracking which client and strategy they belong to.
- Party groups may include both the client (underlying fund) and the broker itself in different roles (for example, Broker of Credit vs. Executing Firm).

From a design standpoint, you should make two decisions explicit and document them:

- For inbound client orders: which field(s) identify the end-client vs. the trading sub-account?
- For outbound venue orders: which field(s) remain stable across parent and child orders so that allocations and drop copies can be reconciled back to the original client flow?

A stable mapping of Account and Party roles across DMA and agency flows greatly simplifies your downstream order-state reconstruction and regulatory reporting.

Where Routing Logic Should Live

Given this context, where should routing decisions be made?

Broadly, you can think of three layers:

- **Upstream OMS / EMS**: Where traders and strategies create orders. This layer knows the business intent and high-level client and strategy identities.
- **Broker or internal FIX gateway**: Where many clients and strategies converge. This layer enforces entitlements, risk checks, and coarse routing rules.
- **Execution venue or smart router**: Where detailed market microstructure decisions are made (venue choice, order types, timing).

Routing context (accounts and Party groups) is primarily the responsibility of the *upstream* side. The rule of thumb:

> *By the time an order reaches the broker's FIX gateway, all fields needed to choose risk limits and downstream pipes must already be present and consistent.*

This implies:

- The client OMS or EMS must assign a correct Account and Party set for every order.
- The broker's gateway must validate these identifiers against its reference data, but not invent or guess them.
- Smart routing and venue-level logic may add or adjust some Party entries (for example, venue member IDs), but should not change the client or sub-account identity.

If routing logic is scattered—some in the upstream OMS, some hidden inside the gateway, some in the router—you will experience:

- Hard-to-debug differences in behavior across connections.
- Inconsistent risk treatment of nominally identical flows.
- Confusion in drop copy or post-trade because the same client or strategy appears under multiple inconsistent codes.

Centralizing routing context construction upstream, and treating the FIX gateway as a validator and enforcer rather than an interpreter, keeps order flows predictable.

Normalization Rules for Account and Party Schemes

Defining a scheme is only half the job; enforcing it consistently is the other half. Firms that do this well typically adopt a small set of simple, rigid rules:

Rule 1: One Primary Account per Order

Every order must have exactly one non-empty Account that points to a single internal risk and booking container. Avoid multi-purpose overloading such as "client-account-strategy" strings unless they are formally structured and parsed consistently.

Rule 2: Stable Meanings Across Flows

The meaning of Account and each Party role must be the same:

- Across asset classes (equities, futures, options).
- Across sessions and counterparties.
- Across the order lifecycle (parent and child orders, replacements, cancels).

If Account means "sub-account/strategy" for new orders, it must still mean that for cancels, corrections, and drop copies.

Rule 3: Explicit Party Roles for All External Entities

Every external entity that could drive risk or reporting should appear as a Party entry, not be embedded in free-form text or encoded indirectly in Account. Typical mandatory roles include:

- Client or Customer.
- Executing Firm.
- Prime Broker or Clearing Firm (where applicable).
- Introducing Broker (in introduce/clear models).

Rule 4: Use a Controlled Set of PartyID Sources

Choose a small, documented set of PartyIDSource values and stick to them. For example:

- BIC for regulated firms.
- LEI for legal entities.
- Proprietary codes for internal books or client short codes.

This avoids messy situations where the same PartyID string could refer to completely different entities depending on context.

Rule 5: Validate All Identifiers at the Gateway

When a new order arrives, the gateway should:

- Check that Account exists, is active, and is allowed on this session.

- Check that mandatory Party roles are present for this type of flow (for example, Client and Prime for prime brokerage).
- Check that all Party IDs map cleanly to known entities, and that combinations of roles (Client + Prime + Account) are permitted.

Reject early and explicitly when these checks fail. Clear error messages about invalid accounts or Party combinations prevent silent misrouting and reduce operational risk.

How Routing Context Drives Risk and Downstream Logic

With a robust account and Party scheme in place, many downstream decisions become simple table lookups instead of ad-hoc logic.

Risk Controls

Given a validated order, your pre-trade risk engine can:

- Look up per-account or per-sub-account exposure limits.
- Aggregate exposure by client across multiple accounts (using the Client party).
- Apply credit checks at the prime or clearing-firm level (using the Prime Broker or Clearing Firm party).
- Enforce product or venue entitlements at the account or client level.

If risk is breached, the engine can generate clear messages such as "max notional for Account FUND_A_STAT exceeded" instead of generic errors.

Routing and Smart Order Logic

A smart router can use the same context to:

- Route certain clients or accounts only to approved venues.

- Apply specific routing strategies or algo parameters per client, account type, or prime.
- Select different clearing arrangements for the same instrument depending on prime broker or account flags.

Again, because context is explicit, these decisions can be declaratively configured instead of hard-coded.

Post-Trade, P&L, and Drop Copy

Finally, consistent account and Party usage:

- Allows your middle office to match fills from drop copy to internal orders without complex guesswork.
- Ensures that P&L is correctly attributed to the right strategy, fund, and client.
- Simplifies regulatory and client reporting, because every trade carries explicit client, account, and intermediary identifiers from front to back.

In the next section, we will build on this routing context to construct complete NewOrderSingle messages. There we will see how order parameters (price, quantity, time-in-force) sit alongside accounts and Party groups to form a minimal but fully routable order that passes both technical and risk validations.

4.2 Order Entry with NewOrderSingle

In the previous section we built the *routing context* for an order: accounts, parties, and intermediaries, all encoded in a consistent way so that risk, routing, and post-trade processes know exactly whose order they are handling. We are now ready to attach *trading intent* to that context.

In FIX, the standard way to introduce a new order into the system is the **NewOrderSingle** message, with MsgType = D. If you think of order flow as a story, NewOrderSingle is where the story begins. Every cancel, replace, or fill traces back to one initial D message.

This section walks step by step through:

- What a "minimal viable order" looks like in FIX.
- How the main field groups of a NewOrderSingle fit together.
- How to add optional–but practically required–fields such as handling instructions, capacity, and algo hints.
- Common venue-specific nuances that often surprise new implementers.
- Typical reasons why orders are rejected, and how to design defensively so most bad orders never leave your system.

Throughout, we assume the account and Party conventions from the previous section. We will not repeat that material, but we will use it as a given: by the time you construct a NewOrderSingle, you already know which account, client, and intermediaries apply.

The Minimal Viable Order

Conceptually, a NewOrderSingle answers four basic questions:

1. **What** do you want to trade? (instrument)
2. **Which way** do you want to trade it? (side)
3. **How much**? (quantity)
4. **On what terms**? (price logic and time constraints)

On top of that, it carries your routing context:

5. **On whose behalf**? (account, client, intermediaries)

When you strip away all optional elaborations, the minimal viable order in FIX typically includes:

- A unique client order identifier.
- Instrument identification (symbol or security IDs).
- Side (buy, sell, short sell, etc.).
- Order quantity.
- Price information, or an indication that it is a market order.
- Time-in-force or default day order behavior.
- Account and Party identifiers, as defined earlier.

Even though the FIX standard defines many more fields, it is useful to keep this minimal mental model: if any one of these is missing or inconsistent, the order is not truly defined.

Structural View of a NewOrderSingle

Before diving into individual fields, it helps to see the message as composed of three major groups:

1. **Core order parameters**: what, side, quantity, and pricing/-time instructions.
2. **Routing and risk context**: account, parties, capacity, and any tags that control which risk limits and books the order hits.
3. **Strategy and handling extensions**: how the broker or venue should treat the order (DMA vs. worked, algo parameters, special instructions).

The following diagram lays out these groups visually.

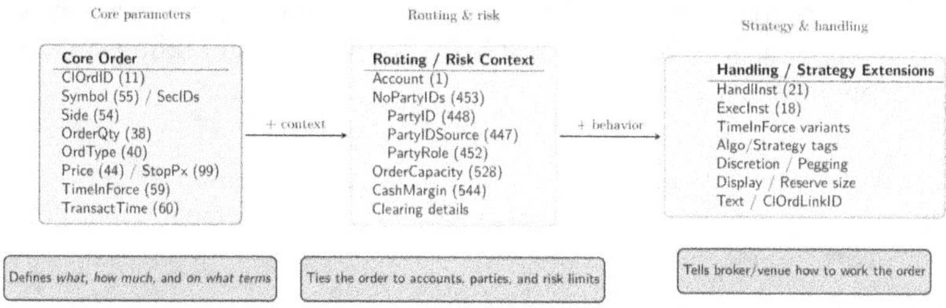

You can think of building a NewOrderSingle from left to right:

1. Start by defining the clean, minimal description of what you want to trade.

2. Attach the correct account and parties so the broker knows whose trade it is.

3. Optionally, refine how the order should be handled and executed.

We now go through these parts in more detail.

Core Order Parameters

Client Order Identifier

Every order needs a unique label from the client:

- **ClOrdID (11)**: The primary key from the client side. It is how the client will later refer to this order when sending cancels or replaces.

Good practice is to:

- Make it unique at least per trading day and per connection.

- Use a structured scheme that encodes the trading system and maybe a time-based component, but avoid embedding sensitive business data.

If two active orders share the same ClOrdID, the broker or venue will typically reject the second one to avoid ambiguity, or treat it as a potential error.

Instrument Identification

At a minimum:

- **Symbol (55)**: A human-readable ticker. Some venues rely heavily on this; others treat it as secondary.

For robustness, especially across regions and asset classes, you should include one or more security identifier fields (for example, ISIN or exchange-specific codes) in addition to Symbol. The exact tags vary by asset class and FIX version, but the principle is the same: do not rely solely on a free-form ticker when precise security IDs are available.

Side and Quantity

Two simple but critical fields:

- **Side (54)**: Buy, sell, sell short, buy to cover, and so on. Downstream systems heavily depend on this being correct.
- **OrderQty (38)**: The total number of shares or contracts requested.

Remember that OrderQty is the *total* order size, not the remaining quantity or last fill. Those will be reported in ExecutionReports.

Order Type and Price Information

Next, you define *how* the order should interact with the order book:

- **OrdType (40)**: Market, limit, stop, stop-limit, and other specialized types.
- **Price (44)**: The limit price, when applicable.

- **StopPx (99)**: The trigger price for stop or stop-limit orders.

The combination of OrdType, Price, and StopPx must be coherent:

- Market orders: OrdType indicates market; no limit Price is needed or allowed.
- Limit orders: OrdType indicates limit and a finite, valid Price is required.
- Stop orders: StopPx is required, and rules on Price depend on whether it is a stop-market or stop-limit variant.

Venues often enforce price bands: if the limit price is too far from the current market or violates price increment rules (ticks), the order may be rejected.

Time Constraints

Time constraints control how long the order should remain active:

- **TimeInForce (59)**: Day, immediate-or-cancel, fill-or-kill, good-till-cancel, and others.
- **TransactTime (60)**: The time the order was initiated from the client's perspective.

Some venues treat the absence of TimeInForce as "Day" by default; others may require it explicitly. Including it avoids ambiguity.

Routing and Risk Context in NewOrderSingle

All the routing and risk logic from the previous section comes into play here. In a NewOrderSingle, at minimum, you should expect to set:

- **Account (1)**: The primary risk and booking container at the broker.
- **Parties (453, 448, 447, 452)**: One or more entries specifying the client, prime broker, executing firm, and any other intermediaries.

In addition, orders often carry:

- **OrderCapacity (528)**: Indicates whether the firm is trading as agent, principal, or in some other capacity. This is important for both regulatory reasons and routing behavior.
- **CashMargin (544)** or equivalent: Distinguishes between cash and margin accounts when required.
- Clearing-specific fields: For example, details needed for give-ups or clearing arrangements in derivatives markets.

From an implementation perspective, you want to make this portion of the message as deterministic as possible:

- Given a user, strategy, and client, your OMS should always populate the same Account and Party combination.
- Your FIX gateway should validate those fields, not reinterpret them.

The key is that by the time the order hits the broker's risk engine, all the information necessary to select risk limits and venue routes is already present and consistent.

Handling and Strategy Extensions

Once the core order and context are in place, you can refine *how* the order should be handled.

Handling Instructions

- **HandlInst (21)**: Historically indicated whether the order was handled manually, by an automated system, or was a DMA order.

Some markets still rely on this tag to distinguish DMA from non-DMA flow or to decide where to direct the order internally. Others use additional, more modern flags. In any case, you should align your use of HandlInst with your broker's documented expectations.

Execution Instructions

- **ExecInst (18)**: A flexible field that can encode additional instructions, such as participation constraints, display preferences, and interaction with dark pools.

The content of ExecInst is often venue- or broker-specific. For example, one broker might use it to request "participate but do not initiate" behavior, while another uses proprietary combinations for special auction handling. Your implementation should treat it as a list of documented flags, not free text.

Algo and Strategy Parameters

Algo orders and more complex strategies typically introduce additional tags:

- Named strategy identifiers.
- Parameters controlling urgency, schedule, or participation rate.
- Minimum or maximum participation constraints.

While these are not standardized across all brokers, the design principle is the same:

- Keep mandatory risk and routing fields separate from optional strategy hints.
- Treat missing or unrecognized strategy parameters in a safe way, ideally reverting to well-documented defaults rather than guessing.

Display and Reserve Size

Many venues support iceberg or reserve orders, where part of the order is visible and part is hidden. In FIX, this can be represented by:

- The main OrderQty (total size).
- Additional tags indicating how much to display at a time.

Once again, details differ by venue, but a common mistake is to confuse display size with total order size. Your pre-trade checks should ensure that display size does not exceed total size and that venue-specific constraints on minimum display are respected.

Venue-Specific Nuances

The FIX standard is broad, but each exchange, MTF, or broker implements its own subset and extensions. A NewOrderSingle that is valid for one destination may be rejected by another even though all the core fields are present.

Common venue-specific nuances include:

Required Identifiers and Formats

- Some venues require certain security ID types (for example, a local market code) and ignore others.
- Some impose strict formats on Account or internal client codes.

You should maintain per-venue configuration describing:

- Which identifier tags are required.
- Which ones are optional.
- Which ones must *not* be sent (because they may conflict with venue logic).

Supported Order Types and TimeInForce Combinations

Venues differ in which combinations of OrdType, TimeInForce, and execution instructions they will accept. For example:

- Some do not allow good-till-cancel for certain instruments.
- Others restrict immediate-or-cancel to specific order types.

Your system should know, for each venue:

- The allowed order types.
- The allowed time-in-force values.
- Any disallowed combinations.

Ideally these are enforced before an order leaves your environment.

Market Sessions and Trading Phases

Many venues have pre-open, continuous trading, and auction phases, each with different rules:

- A limit order type might be valid in the auction, but a particular execution instruction may not be.
- Market orders may be disallowed or treated specially during auctions.

If your router sends orders across sessions, it should be aware of these phase-specific rules and either adjust the order type or delay submission.

Typical Rejection Causes

Even when a NewOrderSingle is syntactically correct, it may be rejected by the broker or venue for business reasons. Understanding these common failure modes helps you design better validation upstream.

Missing or Inconsistent Required Fields

Typical examples:

- ClOrdID missing or duplicated for an active order.
- OrderQty zero or negative.
- OrdType requires a Price, but Price is missing or invalid.
- Symbol and security IDs do not match any known instrument at the venue.

These are the easiest to catch with simple, stateless checks before sending the order.

Price and Quantity Violations

Venues apply a variety of price and volume controls:

- Price bands relative to last trade or reference prices.
- Tick-size rules per instrument.
- Minimum or maximum order sizes, sometimes per client or account.

If you send a limit buy far above the allowable band, or a quantity that exceeds venue limits, the order is likely to be rejected. A robust implementation:

- Maintains instrument reference data (tick size, min/max quantity).
- Applies a pre-trade check against these values.

Risk and Credit Limits

From the broker's perspective, an otherwise valid order may be rejected because:

- The account has reached its notional or position limit.
- The client's credit line with a prime or clearer is exhausted.
- The order would violate concentration or product-specific rules.

These checks depend on current exposures and portfolio state. You cannot fully replicate them on the client side, but you can:

- Query limits where available.
- Implement your own internal limits toward the broker to catch obvious violations.

Entitlement and Regulatory Issues

Orders may also be rejected because:

- The account is not entitled to trade a given market or instrument.

- Regulatory flags (for example, short sale marking) are missing or inconsistent.
- Required client or account documentation is incomplete, prompting the broker to temporarily block trading.

These are largely configuration and onboarding issues, but your system should be prepared to surface such rejections clearly to users and not continue to repeat failing orders.

Defensive Design: Preventing Bad Orders from Leaving

The best place to handle errors is *before* the order leaves your own system. A thoughtful design includes:

Layered Validation

Implement validation in layers:

1. **Basic syntax**: Required fields present, correct data types and ranges.
2. **Instrument and venue rules**: Tick sizes, min/max quantities, allowed order types.
3. **Internal risk and policy**: Firm-specific constraints, such as maximum order size per strategy or product.

Only once an order passes all layers should it be translated into FIX and sent.

Configuration-Driven Rules

Many checks should be configuration-driven rather than hard-coded, for example:

- Per-venue lists of supported order types and TimeInForce values.
- Per-instrument tick sizes and trading phases.
- Per-account and per-client risk limits.

This allows you to adjust behavior as venues change rules without changing application code.

Clear Feedback Loops

When an order is rejected:

- Capture the reject reason from the broker's ExecutionReport or Reject message.
- Map it into user-facing messages and internal metrics.
- Use aggregated statistics on rejections to improve validation over time.

If a particular venue starts enforcing a new rule, recurring rejections will quickly show up in your monitoring, prompting you to tighten your pre-trade checks.

Putting It All Together

A well-constructed NewOrderSingle is not just a random collection of tags. It is:

- A concise expression of trading intent (what, side, quantity, and price/time terms).
- Embedded in a precise routing context (account and parties) that tells the broker whose trade it is and how risk should be managed.
- Decorated with handling and strategy hints that control how the order is worked, without obscuring the core definition.

By building NewOrderSingle messages systematically—first the core parameters, then the routing context, then optional strategy extensions—you make your order flow easier to reason about, debug, and extend.

In the next section, we will see how these initial orders evolve over time through cancel and replace requests, and how to keep that lifecycle safe and coherent using careful ClOrdID and OrigClOrdID discipline.

4.3 Safe Order Modification and Cancellation

By this point in the chapter, we have two pillars in place:

- A clear *routing context*: accounts and parties that tell us whose order it is and how risk should be applied.
- A precise *order entry format*: a well-formed NewOrderSingle with core order parameters, context, and optional strategy hints.

Once an order is accepted, the real world intrudes: prices move, strategies change their mind, risk managers cut limits, or clients simply realize that an instruction was wrong. The order must be modified or cancelled.

At this point, your problem stops being just about message formatting and becomes a *concurrency problem*. Messages travel over a network, sometimes out of order, sometimes delayed. The market may fill the order while your cancellation is still in flight. Multiple systems may try to touch the same order at once.

This section explains how to manage that complexity safely using the standard FIX choreography:

- **OrderCancelReplaceRequest** (MsgType = G) to modify an existing order.
- **OrderCancelRequest** (MsgType = F) to cancel an existing order.
- **OrigClOrdID** and **ClOrdID** discipline to link each modification to its predecessor and preserve an unbroken audit trail.
- A robust mental model for race conditions and defensive patterns that keep your workflow stable, even under high message rates and latency jitter.

Two Basic Moves: Replace vs. Cancel

FIX gives you two distinct moves on a live order:

- **Cancel/Replace**: Adjusts attributes of the order while keeping its economic identity (same client, instrument, side, and usually the same overall business intent). You send an OrderCancelReplaceRequest.
- **Cancel**: Asks the broker or venue to remove whatever quantity remains, stopping any further executions. You send an OrderCancelRequest.

It is helpful to think in terms of a simple rule:

> You *replace* when the order should continue to exist in modified form; you *cancel* when the order should no longer exist.

Behind the scenes, a venue may implement a replace as "cancel old order, create new order" or as an in-place update. From the client's perspective, however, both actions are tied into a single logical order stream, and FIX uses ClOrdID and OrigClOrdID to keep that chain intact.

ClOrdID and OrigClOrdID: The Backbone of the Lifecycle

You have already seen ClOrdID (11) in the context of NewOrderSingle. For safe modification and cancellation, we now add:

- **OrigClOrdID (41)**: "Original client order ID." In replace and cancel messages, it tells the broker which existing order you are referring to.

A simple but powerful discipline emerges:

1. Every *new* order gets a new ClOrdID.
2. Every *replace* or *cancel* request:
    - Gets its own *new* ClOrdID.
    - Uses OrigClOrdID to point to the most recent active ClOrdID in the chain.

In other words, you build a version chain:

$$\text{ClOrdID} = \text{A (New)} \rightarrow \text{ClOrdID} = \text{B, OrigClOrdID} = \text{A (Replace)}$$
$$\rightarrow \text{ClOrdID} = \text{C, OrigClOrdID} = \text{B (Replace)} \rightarrow \ldots$$

At any moment, the broker and client both consider only the latest acknowledged ClOrdID as the active representation of that order. Execution reports for fills and final status (filled, cancelled, rejected) are tied to that evolving chain.

Legal vs. Illegal Changes

Not all changes are allowed. A safe mental model is to divide order attributes into:

- **Identity attributes** that must *never* change, such as:
    - Instrument (symbol and security IDs).
    - Side (buy/sell/short).
    - Client and account identity (in most workflows).
- **Trading attributes** that *may* change, subject to venue rules, such as:
    - Remaining quantity.
    - Limit price or stop price.
    - Time-in-force (within allowed transitions).
    - Certain handling or execution instructions.

Attempting to replace an order while changing identity attributes is often treated as an error. Many brokers will reject such a replace outright, forcing you instead to cancel the original order and submit a new one.

Your client-side order state machine should enforce these rules *before* a replace is sent:

- If a user attempts to change a forbidden attribute, either:
  - Automatically perform a cancel-then-new sequence, or
  - Block the change and inform the user.
- Only generate OrderCancelReplaceRequest messages for changes that are supported and sensible for the destination venue.

The Core Choreography

Let us outline the idealized, race-free choreography for three common actions:

1. **Order entry** (NewOrderSingle).
2. **Order replace** (OrderCancelReplaceRequest).
3. **Order cancel** (OrderCancelRequest).

Order Entry

1. Client sends a well-formed NewOrderSingle with ClOrdID = A.
2. Broker acknowledges and returns an ExecutionReport:
   - Echoes ClOrdID = A.
   - Carries an order ID from the broker or venue.
   - Has status "New" (or "Partially Filled" if an immediate fill occurred).

Order Replace

1. Client decides to change price or quantity.
2. Client sends an OrderCancelReplaceRequest:
   - OrigClOrdID = A.
   - ClOrdID = B (new ID).
   - New order parameters (for example, new price).
3. Broker:
   - Locates the existing order using OrigClOrdID.
   - Verifies that the order can be replaced (not fully filled, not already done-for-day, etc.).
   - Applies the changes at the venue.
   - Returns an ExecutionReport acknowledging the replace, now echoing ClOrdID = B.

At this point, the client updates its local state: order version A is now superseded by version B.

Order Cancel

1. Client decides to cancel the active order.
2. Client sends an OrderCancelRequest:
   - OrigClOrdID = B (the latest active ID).
   - ClOrdID = C (new cancel request ID).
3. Broker:
   - Attempts to cancel the order at the venue.
   - Returns either:
     - An ExecutionReport with status "Canceled" if the cancel fully succeeded, or
     - An ExecutionReport with "Canceled" and a final filled quantity, if part or all of the order had already traded, or
     - A reject if the cancel could not be applied (for example, the order was already filled or not found).

In this race-free world, events line up neatly. Real trading, however, is full of boundary cases, which is why we must think carefully about race conditions.

Where Race Conditions Come From

Race conditions arise whenever two or more actions related to the same order overlap in time and their outcomes depend on ordering or delays. In FIX-based order flows, the main culprits are:

- **Network latency and jitter**: Messages do not arrive instantly and may be momentarily delayed or reordered by network paths and intermediaries.
- **Asynchronous venue behavior**: An exchange may receive a cancel and a matching order at nearly the same time. Depending on microsecond-level timing, the trade may still occur even after you "sent a cancel."
- **Multiple decision makers**: A risk system may cancel an order at the same time a trader attempts to replace it, or different applications may act on the same order concurrently.

This leads to patterns such as:

- "I thought the order was cancelled, but it still got filled."
- "The replace was accepted by the broker, but the fill we received appears to use the old price."
- "We sent two cancels; one was accepted, one was rejected; now we are not sure of the final status."

Your goal is not to eliminate all races (that is impossible), but to:

1. *Make them explicit* and handle them deterministically.
2. *Design idempotent workflows* where repeated or out-of-order messages do not corrupt your internal state.

A Timeline View of Common Races

To build intuition, it is helpful to visualize the message timeline between client and broker. The following diagram shows a simplified sequence with a new order, a replace, and a cancel, together with fills that interact with them.

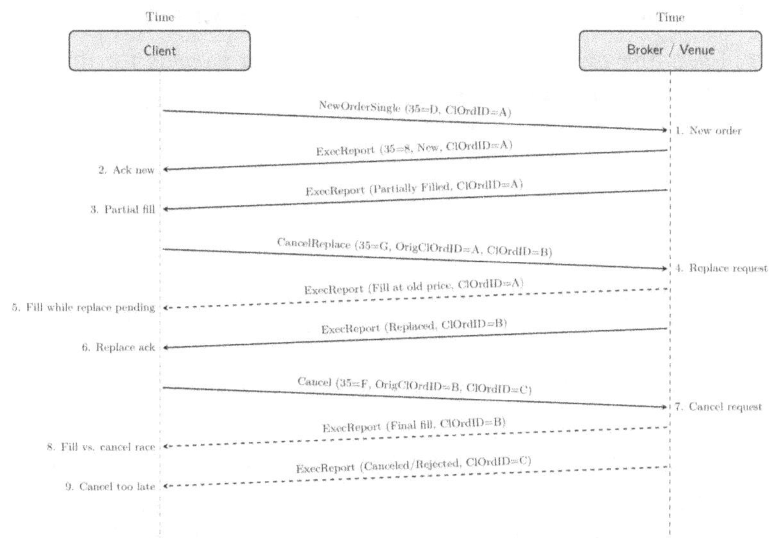

This diagram illustrates two typical races:

- A fill arriving while a replace is in flight.
- A final fill arriving while a cancel is in flight, causing the cancel to be effectively "too late."

Both situations are valid outcomes from the venue's perspective and must be handled gracefully by your client-side order state machine.

Designing a Robust Client-Side State Machine

A state machine turns this complex stream of messages into a clean internal view of the order: current quantity, price, and status. For modification and cancellation, a few practical design rules go a long way.

Rule 1: One Outstanding Action per Order Chain

Avoid sending multiple concurrent modifies or cancels for the same active ClOrdID. A safe pattern is:

- Treat each order chain as having a current *version state*: for example, "Active," "Replace Pending," "Cancel Pending," "Completed."
- When a replace is in flight, block further user modifications until an ExecutionReport confirms acceptance or rejection.
- When a cancel is in flight, block further replaces for that chain.

This prevents your own systems from generating self-conflicting instructions.

Rule 2: Always Refer to the Latest Accepted ClOrdID

Your local state should track:

- The latest *acknowledged* ClOrdID for each logical order.
- Any pending requests that have not yet been confirmed or rejected.

When creating a new replace or cancel:

- Set OrigClOrdID to the latest *acknowledged* ClOrdID.
- Use a brand new ClOrdID for the new request itself.

If a replace is rejected, the previously acknowledged ClOrdID remains active; subsequent actions should continue to refer back to that ID.

Rule 3: Idempotent Handling of Late and Duplicate Messages

Because of network effects, you may receive:

- Duplicate execution reports.
- Late acknowledgements relative to subsequent events.

Your state machine should therefore be idempotent, meaning that applying the same event twice does not change the final order state beyond the first application. Practical techniques include:

- Tracking cumulative executed quantity and verifying that each new fill increases it monotonically.
- Ignoring repeated status transitions that do not change cumulative quantity or leaves quantity.
- Logging but safely discarding any message whose ClOrdID does not correspond to a known active or recently closed order chain.

Rule 4: Explicit Handling of "Too Late to Cancel"

A frequent outcome is that a cancel request is rejected as "too late to cancel" because the order is already fully executed or otherwise no longer cancellable. Rather than treating this as an error, your state machine should:

- Recognize it as a valid terminal event for the cancel request.
- Confirm that the underlying order's final status and filled quantity are consistent with the broker's view.

From a user perspective, it is important to communicate that the cancel was applied as far as possible, but could not prevent some or all remaining fills.

Defending Against Multi-Source Conflicts

In many real environments, more than one system can act on the same order:

- A trader's front-end GUI may allow manual cancels and replaces.
- A risk engine may automatically cancel orders that breach limits.
- A supervisory tool may issue mass cancels for whole accounts or symbols.

Without coordination, these sources can generate conflicting instructions that arrive at the broker in arbitrary order. To defend against this, consider:

Single Point of Decision per Order

Designate a single logical "owner" per order chain. All user actions and automated triggers must flow through that owner, which is responsible for:

- Serializing actions (no overlapping replaces and cancels).
- Ensuring ClOrdID/OrigClOrdID sequences remain consistent.

Other systems can request actions, but the owner decides in what order to apply them.

Priority Rules for Automated vs. Manual Actions

In some shops, a risk engine override should always win over trader intent. In others, manual supervisor actions may trump algorithmic behavior. Whatever your policy, codify it explicitly:

- Define which sources can initiate cancels or replaces.
- Define what happens if a lower-priority source issues a conflicting request while a higher-priority action is in flight.

Your state machine can then handle these as orderly transitions instead of ad-hoc exceptions.

Interaction with ExecutionReports

Every modification or cancellation is ultimately confirmed or denied via ExecutionReport messages, not simply by the absence of an error. For each order chain:

- ExecutionReports signal:
  - Acceptance of a replace (order status moves to "Replaced" or remains "New" with updated parameters).
  - Acceptance of a cancel (status moves to "Canceled").
  - Rejection of a replace or cancel, with reasons.
  - Fills and partial fills.
- Your system must process them in the context of:
  - The order version (which ClOrdID they refer to).
  - Any outstanding pending requests (replace or cancel in flight).

When a replace is acknowledged:

- Update the order's parameters (for example, new price).
- Mark the previous version as superseded.

When a replace is rejected:

- Retain the previous version as still active.
- Optionally notify users or systems that requested the change.

When a cancel is acknowledged or rejected as too late:

- Move the order to a terminal state (canceled or fully filled).
- Ensure no further actions are generated for that chain.

We will return to ExecutionReports in the next section in more depth, treating them as an event stream that drives a complete state machine across all orders. For now, the key idea is that safe modification and cancellation rely on taking ExecutionReports seriously as the ultimate source of truth about what the broker and venue actually did.

Safe order modification and cancellation in FIX rest on a few core ideas:

- **ClOrdID and OrigClOrdID form a version chain** that uniquely identifies each step in an order's lifecycle.
- **Replace and cancel requests are separate actions** with clear semantics: continue the order in modified form, or stop it altogether.
- **Race conditions are inevitable**, but you can design your workflows and state machines to be deterministic, idempotent, and robust under delayed or overlapping messages.
- **Only one outstanding action per order chain** and a clear ownership model help avoid self-inflicted conflicts.
- **ExecutionReports close the loop**, confirming or rejecting your intentions and telling you what actually happened at the venue.

With this choreography in place, you can safely evolve orders over their lifetime without losing track of which version is active, how much has traded, or why a particular cancel did or did not take effect. The next section builds on this by treating the entire stream of ExecutionReports as a driving event log for your internal order state machine, turning noisy FIX traffic into clean, queryable records for P&L, risk, and drop copy.

4.4 ExecutionReport Event Stream

In the previous sections we worked from the *front* of the order workflow:

- We defined the routing context (accounts and parties) that anchors every order to a clear economic owner.
- We learned how to construct a valid NewOrderSingle that encodes trading intent.
- We saw how cancel and replace requests, tied together with ClOrdID and OrigClOrdID, safely evolve an order over time.

We now turn to the other side of the conversation: the broker or venue's ongoing responses. In FIX, those responses arrive primarily as **ExecutionReport** messages (MsgType = 8). These messages are the narrative of the order's life. If you string them together for a given order, you get a complete story: accepted, partially filled, modified, finally filled, cancelled, or rejected.

This section treats ExecutionReports as an event stream and shows how to:

- Read the key fields that tell you what just happened.
- Translate each report into a transition in a small internal state machine.
- Maintain a clean, queryable view of each order and its fills, even when the underlying FIX traffic is noisy.

The goal is that by the end of this section you can look at an arbitrary sequence of ExecutionReports and confidently reconstruct the economic outcome: what traded, what did not, and why.

ExecutionReport as an Incremental Event

An ExecutionReport is not a full restatement of everything about an order. Instead, it is an *incremental event* that tells you:

- What just happened (*event type*).
- What the order's status is now (*resulting status*).

- How the executed quantities and prices have changed (*deltas and aggregates*).

The most important fields for building a state machine are:

- **ExecType** A fine-grained classification of the event: new, partial fill, fill, cancel, replace, reject, and so on.
- **OrdStatus** The resulting overall status of the order after this event: new, partially filled, filled, cancelled, rejected, etc.
- **OrderID / ClOrdID / OrigClOrdID** References tying this event to a specific order chain and version, as discussed in the previous section.
- **LastQty / LastPx** The quantity and price of the *most recent* execution, if this event includes a trade.
- **CumQty** The *cumulative* quantity executed so far on this order.
- **LeavesQty** The remaining quantity that could still be executed.
- **TransactTime** The time the event occurred from the broker or venue's perspective.
- **Text / ExecRestatementReason / other reason codes** Human-readable or coded explanations of rejections, cancels, corrections, and restatements.

A good mental model is:

> Each ExecutionReport is a timestamped event that moves the order from one state to another and adjusts your view of cumulative and remaining quantity.

Your internal order representation should therefore be driven by *consuming* these events in order, not by re-deriving state from scratch each time.

Key ExecType and OrdStatus Values

The FIX standard defines many values for ExecType and OrdStatus, but a small subset appears in almost every equity or futures workflow. It is worth internalizing how they relate.

ExecType: What Just Happened

Typical values include:

- **New** – The order has been accepted and is now live.
- **Partially Filled** – A trade occurred, but the order still has remaining quantity.
- **Filled** – The order is fully executed; no remaining quantity.
- **Canceled** – The remaining quantity, if any, has been cancelled.
- **Replaced** – A cancel/replace request was applied, updating order parameters.
- **Rejected** – An order, replace, or cancel has been rejected.
- **Trade Cancel / Correct** – A previous trade has been busted or corrected.

OrdStatus: What Is the Order's Overall State Now

Typical values include:

- **New** – Live, with no fills yet.
- **Partially Filled** – Live, with some fills and remaining quantity.
- **Filled** – Fully executed; terminal.
- **Canceled** – Stopped with some remaining quantity unused; terminal.
- **Rejected** – Never became live; terminal.
- **Pending Cancel / Pending Replace** – A cancel or replace request has been received but not yet fully processed.

The pair (ExecType, OrdStatus) together gives you a precise picture:

- ExecType = New, OrdStatus = New: order just accepted, no fills yet.
- ExecType = Partially Filled, OrdStatus = Partially Filled: additional fill happened, order still live.
- ExecType = Canceled, OrdStatus = Canceled: cancel went through and the order is no longer live.
- ExecType = Trade Cancel, OrdStatus = Partially Filled: a previous execution was busted, but the order still has some other fills and remains live.

Your internal state machine should not attempt to deduce status purely from OrdStatus. It should interpret ExecType as the incoming event and treat OrdStatus as a sanity check on the resulting state.

From Events to a State Machine

We now move from reading individual reports to designing a finite set of internal states and transitions. The idea is simple but powerful:

> Define a small set of internal order states, and for each possible ExecType/OrdStatus combination, specify how that event moves the order from one state to another and how it updates quantities.

A practical internal state set might include:

- **PendingNew** – Order has been sent, no acknowledgement yet.
- **New** – Live with zero fills.
- **PartiallyFilled** – Live with some fills.
- **Filled** – Fully executed; closed.

- **Canceled** – Stopped; some or all quantity may have traded earlier.
- **Rejected** – Never live; closed.
- **PendingCancel** – Cancel requested, waiting for outcome.
- **PendingReplace** – Replace requested, waiting for outcome.
- **Suspended / Halted** – Temporarily untradeable due to venue action (optional, depending on asset class and venue).

Your application may use slightly different names or include additional nuances, but the important point is that you commit to a *finite* set of internal states and define transitions explicitly.

Typical Event Sequences

Let us look at a few common sequences and how they traverse this state machine.

Simple Fill

1. You send a NewOrderSingle. Internally: **PendingNew**.
2. You receive an ExecutionReport: ExecType = New, OrdStatus = New. Internally: transition to **New**. Set CumQty = 0, LeavesQty = OrderQty.
3. You receive an ExecutionReport: ExecType = Filled, OrdStatus = Filled, with LastQty = OrderQty. Internally:
   - Update CumQty to full size.
   - Set LeavesQty = 0.
   - Transition to **Filled**.

Partial Fills Then Cancel

1. Start as before: **PendingNew** → **New**.

2. Receive partial fill: ExecType = Partially Filled, OrdStatus = Partially Filled, with LastQty = x. Internally:
   - Increase CumQty by x.
   - Decrease LeavesQty by x.
   - Transition to **PartiallyFilled**.
3. Trader decides to cancel remaining quantity. Client sends cancel request. Internally: **PartiallyFilled** → **PendingCancel**.
4. Broker acknowledges cancel: ExecType = Canceled, OrdStatus = Canceled. Internally:
   - CumQty unchanged.
   - LeavesQty = 0.
   - Transition to **Canceled**.

Reject on Entry

1. You send a NewOrderSingle. Internally: **PendingNew**.
2. Broker rejects it: ExecType = Rejected, OrdStatus = Rejected, with a reason code. Internally:
   - CumQty = 0.
   - LeavesQty = 0.
   - Transition directly to **Rejected**.

Importantly, orders in **Rejected**, **Filled**, or **Canceled** should be treated as terminal: no further actions should be initiated for that chain.

Dealing with Corrections and Venue-Generated Events

Real markets introduce less common, but important, events:

- **Trade busts** After a fill has been reported, the exchange later cancels the trade (for example, due to an error or erroneous price).
- **Trade corrections** A fill is adjusted to a different price or quantity.
- **Venue-initiated cancels** The venue cancels the order unilaterally, for example due to instrument halts or system issues.
- **Repricing / Routing events** The broker or venue alters the order's characteristics (such as price or destination) for technical reasons.

In FIX, these typically appear as ExecutionReports with specific ExecType or reason codes, sometimes reusing the same OrdStatus as before. To handle them safely:

- Treat **trade busts** as negative fills: you receive an event indicating a bust, with LastQty and LastPx matching (or referencing) the original trade. Internally, decrease CumQty by the busted quantity, and adjust P&L accordingly.
- Treat **trade corrections** as a combination of a bust and a new fill: the original execution is reversed, then a replacement execution is applied.
- Treat **venue-initiated cancels** as events transitioning the order to **Canceled**, often with specific reason codes. Your system should surface these reasons and close the order.
- For **repricing** or similar events, treat them as ExecType = Replaced and update your local order parameters in line with the broker's view.

These events emphasize why a state machine driven by the *event stream* is more robust than simply assuming a one-way flow from new to fill/cancel. The venue has the right to alter or reverse previous outcomes, and your system must be able to replay those changes correctly.

Quantity Accounting: CumQty, LastQty, and LeavesQty

Reliable quantity accounting is central to both risk and P&L, and ExecutionReports give you all the pieces you need:

- **OrderQty** (from the original order) is your starting total.
- **LastQty** is the increment: how much traded (or was busted) in this event.
- **CumQty** is the running total that the broker or venue believes has traded so far.
- **LeavesQty** is what the broker thinks is still live and available to trade.

A disciplined implementation should:

- Use LastQty and LastPx to book individual fills (to positions, P&L, and downstream consumers).
- Use CumQty and LeavesQty as cross-checks, confirming that your aggregation matches the broker's running totals.
- Flag any discrepancies between your computed cumulated quantity and the reported CumQty. Such mismatches are early warning signs of missed or double-counted events.

This approach naturally supports corrections: a bust event with negative LastQty will reduce your total, and a subsequent correction event will increase it again.

Building the State-Transition Chart

We are now ready to codify all of this in a compact visual form: a state-transition chart. The chart:

- Lists internal states such as New, PartiallyFilled, Filled, Canceled, Rejected.

- Draws arrows labeled with key ExecType/OrdStatus combinations.
- Emphasizes which states are terminal and which are intermediate.

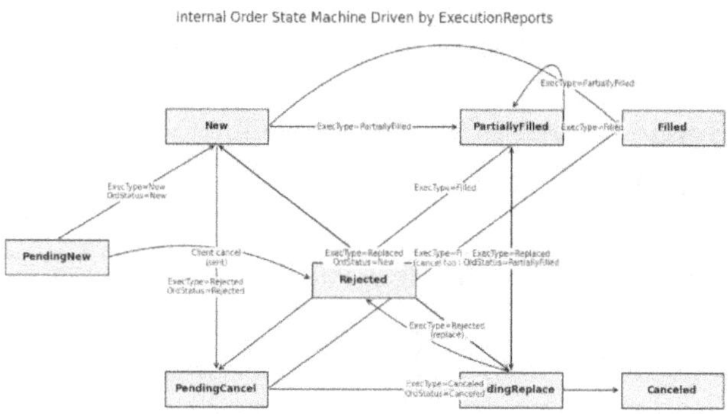

This chart is intentionally simplified, but it captures the main patterns:

- From **PendingNew**, you either become **New** or **Rejected**.
- From **New** or **PartiallyFilled**, you can:
  - Move through repeated partial fills toward **Filled**.
  - Enter **PendingCancel** or **PendingReplace** based on client actions.
- From **PendingCancel**, you either reach **Canceled** or, if fills overtake your cancel, you may reach **Filled**.
- From **PendingReplace**, you may end up back in **New** or **PartiallyFilled** with updated parameters, or see the replace rejected and transition to **Rejected** for that replace request.

In practice, you will expand this chart with additional states or transitions for your specific asset classes, but the discipline remains: define the finite set of internal states and the allowed transitions driven by ExecutionReport events.

Practical Implementation Tips

Finally, a few practical guidelines for turning this conceptual state machine into robust code:

Use a Single Source of Truth per Order

Store, for each order chain:

- Current internal state (New, PartiallyFilled, etc.).
- Latest acknowledged ClOrdID.
- Cumulative executed quantity and average price.
- A list of individual fills (from LastQty/LastPx) to support P&L and reconciliation.

Treat incoming ExecutionReports as the only authoritative source of changes to these fields.

Process Events in a Deterministic Order

To the extent possible:

- Process ExecutionReports in sequence number order (from the FIX session layer) to reduce out-of-order surprises.
- If you must handle truly out-of-order delivery (for example, from multiple connections), use TransactTime and your own ordering rules to reconcile them.

Validate Consistency on Each Transition

For each incoming event:

- Check that the transition from current state to new state is allowed in your chart. If not, log and flag it; do not silently force it.
- Compare your computed CumQty and LeavesQty to the values in the message. Small discrepancies indicate bugs or missed events.

Design with Downstream Consumers in Mind

Risk engines, drop copy listeners, and P&L systems all read from the order and fill records your state machine produces. A clean, well-defined state machine makes their lives easier:

- Risk systems can rely on LeavesQty and state to decide how much exposure is still live.
- P&L systems can rely on the list of fills and busts to compute realized and unrealized gains.
- Supervisory tools can quickly answer questions like “Which orders were rejected today and why?” or “Which orders were cancelled by the venue?”

ExecutionReports are more than acknowledgements; they are the event stream from which all order state, fills, and outcomes should be derived. By:

- Understanding the meaning of ExecType and OrdStatus,
- Defining a small set of internal states and explicit transitions,
- Using quantity fields consistently to track fills and busts,

you transform noisy FIX traffic into a deterministic, auditable view of trading activity. This view is the bedrock on which risk, P&L, client reporting, and drop copy all rest.

In the next section, we will zoom out from individual orders to portfolio-level control, and see how mass cancel and mass status workflows reuse the same routing context and event-stream thinking to manage risk across many orders at once.

4.5 Bulk Risk Controls via Mass Actions

Up to this point in the chapter we have focused on *single-order* workflows: creating a well-formed NewOrderSingle, modifying or cancelling it safely, and interpreting its stream of ExecutionReports as a coherent lifecycle. In live trading, however, you are often not worried about one order, but about *hundreds or thousands* at once.

Consider a few examples:

- A strategy goes haywire and starts firing orders aggressively across multiple symbols.
- A venue experiences a technical issue or a market-wide trading halt is announced.
- A risk officer decides that a particular client, strategy, or account must stop trading immediately.

In all these cases, managing orders one-by-one is too slow and too error-prone. You need **bulk controls**: the ability to query, cancel, or otherwise act on many orders at once, based on routing context (accounts, parties) and other attributes (symbols, sides, sessions).

This is where the FIX *mass action* messages come in. In this section we will:

- Explain the role of mass cancel and mass status messages as portfolio-level risk controls.
- Show how they reuse routing context (accounts and Party groups) as selection filters.
- Describe how the resulting ExecutionReports update your internal order book.
- Discuss practical safeguards so these powerful tools are decisive in emergencies yet predictable and auditable.

From Single-Order Control to Portfolio-Level Control

Recall the single-order tools:

- OrderCancelRequest requests that an individual order be stopped.
- OrderCancelReplaceRequest adjusts the parameters of an individual order.

These are ideal for routine trader actions on specific orders. But from a risk perspective, you might ask more global questions:

- "Cancel all live orders for Account FUND_A_STAT."
- "Cancel all live orders for Client Alpha Capital across all accounts."
- "Cancel all live orders in symbol AAPL and related options."
- "Cancel all orders on Venue X for this firm, right now."

Implementing these behaviors by iterating through local order records and sending thousands of single cancels is problematic:

- It is slow and may not complete before the market moves further.
- It risks hitting message-rate limits at the gateway or venue.
- It can leave gaps if your internal view of live orders is slightly stale.

Mass actions address this by moving the selection logic *to the broker or venue*, which has the authoritative list of live orders and can cancel directly at the source.

Mass Cancel: The Risk "Kill Switch"

At the heart of bulk risk control is the **mass cancel** workflow. Conceptually, a mass cancel is:

> A single instruction that asks the broker or venue to cancel *all* open orders matching a specified set of criteria.

Those criteria can include:

- Account or group of accounts.
- Client or Party identifiers.
- Symbol, security type, or product complex.
- Trading session (for example, regular vs. extended hours).
- Sometimes side (buy vs. sell) or other flags.

The broker or venue receives the request, searches its own live-order book for orders that meet the criteria, and attempts to cancel each one. The outcome is reported back through:

- An immediate acknowledgment or rejection of the mass-cancel *request* itself.
- A stream of individual ExecutionReports for each affected order (typically with ExecType = Canceled, OrdStatus = Canceled).

From your system's point of view, a successful mass cancel is effectively a batch of normal cancels, except that you did not have to enumerate every order.

Selection by Routing Context

The big design theme in this chapter has been *routing context*: accounts and Party groups as a precise identifier of who owns which orders. Mass actions heavily reuse this machinery.

By Account

The most common selection key is **Account**. A risk officer might instruct:

> "Cancel all working orders for account FUND_A_STAT."

In FIX terms, this means sending a mass-cancel message that specifies:

- The appropriate command for mass cancel.
- Account set to FUND_A_STAT.
- A scope indicating "all open orders for this account".

At the broker, this typically becomes:

- Query internal order records where Account = FUND_A_STAT and status is live.
- Issue cancels for each of those orders at the venue(s).

By Client or Party

Sometimes, accounts alone are not enough. For example, you might want to halt all trading for a client that uses multiple accounts, or you may operate as an intermediary with sub-clients and need to stop all their orders.

In that case, selection can be based on Party roles:

- Include in the mass-cancel request a Party entry for the client or sub-client with the correct PartyRole.
- The broker or venue uses that Party role and identifier to filter live orders.

This only works cleanly if your order-entry messages have been consistently populating those Party fields, as recommended earlier. If Party usage is inconsistent, mass actions based on them will be unreliable.

By Symbol or Product

Another common risk action is product-based:

"Cancel all live orders in AAPL" or "Cancel all orders in this futures contract and its options."

In this case, the selection criteria include:

- Symbol or security identifier fields for a specific instrument.
- Optionally, broader product filters (for example, all options on a given underlying).

The broker or venue will match open orders against these fields in its order records and cancel those that match.

By Venue or Session

Finally, you may need to act at the venue or session level:

- Cancel all orders on a particular exchange or MTF.
- Cancel all orders in a given trading session (for example, closing auction only).

This uses session identifiers or custom fields depending on the venue's FIX specification. Again, the key is that the selection is made at the destination that actually knows which orders are live in which sessions.

Mass Status: Seeing the Whole Board

Closely related to mass cancel is **mass status**: instead of cancelling orders, you ask for a *snapshot or enumeration* of live orders matching certain criteria. This is essential for:

- Confirming what is actually live at the broker or venue when your internal view may be stale (for example, after a disconnect or failover).
- Auditing that a previous mass cancel indeed took effect.
- Reconciling differences between your internal state machine and the broker's view.

A mass-status request typically specifies:

- A selection key (for example, by account or client).
- A scope (for example, all open orders vs. all orders including closed).

The broker replies with:

- A series of status messages or ExecutionReports enumerating matching orders.
- Each message includes the current OrdStatus, quantities, and identifiers.

Your system can then:

- Compare the broker's enumeration with your own internal records.
- Fill in gaps (for example, orders you believe are live that the broker does not know about, or vice versa).

Used together, mass status and mass cancel give you visibility and control: first, see what exists; second, act on it at scale.

How Mass Cancels Flow Through ExecutionReports

From the perspective of your existing order state machine, mass cancels do not introduce new types of ExecutionReport. Each affected order typically receives:

- An ExecutionReport with ExecType = Canceled.
- OrdStatus = Canceled, LeavesQty = 0.
- CumQty unchanged from before the cancel.

- Optional fields indicating that the cancel was part of a mass action or providing a reason code.

Your logic for updating each order on receipt of a cancel report is exactly the same whether the cancel was:

- Initiated by a trader via single-order cancel.
- Initiated by your risk system via mass cancel.
- Initiated by the broker or venue (for example, due to a trading halt).

The only difference is the *origin* of the cancel request and perhaps some additional tags describing the action. Internally, you should:

- Mark the order as canceled with the appropriate final CumQty.
- Attribute the source of the cancel (trader, risk system, supervisor, venue) in your own audit fields.

This reinforces an important design principle: downstream consumers of the order book (risk, P&L, reporting) do not need to know whether a cancel was "mass" or "single". They just need a consistent end state. The fact that it was a mass action is primarily relevant for operational audit and control.

Risk Mitigation Scenarios

Let us now connect mass actions to concrete risk and operational scenarios.

Broken Strategy or Algo

A strategy starts sending obviously bad orders—perhaps due to a bug, a data-feed issue, or misconfiguration. A risk engine detects abnormal behavior, for example:

- Excessive order rate.

- Orders at extreme prices relative to market.
- Rapid accumulation of undesirable position.

A typical response chain is:

- Risk engine triggers a *mass cancel* for the affected account(s) or strategies.
- Broker or venue cancels all open orders matching the selection.
- ExecutionReports confirm each cancel.
- Risk engine optionally blocks further new orders for these accounts until manual investigation.

Acting at the mass level ensures that even if you briefly lose exact track of how many orders the strategy has already sent, all live orders held by the broker or venue are swept up in one move.

Market or Venue Halt

An exchange announces a trading halt in a particular instrument, sector, or the entire market. Various responses are possible:

- The venue may automatically cancel all open orders and send cancel ExecutionReports.
- Your firm may choose to issue mass cancels for affected symbols or venues across your internal order book, ensuring you are flat in terms of live orders when trading resumes.

Mass status can be useful immediately after such events:

- Request a status snapshot for affected accounts or symbols.
- Verify that no stray orders remain live.

Client-Level Risk Actions

Suppose a client breaches a credit limit or fails an operational check. Your risk team may decide to:

- Cancel all open orders for that client across all accounts.
- Optionally mass-cancel or block further orders routed via that client's prime or clearing arrangement.

In this case, the selection filter is built from routing context:

- Client Party identifiers.
- Related accounts and sub-accounts.
- Possibly prime broker roles, if the issue is with a particular prime arrangement.

This again illustrates how careful design of accounts and Party roles upstream pays dividends when you must act quickly downstream.

End-of-Day Operational Cleanup

Even when there is no immediate risk crisis, mass actions help with housekeeping. For example:

- Before systems shutdown, mass-cancel any day orders that should not carry over.
- Clear out stale GTC (good-till-cancel) orders that are no longer aligned with current strategy.

Instead of relying on each strategy to remember its own leftovers, a central process can:

- Use mass status to enumerate live orders per account.
- Apply firm policies to decide which ones to cancel.
- Issue targeted or broad mass cancels as appropriate.

Operational Safeguards

Because mass actions are powerful, they require strong safeguards. A simple mistake—such as cancelling the wrong scope—can disrupt trading across many clients or strategies.

Key safeguards include:

Authentication and Entitlements

Not every user or system should be allowed to perform mass actions. At minimum:

- Restrict mass-cancel capabilities to specific roles (for example, risk officers, supervisors, designated system components).
- Enforce per-connection and per-user entitlements: a user with access to one account should not be able to mass-cancel another client's orders.

Confirmation and Two-Step Actions

For high-impact actions (for example, cancel all orders for the entire firm), consider:

- Requiring a two-step workflow: request followed by confirmation from another person or role.
- Presenting a pre-execution summary based on mass status: approximate number of orders affected, estimated notional, and so on.

This helps catch accidental overreach, such as selecting a broader scope than intended.

Dry Runs and Limited Scope

Where possible, support "dry-run" capabilities in your own systems:

- First, simulate the selection using your internal order book without actually sending the mass-cancel message.
- Show operators which orders would be affected.

- Only then, on explicit confirmation, send the actual mass cancel to the broker or venue.

Even if the FIX layer does not support a formal dry-run flag, you can implement the preview internally.

Rate Limiting and Backoff

Risk systems under stress might try to send repeated mass actions. Brokers and venues protect themselves with throttles. Your design should:

- Respect published message rates and guidelines.
- Avoid sending redundant mass cancels in rapid succession for the same scope.
- Back off if you receive rejections or warnings about rate limits.

Audit Logging

Every mass action should be thoroughly logged:

- Who initiated it (user, system, role).
- When it was requested and when it was sent.
- What scope and selection criteria were used (accounts, parties, symbols, sessions).
- What the broker or venue replied (acknowledgments, errors).
- How many and which orders were ultimately affected (based on subsequent ExecutionReports).

This is essential for post-incident analysis and for demonstrating control to regulators and internal governance.

Testing Mass-Action Logic Safely

Testing mass actions in production is risky by definition. Instead, design a disciplined testing strategy:

- Use dedicated test environments from brokers and venues that support realistic order flow but are isolated from real markets.
- Populate those environments with representative mixes of orders across multiple accounts and symbols.
- Exercise mass status and mass cancel under various scopes, including intentionally invalid or edge-case selections, to verify behavior.
- Verify that your internal order state machines react correctly to the flood of cancel ExecutionReports.

You should also simulate disaster scenarios in controlled settings:

- Strategy runaway with very high order rates.
- Sudden market halt followed by mass cancels from the venue.
- Network partitions that cause intermittent visibility of orders and delayed cancel reports.

Doing so increases confidence that, when a real emergency occurs, your bulk controls will behave predictably.

Mass cancel and mass status messages extend the single-order workflows we have built so far into *portfolio-level control mechanisms*. Properly used, they allow you to:

- Act quickly to mitigate risk when strategies misbehave, markets break, or clients breach limits.
- Maintain a synchronized view of live orders across your systems and those of your brokers and venues.
- Perform end-of-day and periodic cleanup without relying on every individual strategy's memory.

Crucially, these tools depend on the groundwork we laid earlier:

- Consistent routing context (accounts and Party roles) makes it possible to target exactly the orders you intend.

- A robust ExecutionReport-driven state machine ensures that the flood of cancel and status events resolves into a clean, auditable view of which orders were affected.

With these bulk controls, your FIX order flow architecture moves beyond simply placing trades; it becomes a controlled environment in which risk can be managed decisively, yet transparently and safely, even under stress.

Chapter 5

Real-Time Drop Copy Design

Drop copy is your safety net and your black box recorder: when markets go wild, it's often the only clean, real-time view of what actually traded. This chapter shows you how to design drop copy flows that are fast but trustworthy, richly informative but lean enough to scale, and isolated enough that a hungry risk engine can never stall your primary order flow.

5.1 Drop Copy Use Cases and Integration Models

In earlier chapters we focused on the basic FIX plumbing: how NewOrderSingle messages reach a venue or broker, how ExecutionReports walk an order through its lifecycle, and how FIX sessions are established, sequenced, and monitored. We were mostly living in the world of *primary flow*: the messages that directly drive trading.

Real-time drop copy sits to the side of that primary flow. It does not change what is traded or how orders are matched. Instead, it creates a parallel, near-real-time stream of order and trade information whose purpose is *visibility*. The business question behind this section is simple:

> If we already have trading sessions, logs, and back-office reports, why do firms spend real money and engineering effort on real-time drop copy?

The answer lies in the needs of three major groups that care deeply about trading activity but are not themselves driving orders: *risk*, *surveillance*, and *middle office*. Each of these groups needs to see the same underlying events, but with slightly different timing, completeness, and enrichment. Once you understand their consumption patterns, the engineering choice of *how* to publish drop copy—what sessions, what messages, and what routing model—becomes much easier to reason about.

This section therefore does two things:

1. Describes concrete, realistic use cases for risk, surveillance, and middle office, highlighting what they need from drop copy.
2. Maps those needs to provider–consumer integration models: how an execution venue or broker publishes drop copy and how multiple consumer systems subscribe to it safely and efficiently.

Front Office vs. Downstream Consumers

It helps to start by contrasting the front office—the traders, algos, and smart order routers sending NewOrderSingle messages—with these downstream consumers.

Front-office order flow has a few defining characteristics:

- **Speed-sensitive:** Microseconds and milliseconds matter. Extra hops and extra bytes are treated as costs.
- **Minimal payload:** You send what the venue requires to execute and allocate the order, and not much more. Anything that lengthens messages or adds processing is carefully justified.

- **Tight coupling to execution engines:** If the session is slow or misbehaves, trading is directly impacted.

By contrast, risk, surveillance, and middle-office teams prioritize different things:

- **Completeness over raw speed:** They care that they see *all* relevant events and that no events are silently dropped or misordered. Sub-millisecond latency is rarely necessary; a lag of tens or hundreds of milliseconds is often acceptable as long as it is stable and bounded.
- **Enrichment:** They need more than basic FIX fields. They want accounts grouped by legal entity, strategy, and desk; regulatory flags; internal identifiers; and sometimes pre-computed risk metrics.
- **Durability:** They need a record that can be replayed, audited, and used to reconstruct the state of the world at any point in time.

Real-time drop copy is the mechanism that feeds these downstream needs without polluting or overloading the primary trading sessions. It is deliberately designed as a separate flow, even when it carries the same core ExecutionReport or TradeCaptureReport content.

Risk Consumption Patterns

Risk functions make heavy use of drop copy. While overnight risk uses full end-of-day positions and pricing, *intraday* risk relies on seeing order and trade events close to real time.

Pre-Trade and At-Trade Limits

Consider a broker providing DMA (direct market access) to clients. The broker is responsible for ensuring that a client's trading activity stays within agreed credit and risk limits. There are several levels at which this can be done:

- **Pre-trade checks** on a per-order basis, often implemented inline in the order gateway (for example, notional checks, fat-finger price bands).
- **Near-real-time exposure monitoring** across many orders and venues, implemented as a separate risk engine.

The inline gateway checks are rightly constrained: they must be very fast and rely only on local state. The broader exposure monitoring, by contrast, can afford a few additional milliseconds of latency but must see:

- All new orders and significant modifications (quantity changes, price moves, side changes).
- All fills and cancelations.
- Any busts or corrections to trades.

A real-time drop copy feed from the broker's internal execution layer into the intraday risk engine is the natural way to satisfy this need. The risk engine subscribes to all order- and trade-related messages for a set of accounts or clients, aggregates notional and volume, and updates limit usage dashboards. When limits are breached, it may take action (alerts, trading suspensions), but the key point is that it is *fed* by drop copy rather than intercepting the trading sessions directly.

Margin and Credit Utilization

Clearing brokers and prime brokers use drop copy to monitor margin and credit usage across products and venues in real time. For example:

- Every new futures trade updates both the client's margin requirement and available credit lines.
- Equity trades might count against concentration limits in specific names or sectors.

Here, a drop copy stream feeding a margin engine allows the firm to:

- Track exposure evolution as orders fill throughout the day.
- Detect sudden build-ups (for example, a client rapidly building a large short position).
- Drive intraday margin calls or adjustments before risk becomes unmanageable.

Because margin engines work across multiple venues, they often subscribe to a *consolidated* drop copy view: a normalized stream that merges events from all execution platforms used by the broker, not just one matching engine.

Real-Time P&L and Exposure Dashboards

Trading desks and risk managers expect real-time dashboards showing:

- Positions by instrument, sector, and strategy.
- Open orders and unfilled exposure.
- Realized and unrealized P&L.

The calculation of P&L obviously needs prices, but the drivers of position changes are orders and trades. A typical pattern is:

1. A central "positions service" consumes drop copy from execution systems.
2. It updates positions and cash as fills occur or trades are busted.
3. It exposes current holdings and trade history to front-end tools and reports.

Without real-time drop copy, these dashboards would either lag significantly (for example, relying only on periodic batch updates) or require direct, fragile integration with each execution system.

Surveillance and Behavior Analytics

Surveillance teams focus on *how* trading is done: patterns of behavior that might indicate market abuse, manipulation, or other breaches of policy or regulation. Their needs differ subtly from risk:

- They care about the *full lifecycle* of orders, including cancels, partial fills, and replacement messages.
- They care about *who* is behind the orders, in more granular terms than a single account. Strategy identifiers, trading desks, and trader IDs are all important.
- They need *reliable identifiers* to connect orders and trades across systems.

Spoofing, Layering, and Wash Trade Detection

Patterns such as spoofing or layering are typically characterized by sequences of orders that are entered and removed quickly relative to executions, often at multiple price levels. To detect such behavior, surveillance systems must see:

- Every new order (ExecutionReport with a new OrderID or a NewOrderSingle mirrored in drop copy).
- Modifications and cancels.
- All actual executions associated with those orders, including quantity and price.

Drop copy is ideal for feeding this view because:

- It can be structured to include *all lifecycle events*, not just trades.
- It can be enriched with fields that may not be present in raw client-facing flow, such as internal trader IDs or strategy codes.
- It is typically centralized and normalized, making it easier to run behavior analytics consistently across venues.

Similarly, wash trades and cross trades require cross-referencing both sides of a trade, even when routed through different channels. Drop copy events enriched with consistent trade identifiers and account hierarchies give surveillance tools the raw material to perform these analyses.

Behavior Analytics and Profiling

Beyond specific alert types, many firms build behavior analytics platforms that profile:

- Typical order size, frequency, and duration for a given trader or algorithm.
- Time-of-day patterns.
- Reaction to market events.

Again, these rely on complete, consistent drop copy streams. Late or missing events can distort the picture. For this reason, surveillance consumers tend to prioritize *completeness and ordering* over ultra-low latency. A batch arriving 200 milliseconds later but complete is more valuable than a partially delivered stream.

Middle Office and Trade Lifecycle Management

The middle office is the bridge between front-office activity and back-office settlement. It is concerned with:

- Trade capture and validation.
- Allocations to funds or underlying clients.
- Trade confirmations and statements.
- Exception workflows: breaks, mismatches, and corrections.

Trade Capture and Allocations

Middle office systems often treat trades, not orders, as their primary objects. They ask questions such as:

> What trades did we execute for Fund A today, and how should they be allocated across underlying client accounts?

A drop copy stream feeding middle office will therefore often emphasize:

- Trade-centric messages (for example, TradeCaptureReport or fill ExecutionReports).
- Allocation-related fields (for example, account, sub-account, give-up details).
- Post-trade enrichment (for example, fee rates, commission flags).

This does not mean middle office never cares about orders. For example, they may need order-level information to explain partial fills or to support client inquiries. But their core operational processes usually hinge on a consolidated view of trades and allocations, which can be derived from, or directly published as, a specialized drop copy feed.

Confirmations, Reconciliations, and Exceptions

Middle office also uses drop copy to:

- Generate or validate trade confirmations before sending them to clients or counterparties.
- Reconcile internal books and records with external statements from exchanges, clearing houses, or custodians.
- Drive exception workflows when something does not match or when a trade is canceled or corrected.

In some organizations, the drop copy feed from internal execution systems is treated as the "golden source" of intraday trade data, which is then compared against external drop copy or end-of-day files from venues. In others, it is a corroborating feed used to cross-check client-provided information or back-office data.

From Use Cases to Integration Models

Once you see these different consumption patterns, you can think of real-time drop copy as a *product* with multiple customer segments:

- Intraday risk engines and dashboards.
- Surveillance and behavior analytics platforms.
- Middle-office trade capture and allocation systems.
- Sometimes, external clients who subscribe to drop copy from their broker.

The provider of this product—typically an execution venue or broker—must decide:

- How many drop copy sessions to offer.
- Which messages and fields each session will carry.
- How to route events to the right consumers while enforcing entitlements.
- How to balance per-consumer customization against operational complexity.

At a high level, you can think of two families of integration models:

1. **Direct sessions:** The provider runs separate FIX drop copy sessions directly to each internal or external consumer.

2. **Hub-and-spoke:** The provider publishes drop copy into an internal hub (a message bus, stream, or data lake), from which many consumers read. External clients might still have direct sessions, but internal systems connect via the hub.

Before we explore these models in detail, it is helpful to visualize the landscape of producers, integration layers, and consumers.

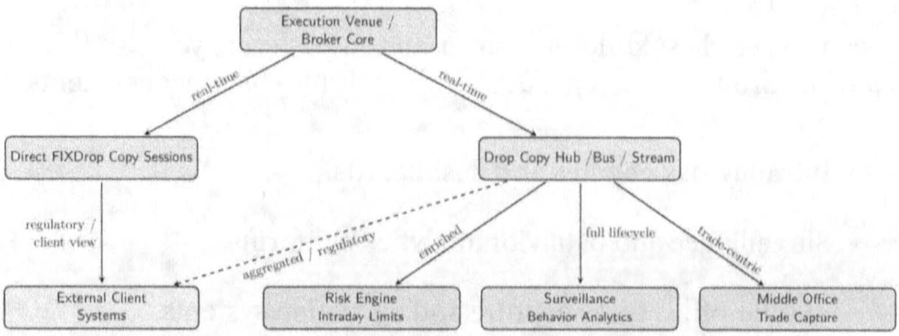

This picture emphasizes three tiers:

1. The **producer**: the execution venue or broker core where orders are matched and trades generated.
2. The **integration layer**: either direct FIX sessions or an internal hub (or both).
3. The **consumers**: risk, surveillance, middle office, and external clients.

Different firms choose different combinations of these patterns, but the fundamental design knobs are common.

Single-Provider, Multi-Consumer Fan-Out

The simplest mental model for drop copy is "one producer, many consumers." The execution system is the sole source of truth for order and trade events. It fans out those events to multiple consumers according to a set of routing and entitlement rules.

Two basic implementation styles are common.

Direct FIX Sessions to Each Consumer

In this model, the execution system (or a drop copy gateway attached to it) establishes a FIX session with each consumer:

- A session to the internal risk engine.
- A session to the surveillance platform.
- A session to middle office.
- Sessions to external clients who subscribe to drop copy.

Each session:

- Has its own sequence numbers and heartbeats.
- Can be tuned independently (message types, throttling, maintenance windows).
- Carries only the subset of events that consumer is entitled to see.

This direct model has some attractive properties:

- **Simplicity:** The mapping from events to sessions is explicit in the execution or routing layer.
- **Isolation:** A misbehaving consumer (for example, one that stops reading) does not directly affect others.
- **Fine-grained entitlements:** It is straightforward to ensure that a given client or internal system only sees its own orders and trades.

However, as the number of consumers grows, direct fan-out can become operationally heavy:

- Every new consumer requires changes in the execution or routing system.
- Replaying history to a consumer may burden the core systems.
- Enrichment logic (for example, adding strategy IDs or risk attributes) can end up duplicated across sessions.

Hub-and-Spoke via a Messaging Bus or Data Lake

To address these scalability and maintainability concerns, many firms introduce an internal integration layer:

- The execution system publishes a single normalized drop copy stream into a messaging hub (for example, a high-throughput message bus or a streaming platform).
- Internal consumers (risk, surveillance, middle office) subscribe to that stream, often via specialized topics or queues.
- External clients may still have separate FIX drop copy sessions, but those are typically fed from the hub rather than directly from the matching engine.

This hub-and-spoke model offers:

- **Decoupling:** Execution developers can focus on correctness and performance of a single publishing path, while downstream teams evolve independently.
- **Shared enrichment:** Common transformations and enrichment (for example, mapping internal account IDs to legal entities, tagging orders with strategy codes) can be performed once at the hub.
- **Replay and durability:** The hub can be designed to retain history and support replays without reloading the execution engine.

The trade-off is that the internal architecture becomes more complex, and you must design clear contracts between the execution system and the hub: message schemas, allowed latencies, and failure modes.

Specialized Feeds for Different Consumer Classes

Even within a given integration model, you will rarely have a single "one size fits all" drop copy feed. Instead, you define a small number of *profiles* tailored to the needs of different consumer classes.

Risk and Exposure Feeds

Risk-oriented feeds typically:

- Include all order lifecycle events and trades.
- Contain account, desk, and sometimes legal-entity information.
- May include derived fields, such as notional value per fill, risk weights, or bucketed exposure tags.

They prioritize:

- **Completeness:** No missing events.
- **Predictable, bounded latency:** For example, "events visible within 100 milliseconds of execution."

Surveillance Feeds

Surveillance-oriented feeds:

- Emphasize full lifecycle detail and stability of identifiers (ClOrdID, OrderID, ExecID, and internal IDs).
- May include additional confidential data, such as trader IDs or strategy names.
- Often require long retention windows or easy replay to reconstruct timelines of behavior.

Their design choices may lean toward:

- Higher tolerance for latency, as long as the order of events is preserved.
- More verbose payloads to capture context around each event.

Middle-Office and Client Feeds

Middle-office and external client feeds are often:

- **Trade-centric:** Less focus on every intermediate state of an order; more focus on executed trades, allocations, and corrections.
- **Regulatory-aware:** Including fields needed for confirmations, regulatory reporting, and client statements.

They usually:

- Need to be stable and well-documented, as changes can impact external parties.
- Prioritize clarity and robustness over sheer throughput.

Entitlements, Data Minimization, and Regulatory Views

An important dimension across all integration models is *who is allowed to see what.* Drop copy can easily become a data-leak risk if not carefully designed.

Client Segregation and Privacy

External clients must only see:

- Their own orders and trades.
- Possibly some anonymized aggregate metrics if explicitly agreed (for example, benchmark data).

The integration model must enforce this at the routing level:

- Separate FIX sessions per client, with filters based on client IDs or account codes.
- No accidental fan-out of other clients' data through shared hubs without proper access controls.

Internal Separation of Views

Even within a firm, not all fields should be visible to all consumers:

- Surveillance might see trader IDs and strategy labels that are not exposed to some middle-office teams.
- Risk may see aggregated exposure across clients while middle office handles client-specific positions.

This leads to patterns such as:

- Multiple logical feeds over the same physical hub, each with its own schema and field set.
- Field-level entitlements enforced at the hub or gateway level.

Regulatory vs. Proprietary Fields

Some drop copy feeds are explicitly designed to satisfy regulatory reporting or audit requirements. These must:

- Contain certain mandatory fields (for example, client identifiers, timestamps, venue codes).
- Be retained and replayable for specified time periods.

At the same time, firms will want to protect proprietary fields that encode alpha, such as detailed algorithm parameters or internal risk scores. These might be suppressed or anonymized for regulatory feeds while retained in full for internal analytics.

Choosing an Integration Style: A Checklist

By now, the connection between use cases and integration models should be clearer. To close this section, it is helpful to summarize a practical checklist:

1. **Identify your consumers:** List all internal and external systems that need real-time visibility of orders and trades.

2. **Clarify their priorities:** For each consumer, decide whether latency, completeness, enrichment, or durability is most important.

3. **Define feed profiles:** Group consumers with similar needs into a small number of feed types (for example, risk, surveillance, middle office, client).

4. **Pick a fan-out model:** Decide whether to push events directly from the execution system to each consumer, to introduce a hub-and-spoke architecture, or to combine both (for example, hub for internal consumers, direct sessions for clients).

5. **Design entitlements and schemas:** For each feed, specify which events and fields are included and how entitlements are enforced.

6. **Plan for growth and replay:** Ensure that adding new consumers or replaying history does not impose unacceptable risk or load on the execution system.

The remainder of this chapter builds on these ideas. In subsequent sections we will examine how the choice between ExecutionReport-based and TradeCaptureReport-based drop copy shapes these feeds, how to design the underlying FIX session and routing topologies, and how to engineer sequencing and latency guarantees appropriate to each consumer class. Here, the key takeaway is that real-time drop copy is not just a technical mirror of trading flow; it is a deliberately designed product that serves multiple constituencies, each with its own view of what "good" looks like.

5.2 Choosing Between ExecutionReport and TradeCaptureReport

In the previous section we treated drop copy as a business product: a fan-out of trading events to risk, surveillance, middle office, and sometimes external clients. We intentionally stayed at the level of *who* consumes drop copy and *how* they use it.

We now move one level down in detail and ask a more technical but equally important question:

> What should the *primary message type* be for my drop copy: ExecutionReport, TradeCaptureReport, or some combination of both?

This choice shapes everything that follows. It determines:

- How much of the *order lifecycle* appears in drop copy.
- Which *identifiers* are naturally available for correlation and audit.
- How easy it is to *enrich* the stream with risk, strategy, and regulatory data.
- How well the feed serves different *downstream consumers*.

This section will:

- Contrast order-lifecycle views (ExecutionReport) with trade-centric views (TradeCaptureReport).
- Examine the identifiers that live in each world and how to cross-link them.
- Discuss enrichment patterns and the impact on payload size and confidentiality.
- Present a visual comparison matrix.
- Offer practical patterns and heuristics: when to choose one, the other, or both.

Order-Lifecycle vs. Trade-Centric Designs

Before we talk about FIX message types, it helps to think in terms of mental models.

- An **order-lifecycle** model asks: *What happened to this order from birth to death?* It cares about the initial NewOrderSingle, all partial fills, cancels, and replacements, and finally, how the order ended up (fully filled, canceled, expired, rejected).
- A **trade-centric** model asks: *What trades happened today, and what are their attributes?* It treats trades as the primary events and gives less attention to the steps that led to them.

ExecutionReport messages are naturally aligned with the order-lifecycle model. Each ExecutionReport corresponds to an event in the life of an order: new, partially filled, filled, canceled, replaced, rejected, busted, and so on. If you string them together by OrderID and ClOrdID, you can replay the entire story of that order.

TradeCaptureReport messages are naturally aligned with the trade-centric model. Each TradeCaptureReport describes one or more trades: price, quantity, side, parties involved, and related identifiers. They may contain some order identifiers, but their focus is on completed (or corrected) executions.

A real-time drop copy service can be built around either of these, or a hybrid. Your choice should be guided by who your consumers are and what questions they need to answer.

ExecutionReport-Based Drop Copy

An ExecutionReport-based design says: *Drop copy will mirror the same order lifecycle that is visible on primary trading sessions, possibly with extra enrichment.*

Lifecycle Coverage

With ExecutionReports you naturally get:

- **Order entry:** The acknowledgement of a new order, with assigned OrderID.

- **Working state changes:** Replacements, partial fills, and status transitions (for example, from "new" to "partially filled" to "filled" or "canceled").
- **Fills and busts:** Each execution event, including later corrections or cancellations.
- **Rejections:** Rejected orders and amendments, along with reason codes.

For surveillance and some risk use cases, this granularity is extremely valuable. For example, to analyze layering behavior, you need to know how many orders were entered and quickly canceled versus how many actually resulted in fills. ExecutionReport sequences give you that history.

Identifiers in ExecutionReports

ExecutionReports typically carry a rich set of identifiers:

- **ClOrdID:** The client order identifier, often assigned by the buy-side or upstream system.
- **OrderID:** The order identifier assigned by the broker or venue; often acts as the internal primary key in the matching engine.
- **ExecID:** A unique identifier for each execution event; useful for deduplicating fills and referencing specific executions.
- **Secondary IDs:** Depending on the implementation, additional fields may link to trade reports, clearing references, or external systems.

Because ExecutionReports appear at each step of the lifecycle, these identifiers give you a strong chain of evidence. For example:

- You can join all ExecutionReports with the same OrderID to reconstruct the full lifecycle.
- You can use ExecID to confirm that a particular fill was recognized by all downstream systems (risk, middle office, client).

Benefits for Downstream Consumers

ExecutionReport-based drop copy is particularly attractive for:

Surveillance and Behavior Analytics

These systems thrive on lifecycle detail. They want to know:

- How many orders a strategy submitted and canceled without execution.
- How many times an order was resized or re-priced before filling.
- The sequence of actions leading up to a suspicious trade.

ExecutionReports provide that narrative by design.

Intraday Risk and Limit Monitoring

Risk engines, especially those doing fine-grained limit checks, benefit from seeing:

- New orders as soon as they are acknowledged, to anticipate potential exposure.
- Reductions in order size or cancelations, to reduce expected exposure.
- Partial fills as they occur, to update realized exposure and P&L.

All of this can be driven from ExecutionReports. The engine can treat each order as a state machine, transitioning its internal exposure as ExecutionReports arrive.

Trade-Offs of ExecutionReport-Centric Designs

The strengths come with costs:

- **Higher message volume:** A single order may generate many ExecutionReports: ack, partial fills, cancel requests, final status. For high-volume clients or venues, this can be a lot of data.
- **More complex consumers:** Downstream systems must understand order states and aggregate across multiple events to form a picture of trades and positions.

- **Payload sizes:** If you add enrichment (strategy IDs, risk attributes, desk codes) to every ExecutionReport, overall bandwidth and processing overhead can grow quickly.

For some consumers, especially middle office and external clients, this level of detail is unnecessary. They may prefer a concise list of trades, with corrections, rather than a play-by-play of every order action.

TradeCaptureReport-Based Drop Copy

A TradeCaptureReport-based design says: *Drop copy will focus on trades as the primary events and capture their key attributes cleanly and compactly.*

Lifecycle Coverage

TradeCaptureReports tend not to carry the full order history. Instead, they give you:

- **Executed trades:** Price, quantity, side, and usually some notion of execution time.
- **Allocations:** In many implementations, they include allocation or give-up details, such as how a block trade is broken down by fund or client account.
- **Corrections and cancellations:** When a trade is corrected or busted, a TradeCaptureReport can carry the details of the change.

From the point of view of middle office or reconciliation teams, this is often exactly what they need. Their driving questions are:

> What trades did we do? For whom? At what prices and quantities? How should they be booked and settled?

They are less interested in how many times the order was resized or re-priced along the way.

Identifiers in TradeCaptureReports

TradeCaptureReports use a slightly different identifier set:

- **TradeID or TradeReportID:** A unique identifier for the trade or trade report.
- **Secondary trade references:** IDs from clearing houses, counterparties, or internal systems.
- **Linked order information:** Some implementations carry OrderID, ClOrdID, or lists of orders contributing to the trade, especially when an execution matches multiple orders.

These identifiers are excellent for:

- **Reconciliation:** Matching internal trades to exchange or clearing statements.
- **Client reporting:** Presenting clients with stable, referenceable IDs for their trades.
- **Back-office processing:** Linking trades to settlement instructions and accounting entries.

However, because TradeCaptureReports do not convey every lifecycle step, you cannot, by using them alone, reconstruct the full history of each order.

Benefits for Downstream Consumers

TradeCaptureReport-based drop copy is particularly well-suited to:

Middle Office and Operations

These teams care most about:

- Capturing trades reliably and promptly.
- Performing allocations and bookings.
- Sending confirmations and regulatory reports.

They appreciate:

- **Compactness:** Fewer messages, each aligned with the operational unit of work (a trade).

- **Stability:** Trade IDs and related references that can be relied upon during reconciliation.

External Client Confirmations and Statements

External clients receiving drop copy may also prefer a trade-focused feed. It:

- Reduces noise for clients who do not care about intra-day order changes.
- Aligns more directly with how they book and report trades internally.

Trade-Offs of TradeCaptureReport-Centric Designs

Focusing only on TradeCaptureReports has its own downsides:

- **Limited behavioral visibility:** Without order-level events, it is harder to detect certain abusive patterns or to analyze algorithm behavior.
- **Reduced pre-trade context:** Risk systems relying solely on trade data see exposure only after fills, not as orders are working in the market.
- **Potential gaps in lifecycle understanding:** When trades are corrected or busted, you need careful handling to keep all downstream systems in sync.

For risk and surveillance, TradeCaptureReports alone are usually not enough. They may serve as a good complement to ExecutionReports, but rarely as a full replacement.

Comparing the Two: A Visual Matrix

To bring these ideas together, it helps to see a side-by-side comparison across key dimensions: lifecycle detail, payload size, latency sensitivity, suitability for different consumers, and reconciliation ease.

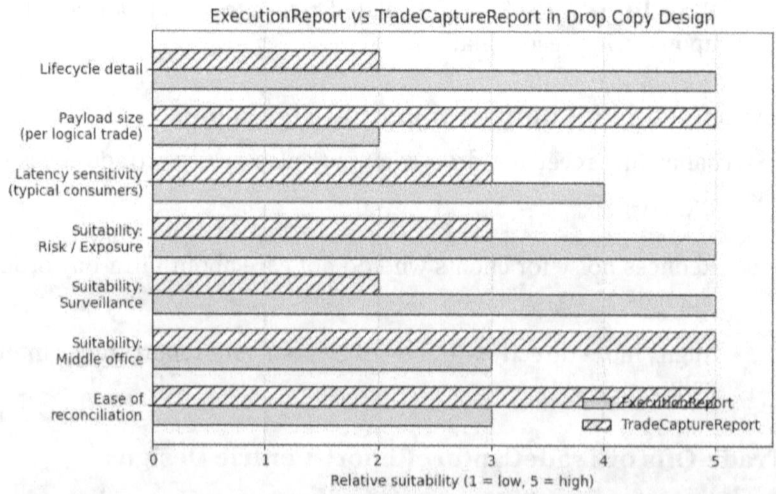

Figure 5.1: Qualitative comparison of ExecutionReport- and TradeCaptureReport-based drop copy designs across key dimensions.

This chart is not meant to be numerically precise; it is a way to summarize our discussion in a form that you can adapt to your own environment.

Identifiers and Cross-Referencing Between Worlds

In practice, you will often need to connect the order-lifecycle world (ExecutionReports) with the trade-centric world (TradeCaptureReports). Even if your drop copy focuses on one type, your internal systems may use both.

Core Identifier Flows

In an ExecutionReport-based flow:

- **ClOrdID** originates from the client or upstream system and is echoed back in ExecutionReports.

- **OrderID** is created by the broker or venue and used as the internal key for the order.
- **ExecID** is generated per execution; several ExecutionReports for the same order will share the same OrderID but have different ExecIDs.

In a TradeCaptureReport-based flow:

- **TradeID or TradeReportID** is assigned to each trade or trade report.
- Some implementations also carry **OrderID** and **ClOrdID**, especially if a trade corresponds to a single order.
- When a single trade aggregates multiple orders, an array or repeating group of order references may be included.

Designing Stable Cross-References

To preserve a stable cross-reference between orders and trades:

- Ensure that TradeCaptureReports include at least one of the key order identifiers (OrderID, ClOrdID) when possible.
- Consider introducing firm-specific identifiers that are consistent across both message types (for example, an internal "Execution Key" that links a fill ExecutionReport and its corresponding TradeCaptureReport).
- Document clearly which identifiers are guaranteed unique, which are unique only per day or per session, and how long they are retained.

When this is done well:

- Surveillance can start with orders (ExecutionReports) and jump to the corresponding trades (TradeCaptureReports) when needed for reconciliation.
- Middle office can start from trade references and, when investigating issues, pull up the underlying order history.

Enrichment Patterns and Payload Considerations

Regardless of which message type you emphasize, drop copy rarely consists of raw, venue-style messages. Firms almost always enrich the messages before publication.

Common Enrichment Fields

Typical enrichments include:

- **Account and desk metadata:** Links from the trading account to legal entities, desks, regions, and strategies.
- **Risk and credit attributes:** Risk buckets, margin classes, regulatory capital charges.
- **Strategy and algorithm identifiers:** Which algo or strategy generated the order or trade.
- **Regulatory flags:** Short-sale indicators, liquidity provision flags, client vs. house flags, and so on.

These may be carried in standard FIX tags where available, or in firm-specific custom tags.

Impact on ExecutionReport vs. TradeCaptureReport

With ExecutionReports:

- Enrichment is applied to many more messages, increasing total bandwidth and processing load.
- However, you get fine-grained context at each lifecycle stage, which can be powerful for risk and surveillance.

With TradeCaptureReports:

- Enrichment is applied primarily to trades and, in some designs, allocations, meaning fewer messages overall.
- Middle office and client reporting get richly annotated trades without dealing with every order event.

A pragmatic approach is to:

- Keep enrichment on ExecutionReports focused on fields that matter for intraday risk and surveillance.
- Put heavier enrichment related to allocations, fees, and regulatory reporting on TradeCaptureReports or on separate middle-office feeds derived from them.

Matching Message Choice to Consumers: Patterns

We can now return to the business-driven perspective from the previous section and overlay these technical choices.

Pattern 1: Pure ExecutionReport Drop Copy

In this pattern, drop copy is built entirely around ExecutionReports. All consumers—risk, surveillance, middle office, clients—receive variants of the same lifecycle-based feed.

This is:

- **Simple conceptually:** One message type, one primary source of truth.
- **Strong for risk and surveillance:** All lifecycle detail is available.

But:

- Middle office and external clients may be overwhelmed by lifecycle noise.
- Additional internal work is needed to aggregate execution events into trade-level objects for booking and reporting.

This pattern is most appropriate when:

- Your consumer base is dominated by risk and surveillance.

- Volumes are manageable, or you have strong infrastructure to cope with the message rates.
- Middle office systems are comfortable working with order events or you have a robust internal trade-construction layer.

Pattern 2: Pure TradeCaptureReport Drop Copy

Here, drop copy is built exclusively around TradeCaptureReports. Risk, surveillance, and middle office all consume trade-centric events.

This is:

- **Lightweight:** Fewer messages and simpler consumer logic.
- **Aligned with middle office and reconciliation:** Trades are the core unit.

But:

- Surveillance and behavior analytics are handicapped by lack of lifecycle detail.
- Risk can only react to exposure after trades are completed, not while orders are working.

This pattern is most suitable when:

- Your primary goal is to support middle office, confirmations, and reconciliations.
- Surveillance and risk get their detailed lifecycle data from other sources (for example, internal logs or dedicated feeds).

Pattern 3: Dual Feeds for Different Consumers

Many firms adopt a dual approach:

- An **ExecutionReport-based feed** for internal risk and surveillance.

- A **TradeCaptureReport-based feed** for middle office and external clients.

In this model:

- Internal systems can use the full lifecycle detail.
- Middle office and clients get concise, trade-centric data.
- Careful design of identifiers and enrichment ensures that the two feeds are consistent and reconcilable.

The main challenges are:

- Maintaining consistent schemas and identifiers across both feeds.
- Ensuring that corrections and busts are handled coherently in both worlds.

Pattern 4: Hybrid ExecutionReport with Trade Promotion

A useful variation is to treat ExecutionReports as the *raw event stream* and to "promote" trades into TradeCaptureReports for downstream systems. In other words:

- The execution engine or a nearby service emits ExecutionReports to a hub.
- A transformation layer consumes those ExecutionReports, constructs trade objects (for example, by aggregating fills where appropriate), and emits TradeCaptureReports into middle-office topics or sessions.

This hybrid pattern gives you:

- A single primary representation of events (ExecutionReports) from the execution system.
- Trade-centric views for consumers who prefer them, built in a consistent and auditable way.

It does introduce operational complexity—there is now an additional transformation component to monitor and maintain—but it often provides the cleanest separation of concerns.

Practical Heuristics

To close this section, here is a set of simple heuristics you can apply when designing or reviewing a drop copy service:

- If a consumer cares about **behavior, patterns, and full history of orders**, it probably needs ExecutionReports.
- If a consumer cares primarily about **what was traded and how to book it**, it probably prefers TradeCaptureReports or a trade-derived feed.
- If you need **real-time limit monitoring** that reacts to working orders as well as trades, ExecutionReports should be part of the solution.
- If your main pain point is **reconciliation and client statements**, TradeCaptureReports will feel more natural.
- If both sets of needs are strong and you have the engineering capacity, consider a **dual or hybrid** approach, with clear identifier schemes and enrichment policies that tie the two views together.

In the next section we will move from message choice to wiring: how to design FIX session and routing topologies that isolate drop copy from primary flow, enforce entitlements, and scale to many consumers. The concepts from this section—especially which feeds serve which users—will guide those session-level design decisions.

5.3 Session & Routing Topologies for Drop Copy

In the first two sections of this chapter we took two important steps. First, we treated drop copy as a business product and identified its main consumers: risk, surveillance, middle office, and clients. Second, we chose the basic "language" of that product by deciding how much to emphasize ExecutionReports versus TradeCaptureReports.

We now move from *what* we publish to *how we wire it*. In other words:

> How should FIX sessions and routing be structured so that real-time drop copy is robust, secure, and scalable, without putting primary trading flow at risk?

This is not just a plumbing question. Session and routing design directly affects:

- How easily you can add new consumers.
- How safely you can enforce entitlements and privacy.
- How resilient trading is when a downstream consumer misbehaves.
- How quickly you can investigate incidents and replay history.

We will proceed in four steps:

1. Explain why drop copy sessions should be separate from primary execution sessions.
2. Introduce canonical topology patterns for drop copy.
3. Discuss addressing and routing using CompID, SubID, and LocationID.
4. Connect these patterns to entitlements, scaling, and operational practices.

Throughout, keep in mind the mental model from earlier: a single producer (the execution engine or broker core) and many different consumers, each with its own view of what "good" looks like.

Why Separate Drop Copy from Primary Flow?

It is technically possible to imagine a design in which a client or internal system receives everything it needs from a single FIX session: both order-entry traffic and any drop copy messages. In small or legacy environments you still see this.

However, as volumes and consumer counts grow, this unified model becomes fragile. Separate, dedicated drop copy sessions exist for three main reasons.

Protecting Trading from Noisy or Fragile Consumers

Primary execution sessions are the arteries of your trading system. If they stall, the business is immediately impacted. You therefore want to minimize the number of ways in which downstream systems can accidentally interfere with those sessions.

If you try to push drop copy over the same sessions:

- A slow-reading consumer can cause TCP back pressure, delaying critical ExecutionReports that traders and algos depend on.
- Complex entitlement logic (for example, filtering which messages each consumer should see) must run in-line with trading messages, raising latency and risk.

By moving drop copy onto separate FIX sessions (or even separate gateways), you create a safety buffer. If a risk engine goes offline, for example, you may lose its drop copy feed temporarily, but the core trading sessions can continue.

Independent Capacity Planning and SLAs

Drop copy traffic has different characteristics from order-entry traffic:

- It often fans out to more consumers.
- It may be enriched and therefore larger in payload.
- It may include replay and backfill capabilities that require more storage and bandwidth.

If you run everything through the same FIX sessions and gateways, you tie your hands:

- You cannot scale drop copy independently of trading.
- You cannot tune timeouts and batch sizes specifically for drop copy use cases.

Dedicated drop copy sessions let you size and tune these flows according to their own service-level agreements (for example, "all drop copy events visible within 100 milliseconds of execution") without jeopardizing the ultra-low-latency objectives of primary flow.

Clear Separation of Duties and Entitlements

Finally, having distinct sessions makes entitlements and audits easier to reason about:

- Primary sessions are about *who may send orders and receive their own fills.*
- Drop copy sessions are about *who may observe which subset of all activity.*

By keeping these concerns separate, you reduce the risk that a configuration change for one purpose (for example, adding a new risk consumer) accidentally exposes additional data on a trading session.

Canonical Topology Patterns

With the rationale for separation in mind, we can now explore common ways of wiring drop copy sessions around an execution core. We will work from simpler to more sophisticated topologies.

Single Consolidated Drop Copy Session per Firm

The most straightforward pattern is:

- One or more *primary execution sessions* for order flow.
- A single *consolidated drop copy session* that carries all drop copy events for that firm.

In this model:

- The execution engine or a close gateway duplicates relevant ExecutionReports and/or TradeCaptureReports into this single session.
- The consumer of the session is typically an internal aggregation point (for example, a hub, a risk engine, or an in-house market infrastructure team) that then fans out data internally using non-FIX mechanisms.

Advantages:

- Simple to operate and understand: one drop copy session per counterparty or internal firm.
- Easy to control at a contractual level: the session defines the firm's drop copy entitlement.

Limitations:

- Limited granularity of entitlements if you want to segregate data further (for example, per client or per desk).
- Failure of the consolidated session affects all consumers downstream that depend on it.

This pattern works well when:

- You have a small number of high-capability consumers behind the consolidated session.
- Most downstream fan-out will occur within your own controlled infrastructure.

Per-Venue or Per-Product Drop Copy Sessions

As volume, product diversity, or risk segmentation grows, firms often move to multiple drop copy sessions per relationship, such as:

- Separate sessions for cash equities vs. derivatives.
- Separate sessions for different matching engines or venues.

The execution environment then:

- Routes events for each product set or venue to its dedicated drop copy session(s).
- Uses these boundaries to isolate failures and to apply different capacity limits and maintenance windows.

Benefits:

- **Failure isolation:** If the futures drop copy session is overloaded or down, the equities session can continue unaffected.
- **Granular capacity management:** You can scale sessions that see more traffic (for example, high-frequency equities) independently of others.
- **Sharper entitlements:** You can grant access to some product classes but not others by controlling session access.

This pattern is particularly useful for:

- Execution venues that support many products and want to give participants fine-grained control over which data they subscribe to.
- Brokers separating asset classes for regulatory or operational reasons.

Per-Client or Per-Desk Drop Copy Sessions

The finest granularity is a session whose scope is limited to:

- A single external client (for client-facing drop copy).
- A single internal desk or business unit (for very sensitive data).

Here:

- The execution core (or routing layer) enforces a strict mapping: orders and trades for client or desk X only ever appear on session X.
- Entitlements are expressed directly in the session topology: if you do not have a session, you cannot see the data.

Benefits:

- **Strong segregation:** Near-zero risk of data leaks between clients or desks via shared sessions.
- **Custom SLAs:** You can, for example, agree with a latency-sensitive client that their drop copy session will have tighter monitoring or higher throughput guarantees.

Challenges:

- Operational overhead: many sessions to configure, monitor, and maintain.
- Scaling routing logic: the system must efficiently route events into potentially hundreds or thousands of sessions without impacting core performance.

This pattern is usually reserved for:

- External client drop copy in agency broker models.
- Internal flows where strict walling-off of businesses is required (for example, between prop and agency businesses in some jurisdictions).

Introducing a Central Routing Layer

In the previous section we treated fan-out as if the execution engine itself were directly responsible for sending events to all drop copy sessions. In modern architectures, especially at scale, it is common to insert a dedicated *routing layer* between execution and drop copy sessions.

Conceptually, this layer:

- Receives a single, rich stream of order and trade events from execution systems (often via internal FIX, a message bus, or a streaming platform).
- Applies routing rules based on firm, client, desk, product, and other attributes.
- Applies enrichment and filtering as needed.
- Pushes appropriately filtered messages onto multiple external and internal drop copy sessions.

This separation yields several advantages:

- Execution systems remain focused on their core tasks: matching orders and maintaining primary session state.
- Routing and entitlement logic can evolve more rapidly and more flexibly in a centralized component.
- Horizontal scaling (adding more routing instances) is easier than scaling a monolithic execution engine.

After we introduce the main topology patterns, it is helpful to visualize how primary sessions, the routing layer, and drop copy sessions sit relative to each other.

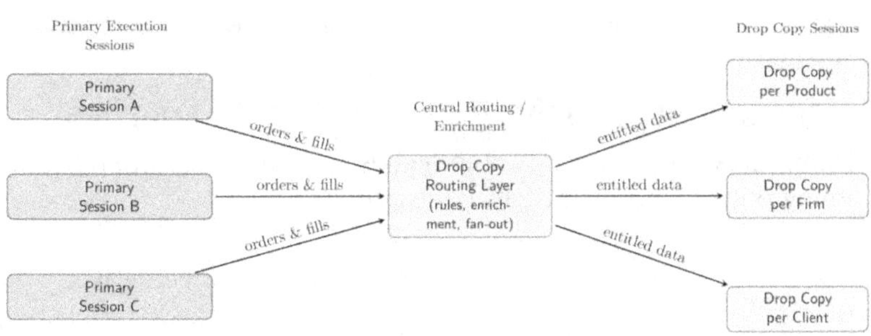

This diagram is deliberately abstract. In a concrete implementation:

- The "routing layer" might be a cluster of FIX gateways, a Kafka-based stream processor, or another internal platform.
- The right-hand boxes might represent sessions going to internal risk systems, surveillance, middle office, or external clients.

The essential idea is that the routing layer lets you separate concerns and express different entitlement scopes through different sets of drop copy sessions.

Addressing with CompID, SubID, and LocationID

Once you have decided on your topology—how many primary and drop copy sessions and what routing layer you will use—you must choose an addressing scheme. In FIX, the core addressing fields are:

- **SenderCompID / TargetCompID:** Identify the primary parties to a session.
- **SenderSubID / TargetSubID:** Optional sub-identifiers that can distinguish desks, environments, or logical flows within a CompID.
- **SenderLocationID / TargetLocationID:** Optional location tags, often used for physical region or regulatory location.

A clean, consistent naming scheme makes routing and operations much easier. A messy one becomes a long-term drag on every change you make.

Encoding Business Semantics without Brittle Coupling

A common pattern is to encode some business meaning into IDs while keeping them stable over time. For example:

- BRKR_LON_EQ for a London equities broker gateway.
- CLIENT123_DC for a client's drop copy session.

- RISK_AGG1 for an internal risk aggregator.

You might then use SubID to represent:

- A specific desk or strategy within a firm.
- An environment (for example, UAT, SIM, PROD).

The key is to:

- **Document** the scheme so that new sessions can be added without guesswork.
- Avoid encoding information that is likely to change frequently (for example, precise team names), because renaming IDs later can be painful.

Routing Rules Based on IDs and Business Fields

The routing layer can use these IDs, along with business fields such as account, symbol, or product, to direct events:

- All drop copy for Client A goes to any session whose TargetCompID starts with CLIENTA_.
- All equity trades go to sessions whose SubID indicates EQ.
- All flows from a given region are tagged with a corresponding LocationID, making it easy to segregate data by geography.

You should be able to express most routing rules as a combination of:

- **Who** (CompID/SubID).
- **What** (account, symbol, product type).
- **Where** (LocationID, region).

A well-chosen addressing scheme prevents these rules from turning into an unmaintainable tangle of special cases.

Entitlements as a First-Class Design Constraint

In previous sections we noted that different consumers should only see the data they are entitled to. Session and routing topology is one of your most powerful tools to enforce that.

Entitlement Scope by Session

Each drop copy session should have a clearly defined *scope*, such as:

- One external client across all products.
- One internal risk system, seeing all products but only at an aggregated legal-entity level.
- One surveillance system, seeing all internal activity including trader identifiers.

For each scope you define:

- Which message types are allowed (for example, ExecutionReport, TradeCaptureReport, some admin types).
- Which accounts, firms, or desks are included.
- Which fields are included, masked, or omitted for privacy or regulatory reasons.

The routing layer then acts as the enforcement mechanism, ensuring that:

- Messages that do not belong in a scope are never sent to that session.
- Sensitive fields are removed or transformed for certain sessions.

Avoiding Data Leaks Between Clients

In client-facing drop copy, the worst failure is a data leak where one client sees another client's orders or trades. Session topology can reduce this risk significantly:

- Use per-client sessions as much as practical.
- Ensure that any shared infrastructure (for example, a routing hub) is tested and controlled with strong unit and integration tests specifically for entitlements.
- Keep entitlement logic simple and transparent rather than embedding it in complex custom code.

Good topology does not replace careful coding, but it does mean that a single misrouted message cannot accidentally "fan out" to dozens of clients.

Scaling and Resilience Considerations

Drop copy fans out the same core events to many consumers. Without careful design, that fan-out can become a bottleneck. Session and routing topologies therefore need to anticipate growth.

Horizontal Scaling of Gateways and Routers

Instead of a single drop copy gateway or router, consider:

- A cluster of stateless routing processes, each handling a subset of sessions.
- A shared, ordered input stream of events from the execution core that all routers read (or partitioned streams if ordering can be relaxed across some dimensions).

Sessions can then be:

- Distributed across router instances, balancing load.
- Migrated between instances during maintenance or failure without impacting the upstream execution engine.

Capacity Sizing and Back-Pressure Management

You should size your drop copy layer with realistic assumptions about:

- Peak message rates during fast markets.
- The additional overhead of enrichment.
- Occasional bursts due to backfills or replay operations.

Mechanisms to manage back pressure include:

- Per-session throttling: slowing or temporarily pausing non-critical sessions if they fall behind.
- Priority tiers: ensuring that internal risk and surveillance receive higher priority than, say, optional analytics consumers.
- Clear error handling: defining what happens when a consumer cannot keep up (for example, session logout and documented replay procedures).

Monitoring, Failover, and Replay

Operationally, your topology should support:

- **Monitoring:** Per-session metrics such as message rate, latency, queue depth, and error counts.
- **Failover:** The ability to move a session from one router instance or gateway to another with minimal interruption.
- **Replay:** The capability to re-deliver a range of events to a given session after an outage, without forcing the execution core to regenerate them.

Replay is where the separation of concerns really pays off. If the routing layer is built on a durable event store or message bus, it can serve historical events to consumers while the execution engine focuses solely on current orders and trades.

Bringing It All Together

At this point in the chapter you have:

- Identified your drop copy consumers and their needs.
- Chosen between ExecutionReport, TradeCaptureReport, or a hybrid as the primary content of your feeds.
- Seen how to lay out FIX sessions and routing layers to keep trading safe, enforce entitlements, and scale to many consumers.

The central design message is that session and routing topology is not an afterthought. It encodes, in a very concrete way:

- Which flows are business-critical and latency-sensitive (primary sessions).
- Which flows are business-critical but can tolerate slightly higher latency in exchange for completeness and enrichment (drop copy).
- How you keep different consumers, clients, and desks safely separated.

In the final section of this chapter we will look more closely at sequencing and latency engineering within this topology: how to ensure that each consumer sees a self-consistent timeline of events, how to manage batching versus per-message delivery, and how to recover cleanly from failures without losing the integrity of the drop copy record.

5.4 Sequencing Guarantees and Latency Engineering

In the earlier sections of this chapter we made three big design decisions:

- We treated drop copy as a business product for risk, surveillance, middle office, and clients.
- We chose the core message shapes (ExecutionReport, TradeCaptureReport, or both).

- We laid out FIX sessions and routing topologies that keep drop copy separate from primary order flow and enforce entitlements.

We now turn to a more subtle but equally important aspect: *time*. When consumers read your drop copy, what can they assume about:

- The **order** in which events arrive?
- The **delay** between execution and visibility in drop copy?
- The **reliability** of these properties during failures and replays?

Answering these questions is the domain of *sequencing guarantees* and *latency engineering*. Our goal is not "zero latency" or "perfect global ordering"—both are unrealistic—but a set of clear, well-documented guarantees that your consumers can safely build on.

We will proceed in five steps:

- Clarify realistic sequencing goals for drop copy.
- Explain independent sequence spaces and correlation keys.
- Discuss clock discipline and the role of timestamps.
- Compare per-message versus batched delivery and their latency effects.
- Examine failure modes and replay strategies, tying them back to design choices.

What Sequencing Do Consumers Really Need?

It is tempting to think in absolutes: "all consumers see exactly the same events, in exactly the same order, at exactly the same time." In a distributed trading environment, this is neither necessary nor feasible at high scale.

Instead, it is more useful to think in terms of *scoped* sequencing guarantees.

Single-Consumer, Single-Session Ordering

Within a single FIX session, the minimal and most important guarantee is:

> Messages are delivered in the order in which the provider sent them.

This is the natural consequence of TCP and of FIX sequence numbers: if a consumer sees message with MsgSeqNum 105 after 104, it can assume that 105 was sent later. If there is a gap (jump from 104 to 107), the consumer knows something is missing and can request a resend.

For most consumers, this per-session ordering is the base they rely on to:

- Reconstruct order lifecycles.
- Apply fills and cancels in a coherent sequence.
- Detect duplicate or out-of-order messages (relative to the session).

Per-Order or Per-Account Consistency

Many risk and surveillance use cases are naturally scoped by order or account. They need to reason about:

- The sequence of events for a particular OrderID.
- All trades and cancels affecting a particular account.

For these use cases, the essential requirement is:

> For any given order (or account), the consumer eventually sees all relevant events in an order that makes sense for that order (or account).

This is weaker than global ordering across all orders. It allows you to partition events by account or instrument and process them separately, as long as:

- Events within each partition are ordered correctly.
- No relevant events are missing.

Why Global Total Ordering Is Rarely Needed

Trying to enforce a single, global timeline across venues, products, and consumers is extremely expensive and often impossible:

- Different venues and systems have their own internal clocks and processing pipelines.
- Network paths differ; messages may arrive in different orders at different consumers.
- Even if you impose a strict ordering at a central hub, it can become a bottleneck.

Most practical designs therefore avoid promising global total ordering. Instead, they promise:

- Session ordering: strictly increasing sequence numbers per session.
- Partition ordering: consistent ordering within natural partitions such as account, firm, or instrument.
- Clear correlation keys so that consumers can reconstruct the views they need.

With this in mind, we can look at how FIX sequence numbers and correlation keys are used to express these guarantees.

Independent Sequence Spaces and Correlation Keys

Earlier in the book we discussed FIX session sequence numbers: each session maintains its own MsgSeqNum, starting from 1 and incrementing for each message. Drop copy sessions fit into this same pattern, but with some important twists.

Why Drop Copy Sessions Use Their Own Sequence Spaces

Drop copy sessions are separate from primary trading sessions. That separation extends to sequence numbers:

- Each drop copy session has its own independent MsgSeqNum space.
- These sequence numbers are not expected to match those on primary execution sessions.

This independence is essential:

- It lets you replay or reset a drop copy session without touching the primary session's state.
- It makes it possible to have different subsets of events on different drop copy sessions (for example, per-client views) without worrying about global alignment of sequence numbers.

The trade-off is that consumers cannot use MsgSeqNum to relate events *across* sessions. That is where *correlation keys* come in.

Correlation via Business Identifiers

Instead of relying on sequence numbers to link events across sessions, consumers use stable business identifiers, such as:

- **Orders:** ClOrdID, OrderID.

- **Executions:** ExecID, possibly combined with OrderID.
- **Trades:** TradeID, TradeReportID, or a firm-specific execution key.
- **Accounts and firms:** Account, PartyID, or firm codes.

These identifiers play three roles:

- **Within a single session**, they let the consumer group events (for example, all ExecutionReports with the same OrderID).
- **Across sessions**, they let a consumer or downstream system reconcile events from primary and drop copy feeds (for example, match a client's on-the-wire ExecutionReport to an internal drop copy record).
- **Across systems**, they allow joins between drop copy and other internal data sources (for example, risk engines, inventory systems).

For sequencing purposes, the key is that you can use these identifiers, combined with session ordering, to reconstruct timelines:

- For a given order, sort all its drop copy events by the order they appear in the session stream; that gives you a coherent lifecycle.
- For a given account, filter and sort all its events; you get a coherent exposure history.

Designing Good Correlation Keys

To support robust sequencing and reconstruction, you should:

- Ensure uniqueness and stability: OrderID, ExecID, and TradeID should be unique in well-defined scopes (for example, per day, per firm) and not be reused in ways that confuse history.
- Use the same identifiers consistently across primary and drop copy sessions.

- When you introduce internal keys (for example, a composite execution identifier), document them and carry them in both primary and drop copy messages.

This gives consumers a set of sturdy "hooks" to hang their own sequences and state machines on.

Clock Discipline and Timestamps

Sequence numbers tell you the order in which messages were sent on a given session. Timestamps try to tell you when events *actually happened*. Both are useful, but in different ways.

What Timestamps Can and Cannot Do

Well-designed drop copy feeds include timestamps at one or more stages:

- **Event time:** When the matching or execution engine believes the order was accepted or the trade occurred.
- **Gateway time:** When the message passed through a gateway or routing layer.
- **Transmission time:** When the message was handed to the network stack.

These timestamps support:

- Latency measurement (for example, how long from execution to drop copy visibility).
- Cross-system comparisons (for example, aligning drop copy with market data or external venue feeds).

However, timestamps are only as good as your clock synchronization:

- If clocks on different machines are not synchronized, timestamps from those machines cannot be safely compared.

- Even with synchronization protocols (such as NTP or PTP), there may be residual error or occasional jumps.

For that reason, it is unwise to promise strict ordering or causality based *only* on timestamps across multiple systems. You should still treat per-session sequence numbers as the primary ordering mechanism and use timestamps for approximate alignment and latency metrics.

Clock Discipline as a Design Constraint

To make timestamps useful while understanding their limits:

- Run a disciplined time-synchronization setup on all machines involved in trading and drop copy.
- Monitor clock offsets and drifts; alert when they exceed specified thresholds.
- Clearly document which timestamp fields are present and what they mean (for example, "this field represents internal matching time measured on the matching engine's clock").

This approach gives consumers realistic expectations: they can treat timestamps as accurate to, say, tens or hundreds of microseconds internally, but know not to infer fine-grained ordering across independent venues solely from them.

Latency Engineering: Per-Message vs. Batching

Earlier, when we discussed business use cases, we saw that:

- Some consumers (for example, intraday risk dashboards) want near-real-time updates.
- Others (for example, middle office) can tolerate a bit more lag in exchange for robustness and efficiency.

The central engineering choice here is how aggressively you push events:

- **Per-message delivery:** Send each event as soon as it is available.
- **Batched delivery:** Collect events into small groups over some time window or count threshold and send them together.

Per-Message Delivery

With per-message delivery:

- Latency from execution to drop copy is minimized; this is attractive for latency-sensitive risk and monitoring.
- The number of FIX messages increases; overhead in connections, parsing, and logging rises.
- Burstiness can increase under stress (fast markets can lead to very high message rates).

This model is well suited to:

- ExecutionReport-based feeds for risk and surveillance.
- Consumers that explicitly need to react within milliseconds to changes.

Batched Delivery

With batched delivery:

- You group events into batches (for example, by number of events or by time slice such as 50 milliseconds).
- You reduce per-message overhead, because multiple events travel together.

- You introduce *jitter*: the time from execution to drop copy visibility now includes the batch wait time.

For many consumers, this is acceptable:

- Middle office platforms do not need each trade the instant it happens; a short delay is fine.
- Some risk systems may only need snapshots every second or so, and can derive them from batched streams.

Latency Budgets and Consumer Classes

A practical approach is to define explicit *latency budgets* by consumer class:

- Internal risk and surveillance: for example, 10–100 milliseconds end-to-end.
- Middle office: for example, a few seconds is acceptable, as long as data is complete and ordered.
- External clients: often somewhere in between, depending on contracts.

You can then:

- Use per-message delivery or very small batches for the tightest budgets.
- Use larger batches or downstream aggregation for the more relaxed ones.

Crucially, these decisions must be *documented*. Consumers should know whether a feed is "near real time" or "best-effort within N seconds" and design their systems accordingly.

Monitoring Latency

Once you establish latency targets, you need to monitor them:

- Embed both event-time and send-time timestamps in messages.
- Measure the difference at the consumer or at an intermediate monitoring point.
- Track distributions (not just averages) to understand tails and spikes.

Alerts can then be based on violations of the agreed budgets (for example, "more than 1% of events delayed beyond 200 milliseconds in the last minute").

Failure Modes, Gaps, and Replay

No matter how carefully you engineer your system, things will go wrong: networks fail, processes crash, disk fills up. Good sequencing and latency design assumes failure and provides a path to recovery.

Message Gaps and Sequence Resets

From a consumer's point of view, the first sign of trouble is usually:

- A gap in MsgSeqNum (for example, 120, 121, 125).
- An unexpected sequence reset (for example, after a session reconnect).

Your protocol for handling this should be explicit:

- When the consumer detects a gap, it requests a resend from the last known good sequence number.
- The provider sends the missing messages (possibly marked as retransmissions) before continuing with new flow.

- If recovery via standard resend is not possible (for example, due to log retention limits), a documented out-of-band replay mechanism is used.

Drop copy sessions should be designed so that:

- Resend requests are expected and handled efficiently.
- Message logs are retained for a reasonable replay window (for example, at least the current trading day).

Network Partitions and Failover

In more severe failures, you may lose a session entirely or need to fail it over to another gateway. Your topology from the previous section comes into play here:

- If you have a routing layer with durable storage, you can re-establish sessions from that layer without involving the core execution system.
- If sessions are per-client or per-desk, you can fail over individual sessions without affecting others.

For sequencing:

- After failover, you should resume MsgSeqNum from the last acknowledged value or perform a controlled sequence reset accompanied by a replay to bring the consumer up to date.
- Consumers need clear documentation on how to handle such resets (for example, ignore previously seen messages, rely on idempotent processing keyed by ExecID or TradeID).

Reconstructing a Coherent Timeline After Failures

The real test of your design comes after an incident. Risk, surveillance, regulators, or clients may ask:

> Can you reconstruct exactly what happened, and when, from your records?

If you have:

- Independent sequence spaces with clear correlation keys.
- Durable logs of drop copy messages and, ideally, primary flow.
- Timestamps from key points in the pipeline.

Then you can:

- Rebuild per-order or per-account histories from ExecutionReports or TradeCaptureReports, using identifiers and sequence numbers.
- Align these histories approximately in time using timestamps, recognizing their limits.
- Explain any gaps or replays by referencing session logs and resend activity.

This is what "coherent timeline" really means in practice: not that every system saw exactly the same picture at the same instant, but that you can, retrospectively, stitch together a consistent narrative from your records.

Balancing Speed, Stability, and Completeness

Across this chapter, a pattern should now be clear:

- **Use cases** (risk, surveillance, middle office, clients) drive
- **Message choices** (ExecutionReport vs. TradeCaptureReport), which drive
- **Topology choices** (session layout and routing), which in turn constrain

- **Sequencing and latency guarantees**.

When engineering sequencing and latency for drop copy, you are constantly trading off:

- **Speed** (how quickly consumers see events),
- **Stability** (how frequently they experience gaps, resets, or replays),
- **Completeness** (how confident they can be that they see all relevant events).

There is no single right answer. What matters is that:

- The trade-offs are deliberate rather than accidental.
- The guarantees you choose are clearly stated and technically enforceable.
- Your identifiers, timestamps, and logs give you the tools to recover from inevitable failures.

With these principles in place, real-time drop copy becomes not only a live view of trading activity but also a reliable audit trail—one that downstream systems and regulators can trust, even under stress.

Chapter 6

Stable Sessions & Resilience Engineering

FIX doesn't blow up when markets are quiet; it fails when everything moves at once-precisely when you can't afford to be blind. This chapter shows how to design FIX sessions that remain predictable under disconnects, restarts, failovers, and panic-driven cancels, so that every reconnection is boring, explainable, and fully auditable.

6.1 Durable State: Persistence & Message Stores

In the previous chapters we treated a FIX session mostly as a live conversation: messages flowing in sequence, heartbeats going back and forth, and sequence numbers increasing monotonically while both sides stay connected. We discussed how the session layer frames and validates application messages such as NewOrderSingle and ExecutionReport, and how sequence number management keeps the two parties in sync.

In production, however, FIX engines do not live in a perfect, always-on world. Processes crash, machines reboot, containers are rescheduled, and network paths flap. When that happens, the critical question is:

After a restart, how does the engine know exactly where the session left off?

The answer lives in *durable state* and *message stores*. This section defines which parts of session state must outlive any single process, how to persist that state safely, and how message stores make deterministic recovery and strong audit trails possible.

Transient vs. Durable State

A running FIX engine maintains a large amount of internal state: some of it can be recomputed cheaply after a restart, and some of it cannot. The key design task is to separate:

- **Transient state** – exists only in memory; if it disappears, you can reconstruct it from durable state and the counterparty.
- **Durable state** – must survive process restarts; losing it would make it impossible or ambiguous to resume the session correctly.

Thinking clearly about this distinction simplifies everything that follows. You do not want to persist *all* state; that would be slow and complex. You only want to persist exactly what you need to make the session and its order flow logically continuous across failures.

Examples of transient state

Typical transient (in-memory only) state includes:

- Current TCP connection handles and network buffers.
- In-memory parsing caches (for example, pre-parsed message templates).
- Short-lived timers for heartbeats and test requests.
- Performance counters and metrics.
- Internal optimization structures (for example, indexes to speed up lookups inside the engine).

If a process dies, we do not mind losing this information. When the engine restarts and reconnects, it can recreate these data structures from scratch.

Examples of durable session state

Durable state is different. If you lose it, you no longer know what has already been sent, what has already been received, or what the agreed sequence numbers are. Durable state for a FIX session typically includes:

- **Inbound and outbound sequence numbers** at the last known good point.
- **Session configuration** for each counterparty:
  - SenderCompID, TargetCompID, and any custom identifiers.
  - Logon parameters: heartbeat interval, encryption or compression flags, FIX version or FIXT transport.
  - Reset policies (for example, daily reset at session boundary or continuous sequence numbers across days).
- **Append-only message store** of the raw FIX messages:
  - Every outbound message as sent to the counterparty.
  - Every inbound message as received from the counterparty.
  - Timestamps and sequence numbers for each stored message.
- **Linkage to application-level state**: identifiers that tie FIX messages to orders, executions, and positions in your internal systems (typically stored in trading or order management databases, not inside the FIX engine itself, but the linkage must be durable).

The minimal requirement is that after a restart you can answer, with certainty:

- What is the next outbound sequence number I should use?

- What is the next inbound sequence number I expect from this counterparty?

- Which messages have I already sent or received at each sequence number?

Without correct answers to these questions, safe recovery is impossible.

Session State Flow and the Message Store

Conceptually, you can picture a FIX engine as a funnel: messages enter from the application on one side, flow through the engine, and leave via the network; inbound messages do the reverse. Along the way, the engine updates in-memory state and, for durable components, writes to persistent storage.

Right after we introduce transient vs. durable state, it is useful to see this flow in a structural diagram.

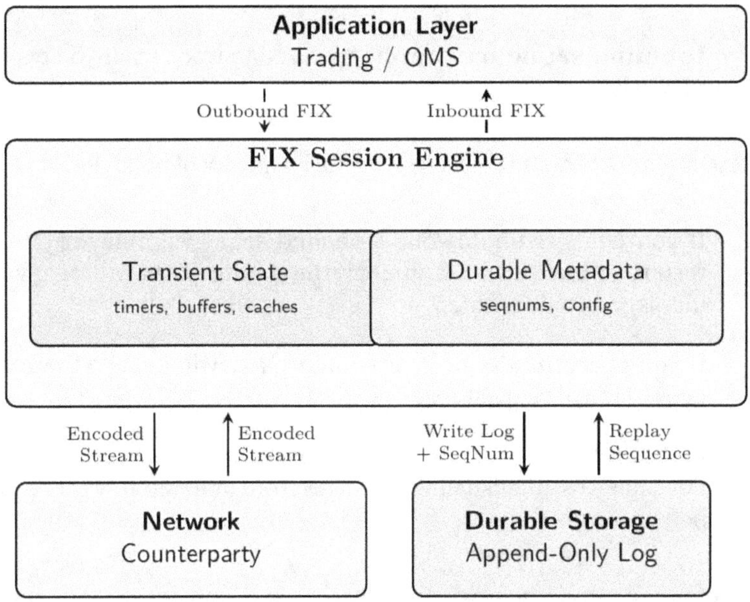

The core idea is that every message that crosses the session boundary is both processed in memory *and* recorded in an append-only store, together with its sequence number and timestamps. The durable metadata (such as the current sequence numbers) is just a compact summary of the full message history.

What Must Survive a Restart?

We now define more precisely which pieces of state must be persisted and when.

Sequence numbers and their semantics

Sequence numbers are the backbone of FIX session semantics. They impose an ordering on messages and allow both sides to detect gaps and duplicates. Two separate counters exist:

- **Outbound sequence number** — used when you send a message.

- **Inbound sequence number** – used to track what you expect to receive next.

These are not cosmetic counters; they drive protocol behavior:

- If you *underestimate* your outbound sequence number after a restart and reuse an old number, the counterparty will treat your message as a duplicate.
- If you *overestimate* it, your counterparty will believe there are gaps and will request resends.
- If you forget which inbound sequence you last processed, you cannot safely distinguish new messages from ones already processed before the crash.

Therefore, **both inbound and outbound sequence numbers must be persisted durably after every successful message processing step**. "Successful" here means:

- For outbound messages: once the engine has accepted the message for send, assigned a sequence number, and written it to the message store.
- For inbound messages: once the engine has validated the message, delivered it to the application (or internal handler), and written it to the message store.

The exact mechanics vary by implementation, but the principle is consistent: the durable sequence numbers must always reflect the state of the message store, not merely what was in memory.

Message histories and deterministic replay

Persisting only the current sequence numbers is not enough. During recovery, you often need to see *which* messages correspond to which sequence numbers:

- To respond to a ResendRequest from the counterparty, you must replay the exact FIX payloads previously sent, with the same sequence numbers.
- To analyze a trading incident, compliance may need to reconstruct the full dialog around a particular order or execution.
- To resolve disputes, you may have to prove what was sent, when it was sent, and what you received in return.

This is the role of the **message store**: an append-only log of all messages in both directions, indexed by session keys and sequence number (and generally timestamp as well). It underpins:

- **Deterministic recovery** – after a crash, the engine can reconstruct its in-memory state by reading the log and applying messages in order.
- **Protocol compliance** – you can replay history to answer resend requests precisely.
- **Auditability** – you have a tamper-evident record of what happened.

Designing the Message Store

A message store does not have to be complicated conceptually; it must be *reliable*, *ordered*, and *queryable*. There are several design decisions to consider.

Append-only vs. mutable stores

Most robust FIX engines treat the store as *append-only*: new messages are only appended; existing records are not modified or deleted during normal operation. Advantages include:

- **Immutability** – once a message is written, it is not altered. This matches how FIX sessions work: a message with a given sequence number is defined once.

- **Simplicity of failure handling** – crashes are easier to reason about; you only worry about whether the last append succeeded, not about half-completed updates.
- **Efficient sequential I/O** – sequential writes map well to disks and log-structured filesystems.

Logically, when a message arrives or is sent, the engine appends a record like:

- Session identifiers (SenderCompID, TargetCompID, and possibly a session instance ID).
- Direction (inbound or outbound).
- Sequence number.
- Receive or send timestamp.
- Raw FIX string (or a compact encoded representation).

Indexes or metadata structures can be kept separately to allow fast lookups by sequence number or time range without disturbing the append-only principle.

File system vs. database vs. log-structured systems

At a physical level, the store can be implemented in several ways, each with trade-offs in latency, throughput, and operational complexity.

Flat files on a filesystem.

The simplest implementation is to write messages into flat files, perhaps one file per session per day. Advantages:

- Very low overhead and high throughput with sequential writes.
- Easy to reason about, easy to back up or rotate.
- Good fit for append-only behavior.

Disadvantages:

- You must build your own indexing scheme to support fast seeks by sequence number or time.
- Concurrency control and corruption detection are your responsibility.

Relational or key-value databases.

Another option is using a database as the backing store:

- Each message becomes a row with columns for session keys, direction, sequence number, timestamps, and payload.
- Indexes allow fast queries by sequence or time.
- The database handles durability, transactions, and basic replication.

This can be attractive when you already operate a robust database platform. However, you must balance:

- **Latency** – database writes can be slower than raw file appends, especially under high volume.
- **Operational load** – schema evolution, maintenance, and tuning become part of your FIX infrastructure.

Log-structured or streaming systems.

Some firms use log-structured systems (such as distributed commit logs) as a central message bus. Advantages include:

- Built-in replication and partitioning for high availability.
- Naturally append-only, with good throughput.
- Same infrastructure can support other trading components.

The complexity here is in integrating the FIX engine with the broader streaming stack and ensuring sequence number semantics are preserved precisely.

Latency, throughput, and sync policies

Regardless of storage technology, you face a classic trade-off: **write safety versus latency**.

- If you *flush every message* synchronously to stable storage (for example, force a disk sync before acknowledging it to the application), you minimize the risk of losing that message in a crash, but incur higher end-to-end latency.
- If you *batch writes* and let the operating system buffer them, you reduce latency but risk losing the last few messages if the process or machine fails before the buffers are flushed.

Production engines typically adopt a middle ground:

- Use an append-only log, where appends are quick and sequential.
- Allow the OS to buffer writes, but force periodic flushes (for example, every few milliseconds, or after $N_{messages}$).
- Ensure that *sequence numbers and message log entries advance together*. That is, you never increment the durable sequence numbers beyond what has been durably written to the store.

The acceptable window of potential data loss (if any) is a business and risk decision. For some flows (for example, low-frequency client order entry), you may opt for strict syncing. For others (for example, very high-frequency market data), you may choose a more relaxed policy.

A Concrete Persistence Model

To make this more tangible, consider a simple but realistic persistence model for a single FIX session.

Outbound message path

When the application sends a new order:

1. The application hands the order to the FIX engine.

2. The engine validates it and assigns the *next outbound sequence number*.

3. The engine builds the raw FIX string, calculates the body length and checksum, and prepares it for the network.

4. Before or concurrently with sending, the engine appends a record to the message store containing:

    - Session identifiers.
    - Direction = outbound.
    - Assigned sequence number.
    - Current timestamp.
    - Raw FIX payload.

5. Once the append is accepted by the storage subsystem (for example, buffered in the OS), the engine updates the *durable outbound sequence number* on disk or in a compact metadata file.

6. The engine writes the message to the network.

Notice the ordering:

- The sequence number is *never* advanced durably if the corresponding message is not in the store.
- If the process fails after writing to the store but before sending on the network, the message is recoverable and may be resent with the same sequence number when the engine restarts.

Inbound message path

When the engine receives a message from the counterparty:

1. The raw bytes arrive from the network and are parsed.

2. The engine verifies that the sequence number is the one expected (or detects a gap).

3. If the message is accepted for processing, the engine appends it to the message store with:

- Session identifiers.
- Direction = inbound.
- Observed sequence number.
- Receive timestamp.
- Raw FIX payload.

4. The engine delivers the message to the application (or internal logic).

5. After successful processing, the engine advances the *durable inbound sequence number*.

Again, the principle is that the durable inbound sequence number always points just beyond the last message that is both *stored* and *processed*.

Restart and recovery

If the process or host fails and later restarts, the engine:

1. Loads session configuration and durable sequence numbers.

2. Opens the message store and replays, if necessary, the tail of the log to confirm that the durable metadata matches the actual content.

3. Re-establishes the TCP connection and initiates a FIX logon with appropriate sequence numbers and flags (for example, ResetSeqNumFlag if a session-level reset is negotiated).

4. Handles any ResendRequest or gap detection by reading from the message store and replaying exactly the relevant outbound messages, in order.

Because the message store is append-only and indexed by sequence number, the engine can respond deterministically: given the same store and the same counterparty behavior, recovery will follow the same path every time.

Making the Store Useful in Operations

Durability alone is not enough. A message store that is technically persistent but operationally painful will frustrate both engineers and business users. Several practices turn the raw store into a powerful operational tool.

Log rotation and retention

FIX traffic is continuous, and message volumes can be large. You must rotate logs to avoid unbounded file growth and to support efficient archival.

Common patterns include:

- One file per session per day, or per session per logical trading session (for example, per market day).
- Retention policies that keep recent logs on fast storage (for example, the last 30–90 days) and move older logs to cheaper archival systems.
- Index files stored alongside log files to speed up searches within a given day or session slice.

Rotation boundaries should align with how you think about trading days and session resets, so that it is easy to fetch "all messages around this incident" without combing through dozens of small files.

Checksums and integrity verification

Message stores must be *trustworthy.* To detect corruption or tampering:

- Include checksums or hashes at the record or block level in the log.
- Periodically run verification tools that scan logs and confirm their integrity.
- Monitor for partial or truncated records at the ends of files, which can occur if a process crashes mid-write.

If corruption is detected, having redundancy (for example, replicated copies of the store) allows you to recover consistent history.

Encryption and access control

FIX logs contain sensitive trading information: orders, prices, and customer identifiers. Good practice includes:

- Encrypting logs at rest, especially when stored on shared or removable media.
- Applying strict access controls: only authorized teams (for example, production support, risk, compliance) should be able to access raw logs.
- Auditing access to logs to support regulatory requirements.

The same care you apply to order and trade data in your databases should apply to message stores.

Replay and search tooling

Finally, to support both everyday support work and rare incident investigations, build tools that let you:

- Search by:
    - Session identifiers.
    - Time ranges.
    - Sequence number ranges.
    - Order IDs or client order IDs inside the FIX payload.
- Replay sequences of messages:
    - To simulate how the engine would behave during recovery.
    - To feed a test environment reproducing a production issue.
- Export selected messages in human-readable form for compliance or client communication.

Such tooling turns the message store into a living asset rather than a write-only archive.

Why Durable State Matters for the Rest of the Chapter

The rest of this chapter will focus on what happens when sessions disconnect and how they recover; on high-availability architectures; and on risk controls such as Cancel-on-Disconnect. All of those mechanisms assume that the FIX engine can:

- Reconstruct the precise state of the session at the moment of failure.
- Prove, via audit trail, what messages were in-flight or pending.
- Coordinate with trading and risk systems using a shared view of history.

That is only possible when durable session state is designed carefully and message stores are robust, append-only, and operationally usable. With these foundations in place, disconnect scenarios become manageable engineering and operational problems instead of sources of mystery and dispute.

6.2 Disconnect Scenarios & Recovery Playbooks

In the previous section we focused on *durable state*: what must survive a restart, how messages are recorded in an append-only store, and how sequence numbers and logs make recovery deterministic and auditable. We now turn to the moments when that durability is actually tested: disconnects, crashes, and mid-session inconsistencies.

From a trading desk's point of view, a disconnect is not merely a technical nuisance. It raises urgent questions:

- Did any orders get lost?
- Did any executions occur that we have not seen yet?

- If we reconnect, how do we avoid duplicating orders or missing fills?

Your FIX engine, together with durable state, should make the answers to these questions *procedural*, not improvisational. This section classifies common disconnect patterns and develops concrete, deterministic playbooks for each:

- How to detect and classify the problem.
- How to use stored sequence numbers and message history to measure gaps.
- When to use resend requests, when to negotiate sequence resets, and when to reset the entire session.
- How to pace recovery, so you do not overwhelm the counterparty or your own systems.

By the end of this section, you should be able to look at any session break and say, "This is scenario X; we follow playbook Y," rather than starting a fresh debate at three in the morning.

A Taxonomy of Disconnects

Not all disconnects are equal. Some are benign and expected; others are sudden and ambiguous. Classifying them helps you choose the right recovery strategy.

Clean, protocol-level closes

A **clean logout** is when one side sends a Logout message and then closes the TCP connection after the peer acknowledges. Common reasons include:

- End of the scheduled trading day or maintenance window.
- Planned restart of a gateway or engine.

- Graceful rejection of a session (for example, wrong credentials).

Here, both sides know the session is ending. Each has a consistent view of sequence numbers and can log the final state. Recovery is straightforward: on the next logon, you typically either:

- Continue sequence numbers from where you left off; or
- Agree to reset sequence numbers (often at the start of a new trading day) as per venue rules.

Sudden network drops

A **sudden network drop** occurs when the TCP connection disappears without a logout:

- Physical network failure.
- Firewall or load balancer resets.
- Counterparty engine crash.

In this case, there may have been messages in flight in either direction when the connection died. Neither side knows exactly which of the last few messages arrived successfully. This is where your durable message store and sequence numbers become critical.

Partial or asymmetric outages

Sometimes, the failure is only on one side or in one component:

- Your internal trading system crashes, but the FIX engine continues to run.
- One of your data centers loses connectivity, while another stays up.
- A gateway between internal systems and the FIX engine fails, but the FIX session itself remains open.

These are especially tricky because the FIX session may appear healthy, yet your application-level state is not. Recovery must reconcile both:

- The FIX session's view of the world (driven by sequence numbers and execution reports).
- The trading system's internal view (orders, trades, positions).

Sequence mismatches discovered mid-session

Even without a clean disconnect, you can discover that sequence numbers have diverged:

- The counterparty sends a message with an unexpected sequence number.
- Your engine detects a gap (for example, you expected 105 but received 110).
- The counterparty complains that your sequence numbers jumped or that they see duplicates.

This class of problems often reveals earlier, smaller issues that went unnoticed, or manual interventions that bypassed normal procedures.

From Event to Playbook: The Recovery Mindset

Before we dive into specific scenarios, it is useful to adopt a consistent mindset about recovery:

1. **Stabilize the situation.** Stop sending new application-level messages (for example, new orders) on a broken or inconsistent session until you understand the state.
2. **Measure the gap.** Use durable inbound and outbound sequence numbers, together with the counterparty's view, to determine:

- Which messages you have sent but are not sure they received.
- Which messages they may have sent but you have not processed.

3. **Choose a repair strategy.** Decide whether to:
   - Issue (or respond to) ResendRequest messages.
   - Negotiate a SequenceReset.
   - Tear down and fully reset the session.
4. **Control the pace.** Limit the rate of replayed messages to avoid flood conditions.
5. **Communicate and coordinate.** Ensure your trading, risk, and operations teams understand what is being replayed and what it means for live orders.

We will now walk through concrete playbooks for the main scenarios, then summarize them in a recovery flowchart.

Scenario 1: Clean Logout and Planned Restart

This is the simplest case and sets a baseline.

Typical sequence of events

1. During regular trading, both sides exchange messages, updating durable sequence numbers and message stores.
2. Near end-of-day (or before planned maintenance), one side sends a Logout indicating the session will close.
3. The other side replies with its own Logout, then both close the TCP connection.
4. Each side records:
   - The final inbound and outbound sequence numbers.
   - The reason and time for the logout.

Recovery playbook

On the next trading day or after maintenance:

1. **Confirm session policy.** Does this session use continuous sequence numbers or daily resets?
2. **Logon with expected numbers.**
    - If continuous, start with outbound sequence equal to last outbound + 1, and expect inbound equal to last inbound + 1.
    - If daily reset is required, both sides agree to reset to 1 (often via a logon parameter or initial SequenceReset).
3. **Verify no gaps.** Since the previous logout was clean, and sequence numbers matched at close, no resend logic should be needed.

In this ideal case, durable state merely confirms that the line was cut cleanly.

Scenario 2: Sudden Disconnect with Possible Message Loss

This is where durability and message stores earn their keep.

Detecting the problem

Indicators of a sudden disconnect include:

- TCP connection closes unexpectedly (for example, reset by peer).
- Heartbeat timer fires; you send a TestRequest but receive no response.
- The counterparty reports they lost connectivity to you.

At this moment, you do not know which, if any, of the last few messages made it across. For example:

- You may have sent a NewOrderSingle that they never saw.
- They may have sent you an ExecutionReport that was in transit when the link died.

Using durable state to measure the gap

Your engine consults durable state:

- **Local outbound sequence** (what you think you last sent).
- **Local inbound sequence** (what you think you last received).

On reconnect, the counterparty does the same. The key step is the *logon handshake*:

1. You send Logon with your current outbound sequence number and your expected inbound sequence number.
2. They respond with their own view.
3. By comparing these, each side can determine if there are gaps:
   - If they report having seen a higher inbound sequence from you than you believe you sent, something is badly inconsistent (often a bug or manual intervention).
   - More commonly, they believe they are missing some of your messages (your outbound numbers jumped), or you believe you are missing some of theirs (your inbound jumped).

Resend versus reset

Once a gap is identified, you face a choice:

- **ResendRequest** — ask the counterparty to replay a specific range of messages you have missed.

- **SequenceReset** – mutually agree to skip a range, telling the peer to advance expected sequence numbers without replaying everything.

The decision depends on:

- **Size of the gap.** A small number of messages can easily be replayed. Very large gaps might take too long to resend in full, especially if each message triggers application-level work.
- **Criticality of complete history.** For order flow, skipping messages can be dangerous; you risk missing executions or cancels.
- **Availability of out-of-band reconciliation.** Sometimes you can tolerate a sequence reset if you have other ways to confirm final positions (for example, end-of-day files).

For typical order entry sessions, the default is:

- Prefer ResendRequest for any gap that could affect live orders or executions.
- Use SequenceReset only under controlled, well-understood circumstances (for example, clearing historical gaps that both sides agree are old and fully reconciled).

Controlled repair pacing

Replays can generate large message bursts. If you simply ask a venue to resend thousands of messages, you may:

- Overload your own engine or downstream systems.
- Contribute to congestion on shared links.

To avoid this, you should:

- **Limit the range of each** ResendRequest**.** For example, request 500 messages at a time, not 50,000.

- **Apply rate limits** on processing of replayed messages to ensure they do not starve live traffic once normal trading resumes.
- **Coordinate with the counterparty** if their documentation suggests particular batch sizes or pacing guidelines.

Your durable message store helps here because you can track which ranges have already been replayed and confirm when the gap is closed.

Scenario 3: Partial or Asymmetric Outages

In a partial outage, the FIX session may stay up while one side's application fails. Suppose:

- Your trading engine crashes, but the FIX engine continues sending heartbeats and responding at the session level.
- During the outage, the venue continues to send ExecutionReport messages (for example, fills from resting orders).

Risk of blind execution

If your application is blind while the session stays up, you risk:

- Missing fills that affect risk and position limits.
- Failing to send cancels or replace requests in response to market changes.

Your recovery plan must assume that the FIX layer and the trading application can be out of sync.

Playbook for application restart with live session

When the trading application comes back:

1. **Pause outbound order flow.** Do not immediately let strategies send new orders.

2. **Rehydrate application state** from durable sources:
   - Internal order and trade databases.
   - FIX message store (replaying all execution-related inbound messages since before the crash).
3. **Compare views.** Ensure that:
   - Every execution report in the message store is reflected in the application's positions and P&L.
   - Any pending cancels or replaces are either completed or explicitly re-issued.
4. **Only then** resume new trading.

If the FIX session itself is deemed unreliable (for example, because it buffered too many messages while the application was down), you may choose to:

- Perform a controlled logout and reconnect.
- Trigger resend of execution reports in a known time or sequence range to confirm the reconstructed state.

Scenario 4: Mid-Session Sequence Mismatches

Finally, consider a case where the session stays up, but you detect a sequence mismatch:

- You expect inbound sequence 201, but receive 204.
- The venue complains that you repeated sequence 310.

Immediate response

The correct response is:

1. **Stop application-level sends** on the affected session to avoid compounding the problem.

2. **Issue (or respond to)** ResendRequest for the missing range.
3. **Use your message store** to ensure any resent messages you generate match the original payloads exactly.

Duplicate handling

When processing replayed messages:

- Your FIX engine must avoid re-applying messages that have already been processed at the application level.
- This is usually achieved by:
  - Recognizing that a resent message has a sequence number less than the current durable inbound sequence.
  - Marking it as a duplicate and routing it only for logging or verification, not for business processing.

This logic depends on the durable inbound sequence number being correct and in sync with the message store.

When to escalate to sequence reset or session reset

If mismatches are large, frequent, or symptomatic of a deeper problem (for example, configuration drift, bugs, or manual tampering), the safer course may be:

- Negotiate a controlled SequenceReset, after both sides agree on a safe point beyond which history is reconciled.
- As a last resort, fully reset the session (log out, clear sequence numbers, and start fresh), combined with out-of-band reconciliation of orders and trades.

These are heavy tools and should be governed by clear procedures and, ideally, pre-agreed with the counterparty.

Visual Summary: Recovery Decision Flow

We have described several recovery choices in words. The following flowchart summarizes the operator's path from detecting a problem to choosing between resend, sequence reset, or full session reset, including pacing considerations.

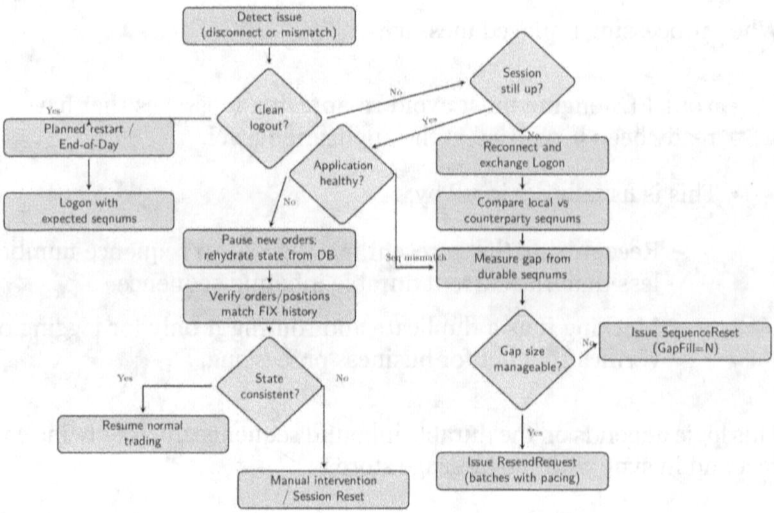

This diagram is intentionally high level. In practice, each box corresponds to more detailed runbook steps and, in many firms, to automated engine behavior supplemented by operator decisions.

Runbooks and Decision Trees in Practice

A well-designed FIX engine will automate as much of this logic as possible:

- Automatically detect gaps and generate ResendRequest messages.
- Recognize resent messages and suppress duplicate application processing.

- Log all recovery actions in enough detail to explain them later.

However, *human operators* still play a crucial role, especially in choosing between competing recovery strategies. To support them:

- **Document playbooks** per venue and session: preferred resend ranges, acceptable use of sequence resets, and any venue-specific quirks.
- **Train support and trading staff** on how to interpret sequence number mismatches and recovery messages.
- **Rehearse scenarios** in test environments, replaying real production message logs to simulate disconnects and validating that the system behaves as expected.

The result is a culture where disconnects are no longer mysterious events but familiar, well-understood workflows, firmly grounded in the durable state and message store model introduced earlier.

6.3 High Availability and Failover Architecture

So far, we have treated a FIX session as if it ran on a single, stable engine: durable message stores protect state, and recovery playbooks tell you what to do when that engine or its network path fails. In a serious trading operation, however, you rarely rely on a single box or process. You design the environment so that:

- A hardware failure does not take down all client connectivity.
- Planned maintenance can occur during trading hours without cutting sessions.
- A single software bug, process crash, or network incident is contained.

This is the role of **high availability (HA)** and **failover** architecture for FIX.

In this section we describe how to architect FIX engines and their surrounding infrastructure so that sessions can ride out failures. We will:

- Explain the *single-writer sequencing constraint* and why it dominates FIX clustering design.
- Show patterns for state replication and their trade-offs.
- Compare *active/passive* and *active/active* architectures, including session pinning and routing.
- Discuss operational issues: split-brain, fencing, and failover drills.

We build directly on the durable state and recovery playbooks from earlier sections: HA is about arranging multiple engines and stores so those same guarantees continue to hold when one component fails.

The Single-Writer Sequencing Constraint

At the heart of FIX HA is a simple but unforgiving rule:

> For a given FIX session and direction, there must be exactly one authoritative writer of sequence numbers at any moment in time.

Why a single writer?

Recall that:

- Outbound sequence numbers identify and order the messages you send.
- Inbound sequence numbers track what you expect to receive.

If two independent processes can both send outbound messages for the *same* session, several bad things can happen:

- They might both try to send using the same next sequence number, producing *duplicates* from the counterparty's perspective.
- They might each increment their own local counter, resulting in *gaps* and inconsistencies when their histories are merged.

Either way, your partner sees a broken sequence and initiates resend procedures, or worse, loses confidence in the connection.

Hence, for each (SenderCompID, TargetCompID, session) pair:

- One and only one engine instance can be the **active sequence owner** at a time.
- All writes of outbound messages and updates to outbound durable sequence numbers must flow through that owner.

This principle shapes HA design more strongly than any particular technology choice.

State Replication: Keeping Standbys in Sync

If only one engine can write for a session, how can others be ready to take over quickly when it fails? The answer is **state replication**: copying (or streaming) the active engine's durable state to one or more standbys.

Two broad layers need replication:

- **Message store and sequence numbers** for each session.
- **Configuration and routing information** that tells engines how to bind sessions to network endpoints and internal applications.

Synchronous vs. asynchronous replication

Replication can be:

- **Synchronous** — the active engine waits for the standby (or shared store) to confirm the write before considering a message committed.

- **Asynchronous** – the active engine writes locally and proceeds; replication to standbys happens slightly later.

Each approach implies a trade-off between:

- **Recovery Point Objective (RPO):** How many messages, at worst, could be missing on the standby at the moment of failover?
- **Latency:** How much extra time is added to each message path by waiting for replication?

Synchronous replication.

- **Pros:** RPO is near zero; when failover occurs, the standby sees nearly the same last committed message and sequence numbers as the old active.
- **Cons:** Outbound message latency includes the time to confirm the write on remote storage or a peer. If network links between data centers are slow or congested, this can be costly.

Asynchronous replication.

- **Pros:** Minimal added latency on the primary path. The engine acknowledges messages once local persistence is done.
- **Cons:** If the active engine or its storage is lost, the standby might be behind by some number of messages, requiring manual gap repair or constrained recovery.

In practice, firms often mix these strategies:

- Use synchronous replication within a low-latency cluster (for example, within a single data center or availability zone).
- Use asynchronous replication to more distant sites, accepting a slightly larger RPO in catastrophic scenarios.

Replicating the message store

There are three common patterns for replicating FIX message logs and sequence numbers:

1. **Shared storage:** active and passive engines both access the same underlying message store (for example, a replicated file system or clustered database).
2. **Engine-level replication:** the active engine writes to its own local store and streams each write to the passive engine's store.
3. **External log or bus:** engines publish messages to a central, replicated log (for example, a distributed commit log), and standbys read from there.

The crucial requirement is that, no matter which mechanism is used:

- The standby can *rely* on the incoming sequence of writes to be ordered and consistent.
- On promotion to active, it can immediately resume sending and receiving with the correct next sequence numbers.

High-Availability Patterns for FIX Engines

With the single-writer constraint and replication basics in hand, we can now discuss architectural patterns. Two major families dominate:

- **Active/passive** with a warm or hot standby per session.
- **Active/active** clusters where multiple engines are live but sessions are *pinned* to a specific engine at any moment.

Active/Passive: One primary, one standby

In an active/passive model:

- A given session lives on a single engine instance, the *active*.

- One (or more) other instances are configured as *passive standbys*, ready to take over.

The standby:

- Either shares the same message store or receives a replicated copy.
- Does *not* send or receive over the TCP connection while passive.
- Tracks metadata (for example, which sessions it could own) and health of the active.

Failover is triggered by:

- Health-check failures (for example, missed heartbeats, failed pings).
- Explicit operator action (for example, planned maintenance).

Promotion to active involves:

1. Ensuring the old active is fully stopped or fenced (so it cannot revive and send conflicting sequence numbers).
2. Bringing up the TCP listener or client connection on the new active.
3. Resuming the session using the latest replicated sequence numbers and message store.

Active/Active: Multiple engines, session pinning

In an active/active model:

- Multiple FIX engine instances are live and handling traffic simultaneously.
- Individual sessions are *pinned* to a particular engine instance, usually via routing at a load balancer, message bus, or specialized gateway.

For example:

- Client A's session might be anchored on Engine 1.
- Client B's session might be anchored on Engine 2.
- Client C might have several sessions distributed across both.

Within each session, the single-writer rule still holds:

- Engine 1 is the sole sequencer for sessions pinned to it.
- If Engine 1 fails, its sessions must migrate to another engine (for example, Engine 2) with an up-to-date view of state.

Compared with active/passive, active/active offers:

- Better horizontal scalability (sessions can be spread across many engines).
- Some resilience: if one engine fails, others continue to handle their own sessions.

However, it requires:

- Robust, per-session state replication or shared storage.
- Careful routing so that, at any given time, client traffic for a session reaches exactly one engine instance.

Topology Comparison: Active/Passive vs. Active/Active

To anchor these ideas, it is helpful to see both patterns side by side, highlighting the single-writer constraint, shared or replicated stores, and traffic flows.

Diagrammatic representation:

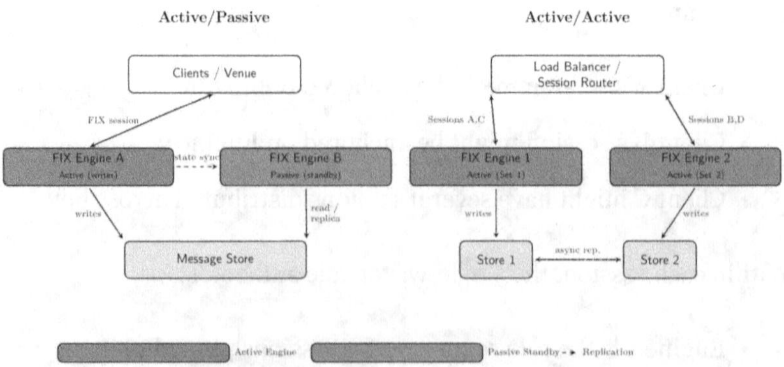

This figure emphasizes that, regardless of topology, each individual session has a single writer at any time, and that message stores — often with some replication — are shared or synchronized to make failover safe.

Failover Mechanics and Split-Brain Avoidance

Designing an HA topology is only half the work; you also need precise rules for how failover is triggered and how you prevent *split-brain* situations.

What is split-brain?

Split-brain occurs when two instances both believe they are the active owner for the same session at the same time. This can happen when:

- The standby loses contact with the active and assumes it has failed.
- In reality, the active is still running and continues sending messages.
- The standby also starts sending, now with conflicting sequence numbers.

To the counterparty, the session appears corrupted: duplicate or out-of-order messages come from apparently the same identity. Recovering from this without significant disruption is difficult.

Fencing and authoritative decisions

Avoiding split-brain requires some form of **fencing**: a guarantee that once a node is demoted or loses its "lock" on a session, it will not be allowed to act as active until explicitly re-admitted.

Typical mechanisms include:

- **External consensus or lock service** (for example, a distributed coordination system) that grants an exclusive lease per session or session group to a specific engine instance.
- **Shared storage-based locks** — a lock record in the shared message store or configuration database that only one engine can hold at a time.
- **Out-of-band infrastructure controls** — the cluster manager disables network paths or TCP endpoints on demoted nodes so they cannot send or accept session traffic.

The pattern is:

1. Before becoming active for a session, an engine acquires the lock.
2. If it loses the lock (for example, because of connectivity loss to the lock service), it must *assume it is no longer active* and stop sending on those sessions.
3. Only an engine with a valid, current lock may accept new logons or continue existing ones.

Health checks and promotion rules

To make failover predictable, define clear rules:

- **Health signals** — how do engines report their health (CPU, memory, connectivity to stores and counterparties)?
- **Timeouts** — after how long without a heartbeat or lock renewal should a node be considered failed?

- **Promotion policy** – which standby takes over, and does it promote all sessions or only a subset?

Ideally, much of this is automated by your clustering or orchestration platform, but the logic must respect FIX's sequencing constraints and durable state.

Multi-Site and Multi-AZ Layouts

So far we have implicitly considered a single data center. In reality, firms often distribute FIX infrastructure across multiple availability zones (AZs) or physical data centers for disaster recovery and local-proximity reasons.

Single primary site with remote DR

In a common pattern:

- One site (Site A) hosts the primary FIX engines and the main message store.
- Another site (Site B) hosts standby engines and a replicated or lagged copy of the store.

Replication from Site A to Site B is usually asynchronous, balancing survivability with the realities of inter-site latency.

If Site A fails:

- Site B promotes its engines to active and resumes sessions where possible.
- Some small number of the most recent messages may need manual reconciliation, depending on replication lag.

Mutual active sites with pinned sessions

More advanced setups run both sites active, with sessions pinned by geography or client:

- European clients connect to a European site.

- U.S. clients connect to a U.S. site.

Each site acts as primary for its set of sessions and as DR for the other's. This spreads load and can reduce latency while still offering continuity if one region fails.

The complexity lies in:

- Cross-site replication of message stores.
- Failing sessions over in a way that preserves (or at least safely repairs) sequence consistency.

Operational Practices: Drills, Visibility, and Limits

A theoretically elegant HA architecture is not enough; it must be tested and operated under real-world conditions.

Planned failover drills

You should schedule regular, controlled failovers:

- Move a subset of production sessions from one engine to another during live trading.
- Monitor how quickly sessions re-establish and whether any sequence anomalies arise.
- Involve both technology and trading teams to confirm that order books and positions stay consistent.

These drills serve two purposes:

- They validate that replication and fencing are working as designed.
- They build operator confidence and muscle memory for real incidents.

Monitoring and alerting

HA without observability is fragile. Key metrics include:

- Health of each engine instance and its connections to:
  - Counterparties (TCP links, heartbeat status).
  - Message stores and replication streams.
  - Lock or coordination services.
- Sequence number anomalies:
  - Unexpected gaps or duplicates.
  - Frequent resend activity outside expected patterns.
- Failover events:
  - Who became active for which session, when, and why.
  - Any errors or slowdowns during promotion.

Alerts should be clear enough that operations and trading staff can quickly answer: "Which sessions are affected?" and "Is order entry or drop copy impaired?"

Capacity and blast radius

Finally, HA architectures must consider what happens when things go wrong in bulk:

- If a large engine or site fails and hundreds of sessions shift at once, can the remaining engines and stores handle the sudden load?
- Is there a mechanism to *throttle* reconnections or resends, so the system does not collapse under its own recovery traffic?

You can reduce blast radius by:

- Sharding sessions across multiple engines even within the same site.
- Designing failover policies that move only a controlled subset of sessions at a time.
- Coordinating with clients and venues during major incidents to limit simultaneous reconnect attempts.

Bringing It All Together

Durable state and message stores, discussed earlier, ensure that a single FIX engine can crash and restart without losing its place. Recovery playbooks, in the previous section, describe how to detect gaps and choose between resend, sequence reset, and full session reset.

High availability and failover architecture extend these concepts across *multiple* engines, sites, and storage systems. The essential goals are:

- Preserve the **illusion of a single, continuous session** to the counterparty, even as engines and infrastructure change behind the scenes.
- Maintain **single-writer sequencing** per session at all times, enforced by clear fencing and coordination.
- Provide **predictable, tested failover paths** with known RPO and latency trade-offs.

When these elements work together, a failure of an individual engine, host, or even a data center becomes a contained event rather than a firm-wide emergency. The FIX connectivity layer remains a dependable foundation for the trading and risk systems that depend on it.

6.4 Cancel-on-Disconnect Protections

The previous sections in this chapter focused on keeping FIX *sessions* stable: persisting state, recovering deterministically after disconnects, and designing high-availability architectures so that failures are contained. In all of those discussions, the main objective was continuity of the conversation.

From a trading and risk perspective, continuity is only half the story. Equally important is *what happens to your orders* when that conversation breaks. A session can disappear at the very moment you have hundreds or thousands of live orders resting on a venue. If your systems are blind, those orders may continue to trade in ways you cannot see or control.

Cancel-on-Disconnect (COD) is a family of mechanisms designed precisely for this problem. COD does not repair connectivity; instead, it limits *exposure* when connectivity breaks. In this section we will:

- Explain the risk that COD addresses and why normal session recovery is not enough.
- Describe how COD is enrolled and configured between client and venue.
- Walk through the lifecycle of a COD event: detection, cancellation, acknowledgement, and logging.
- Show how to reconcile state after reconnect, so that your books and the venue's view agree.
- Highlight operational nuances and best practices.

Throughout, keep in mind the link to earlier material: COD relies heavily on durable message stores and clear recovery playbooks, because you must be able to prove what was cancelled and when.

Why Cancel-on-Disconnect Exists

Imagine a typical day:

- Your algorithms send a burst of NewOrderSingle messages to a venue.
- The venue acknowledges each order with an ExecutionReport (new) and starts working them in the market.
- Suddenly, the FIX session drops due to a network issue.

Several things are immediately true:

- Orders that were accepted by the venue are still live *unless* explicitly cancelled or rejected.

- Your ability to monitor those orders is gone until you reconnect and recover.
- The market continues to move; fills can occur while you are blind.

You do have recovery tools:

- Durable message stores tell you which orders the venue accepted before the crash.
- Recovery playbooks help you request resends and reconcile fills once you reconnect.

But none of that changes what may happen *during* the blind period. COD is intended to put a hard limit on this "unattended risk window."

At a high level, COD is an arrangement where:

> If the session (or gateway) disconnects, the venue automatically cancels some or all of the participant's open orders.

The exact scope of coverage and the triggers vary by venue, but the basic idea is consistent: better a controlled, explainable cancellation than uncontrolled trading while blind.

Dimensions of Cancel-on-Disconnect

Before getting into the mechanics, it helps to identify the key "dimensions" along which COD can be defined. Thinking clearly about these will prevent misunderstandings with venues and internal teams.

What gets cancelled?

COD can apply to different sets of orders:

- **Session-wide COD:** all orders associated with a particular FIX session are cancelled when that session is deemed disconnected.
- **Account- or user-level COD:** all orders for a particular trading account or user ID, possibly spanning multiple sessions or gateways.

- **Instrument- or venue-specific COD:** only certain symbols, markets, or order types are subject to COD.

In practice, many equity venues offer session- or account-wide COD as a basic safety net.

What event triggers COD?

The trigger might be:

- **Session-level disconnect:** loss of the FIX connection, detected at the venue gateway (for example, heartbeats missed, TCP closed).
- **Gateway or port failure:** if an entire gateway process or network segment fails, all sessions through that component are considered disconnected.
- **Manual COD trigger:** operations at the firm or the venue invoke a COD action explicitly (for example, big incident, trading halt).

It is critical to understand whether COD is tied strictly to your own session, or also to the health of shared infrastructure between you and the matching engine.

Is COD automatic or opt-in?

COD policies can be:

- **Mandatory and always-on:** some exchanges require COD for certain client categories or gateways.
- **Optional but recommended:** you may have to sign up via documentation or venue tools.
- **Configurable:** you can specify per-session COD preferences, such as "cancel all orders," "cancel only day orders," or "no COD."

These preferences may be set out-of-band (for example, via web portals) or in-band over FIX, depending on the venue.

Enrolling and Configuring COD

From the perspective of a FIX-connected firm, COD enrollment is a *risk contract* with the venue: you agree that in certain situations the venue can and should cancel your orders automatically. To make this work operationally, three pieces must be clear:

1. How you request or agree to COD.
2. How the venue confirms which orders or accounts are under COD protection.
3. How changes to COD preferences are tracked and auditable.

Out-of-band enrollment

Often, COD is configured outside FIX:

- via customer on-boarding forms,
- account management portals,
- or static configuration files at the venue.

In these cases, your operations or risk team ensures that:

- COD is enabled for specific accounts or sessions,
- choices are documented and reviewed regularly,
- and internal systems are aware of the COD status (for example, storing a flag in an account database).

Your FIX engine may not "see" this configuration directly, but it still needs to know that COD is in effect so that operators interpret disconnects and subsequent cancels correctly.

In-band confirmation and flags

Some venues expose COD-related information over FIX, typically during logon or via dedicated administrative messages. Examples include:

- Flags indicating that the session is COD-protected.
- Fields in ExecutionReport or other admin messages confirming that a mass cancel was triggered due to a disconnect.
- Optional messages that report what COD preferences are currently in force.

Your FIX engine and monitoring tools should capture and surface these confirmations. For instance, when a logon response indicates COD is active, the session dashboard might display a "COD: ON" badge.

Multiple sessions and shared orders

Complications arise when:

- A single account trades through multiple sessions.
- A single session controls orders across multiple sub-accounts.

You and the venue must agree whether COD applies at:

- the session level,
- the account level,
- or both.

For example, if one of several sessions for an account disconnects, does COD cancel *all* account orders or only those linked to that session? This distinction matters greatly for high-volume clients distributing risk across gateways.

The Lifecycle of a COD Event

With configuration in place, we can walk through a typical COD event step by step. Think of it as a time-ordered narrative that your durable message store should be able to replay and prove.

Phase 1: Normal trading

During normal operation:

- Your algorithms send orders, cancel requests, and replace requests over the FIX session.
- The venue sends back ExecutionReport messages reflecting new, partially filled, filled, or cancelled states.
- Durable message stores on both sides capture every message with sequence numbers and timestamps.

COD is configured but inactive; it is simply a standing agreement about what to do if the session disappears.

Phase 2: Disconnect detection at the venue

At some point, something goes wrong:

- Your side loses network connectivity or your engine crashes.
- Heartbeats from your side stop arriving at the venue gateway.
- The venue's timeout logic detects that the session has become inactive (for example, no messages within a configured interval, or TCP disconnect).

Depending on venue policy, there may be:

- A brief grace period (for example, wait a few seconds or heartbeats before triggering COD).
- Additional checks (for example, monitoring multiple redundant links).

Once the venue decides the session is truly disconnected:

- It consults its COD configuration for that session or account.
- If COD is enabled, it moves to cancel affected orders.

Phase 3: Venue-side cancellation of open orders

The venue then cancels eligible open orders according to COD rules:

- This may be implemented as a form of *mass cancel* operation, logically equivalent to sending cancel requests for all qualifying orders.
- For each order, the venue generates a cancellation or update, often as an ExecutionReport with cancelled status.

From a risk perspective at the venue:

- The account's resting exposure is reduced or eliminated.
- Any further fills on those orders are prevented.

At this moment, your firm may still be disconnected and *unaware* that COD has fired, but the market risk has been contained at the venue.

Phase 4: Notification and logging

Next, the venue must make the COD event visible and auditable:

- Internally, it logs the trigger (time, reason, affected sessions/accounts, number of orders cancelled).
- Externally, it communicates what happened:
  - If the session is still up from the venue's side (for example, there was an asymmetric failure), it may send explicit FIX messages indicating that COD was applied.
  - If the session is fully down, this information will be conveyed later upon reconnection (for example, via resend of ExecutionReport messages, special notices, or end-of-day reports).

Your durable message store plays a critical role during recovery: it must capture the COD-related messages once they are sent, so that you can reconstruct and prove the COD event.

Post-Reconnect Reconciliation

When your session recovers after a COD event, the priority shifts from *limiting* risk back to *understanding* exactly what happened and aligning your internal books with the venue.

Step 1: Session recovery and gap detection

Upon reconnect:

- You perform the usual logon handshake and sequence number comparison, as discussed in the recovery playbooks section.
- Gaps are likely: the venue may have generated a stream of ExecutionReport (cancel) messages during the COD mass cancel while you were disconnected.

Accordingly:

- You or the venue initiate ResendRequest messages for the missing sequence ranges.
- The venue replays the COD-related messages, including cancels and any fills that occurred just before COD took effect.

Your message store now fills in the blind period.

Step 2: Order-by-order state alignment

Once you have the complete message history, you must align internal order state with the venue's:

- For each affected order ID or client order ID:
  - Verify the final status (cancelled, filled, partially filled).
  - Confirm the final filled quantity and price if applicable.
- Update your order management and risk systems to reflect:
  - Reduced or zero open quantity on cancelled orders.
  - Realized P&L from any fills that occurred before COD fired.

Because COD happens under stress, you want this process to be as automated as possible:

- Use reconciliation scripts that compare:

  - Venue-side execution reports (from message store or drop copy feeds).
  - Internal order and trade records.

- Flag discrepancies for manual review (for example, orders your system still thinks are live but the venue has cancelled).

Step 3: Decision to resume trading

After reconciliation:

- Risk and trading teams confirm that exposure is understood and within limits.
- Operations confirms there are no unexplained open orders or mismatched fills.
- Only then should you re-enable normal trading on the COD-affected sessions or accounts.

This final decision should be guided by a runbook: COD events are stressful, and clear criteria help avoid hasty or inconsistent choices.

Nuances and Edge Cases

While the basic COD story is conceptually simple, real-world implementations involve several nuances.

Race conditions with manual cancels

Consider:

- Your strategy detects a risk issue and sends a wave of cancel requests.
- Almost simultaneously, the session disconnects and COD triggers at the venue.

Depending on timing:

- Some orders may be cancelled by your explicit requests before COD fires.
- Others may be cancelled by COD after the fact.

From your perspective, the end result (orders are cancelled) is acceptable, but the sequence of events matters for audit and for understanding whether your risk controls or COD were primarily responsible. This is another reason to store and replay the precise message sequence and timestamps on both sides.

Multiple sessions sharing the same account

If COD is configured at the account level, and you have multiple sessions trading that account:

- A disconnect on one session could cancel orders placed via another session.
- Or, conversely, COD might only apply to orders linked to the disconnected session, leaving others untouched.

You must understand and document how each venue handles these multi-session scenarios. Internal monitoring should be able to answer questions like:

> "Session X to Venue Y disconnected at 10:15:23; which orders, across which sessions, were cancelled as a result?"

Interaction with high-availability and failover

Earlier we discussed active/passive and active/active FIX architectures. COD must fit coherently with these:

- If failover between engines is rapid and transparent to the venue, COD might *not* be triggered, because the session appears continuous from the venue's perspective.
- If failover is slow or involves a full disconnect and reconnect, COD might fire during the gap.

Therefore:

- HA designs should consider whether they aim to *avoid* COD triggering (by keeping the session alive) or are comfortable letting COD act as a backstop.
- Runbooks should clearly state, for each type of failure:
  - Whether COD is expected to fire.
  - How operators should respond.

When COD is inappropriate

COD is not always the right choice. For example:

- For certain long-lived, low-liquidity orders, automatic cancellation may be undesirable if it causes you to lose a carefully negotiated position in the order book.
- Some strategies may have their own tightly integrated risk controls and circuit breakers, where COD might interfere with sophisticated hedging or exit logic.

In such cases, firms may choose more selective COD configurations (for example, only for specific product sets or sessions) or rely on other protections.

Best Practices for Using COD Effectively

To make COD an asset rather than a source of confusion, several best practices are helpful.

Treat COD as part of the risk framework

COD is not just a technical feature; it is part of the firm's risk management plan:

- Document which accounts and sessions have COD enabled and at which venues.

- Ensure trading strategies understand that orders may disappear due to COD and must be prepared to re-establish positions or strategies after reconnect.
- Coordinate COD decisions with other risk limits, kill switches, and circuit breakers.

Integrate COD events into monitoring

Your monitoring stack should:

- Detect and alert on COD-related messages or patterns (for example, mass cancels following a disconnect).
- Clearly label COD events in dashboards and post-trade reports.
- Provide easy access to message history around COD incidents for analysis and communication with clients or regulators.

Rehearse COD scenarios

As with failover drills:

- Simulate COD events in test or certification environments, using realistic message flows.
- Practice full lifecycle: disconnect, COD firing at venue, reconnect, resend handling, reconciliation, and restart of trading.
- Validate that tools and procedures (both technical and organizational) behave as expected.

Align COD with client communication

If you are an intermediary or broker:

- Make sure your clients understand when their orders may be subject to COD, and under what conditions.
- Provide explanations and data when COD events occur (for example, exactly which orders were cancelled, at what time, and why).

This transparency helps maintain trust when disruptions happen.

From Stable Sessions to Stable Risk

The journey of this chapter has moved from:

- Persistent, deterministic FIX sessions,
- through structured recovery from disconnects,
- to resilient multi-engine architectures,

and finally to *risk-aware* behavior when sessions fail.

Cancel-on-Disconnect is the bridge between technical resilience and trading resilience. Even the best-engineered session infrastructure cannot guarantee that links will never break. COD acknowledges that reality and provides a pre-agreed emergency brake: when you are blind, it is often safer to be flat than to be unknowingly exposed.

Implementing COD thoughtfully—with clear enrollment, precise triggers, robust reconciliation, and strong operational discipline—turns it from a blunt instrument into a finely integrated layer of your overall risk control stack.

Chapter 7

Operating, Securing, and Monitoring FIX

FIX sessions don't fail in textbooks-they fail at 09:30:01 when the opening auction is crossing and someone's risk limits are on the line. This chapter steps out of the protocol spec and into the engine room: how to pick and tune a FIX engine, lock it down, prove it works with every new counterparty, and watch it well enough that trouble is detected and contained before trades are lost or reputations are damaged.

7.1 FIX Engine Selection & Performance Configuration

In earlier chapters we treated FIX sessions somewhat abstractly: a persistent conversation between your trading system and the outside world, carrying orders, cancels, and execution reports in a strictly ordered sequence. In production, that "conversation" is implemented by a concrete software component: the *FIX engine*.

This section explains what a FIX engine is in operational terms, how to decide whether to build or buy one, which capabilities matter most, and how to configure an engine so that it is both fast and stable under real trading load. The emphasis throughout is practical: we connect each design choice to its impact on order flow, drop copy, and operational risk.

What a FIX Engine Really Is in Production

From an engineering perspective, a FIX engine is a long-lived session manager and message router that sits between your trading logic and your counterparties. It is responsible for:

- Establishing and maintaining FIX sessions (Logon/Logout, heartbeats, sequence numbers).
- Encoding outbound messages from internal objects or data structures into FIX tag–value format.
- Parsing inbound FIX messages into a structured form your trading application can consume.
- Persisting session state and messages so that recovery is possible after failures.
- Enforcing FIX transport rules: sequence number monotonicity, resends, gap fills, and so on.

A helpful mental model is to think of the engine as an *infrastructure appliance* rather than part of your trading strategy. Your trading logic decides *what* orders to send and *how* to react to execution reports; the FIX engine decides *how* to move those messages reliably and efficiently across the network while speaking the FIX dialect your counterparties expect.

Operationally, the engine commonly runs as one or more long-lived processes, often on shared "connectivity" hosts. These processes maintain many concurrent sessions: order-entry sessions to exchanges and brokers, drop-copy sessions receiving post-trade confirmations, and sometimes internal routing sessions between internal components.

Right after this conceptual framing it is useful to anchor the discussion visually.

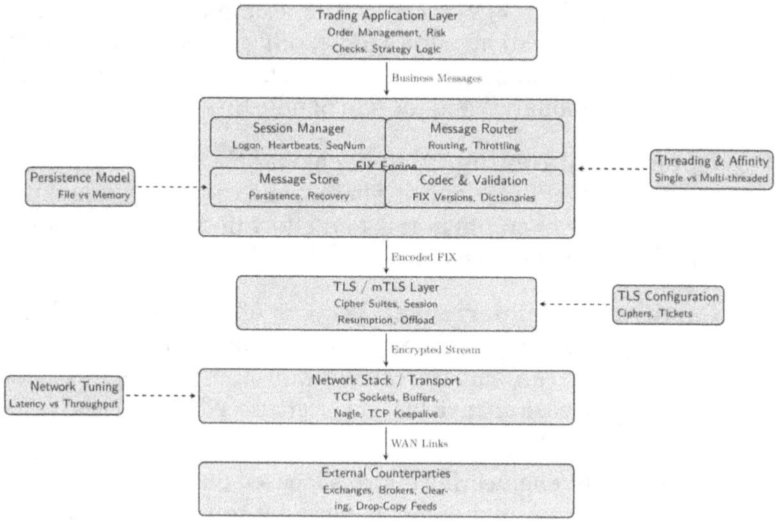

Build Versus Buy: How to Decide

Once you appreciate that the FIX engine is infrastructure, the primary strategic question becomes: *do you build your own, or do you buy or adopt an existing one?* There is no universal answer, but there are clear forces that push in each direction.

When a Commercial Engine Makes Sense

For most firms, especially in the early stages of building a trading platform, a commercial or mature open-source engine is the rational choice. It can save years of development and battle-hardening.

Typical reasons to buy include:

- **Time to market.** Building a compliant, interoperable FIX engine from scratch usually takes far longer than expected: parsing edge cases, handling all session-level behaviors, implementing resends correctly, and passing exchange certifications across multiple venues. A vendor product or proven library gets you to your first live order much faster.
- **Breadth of protocol support.** Many trading environments

require multiple FIX versions (for example, 4.2, 4.4, FIXT 1.1 with application messages 5.0SP2) and venue-specific extensions. Commercial engines often ship with configurable message dictionaries and tools to handle these variants.

- **Operational tooling.** Mature engines come with administration GUIs or APIs, monitoring hooks, and sometimes simulators. These reduce operational risk and effort in day-to-day running and during incident response.

- **Certification experience.** Vendors often maintain relationships with exchanges and brokers, and know the quirks of each venue. This can smooth certification and reduce frustrating rounds of "please change tag X in scenario Y."

In this model, your engineering effort is focused on integrating the engine cleanly into your environment: wiring it to your order management system, risk checks, logging framework, and operational monitoring.

When an In-House Engine Is Justified

Some firms do reach the point where building and owning their own engine makes sense. The typical preconditions are:

- **Extreme latency sensitivity.** If your strategies compete on microseconds and every context switch or memory copy matters, you may want to optimize all the way down to the parser and TCP handling. A general-purpose engine might be too heavy or inflexible.

- **Highly specialized workflows.** Certain venues or asset classes have non-standard workflows that are awkward to force into a generic configuration model. Owning the engine can make it easier to shape the protocol implementation around your internal model.

- **Deep integration with proprietary infrastructure.** If you have custom messaging buses, specialized persistence systems, or co-designed hardware/software stacks, a homegrown engine can integrate more naturally with those.

- **Regulatory or security constraints.** In some environments, there may be policy-driven reasons to avoid external vendor code in the connectivity path, or to maintain full control over cryptographic implementations.

Building an engine is not merely a programming task; it is a commitment to operate and evolve that component over many years. You must be prepared to add features as FIX evolves or venues change, to support new message types, and to respond to subtle interoperability bugs under pressure.

Hybrid Models

A common compromise is a *hybrid model*:

- Use an open-source or commercial core that handles the protocol and session machinery.
- Wrap it in proprietary tooling: configuration management, monitoring, venue-specific adapters, and risk control logic.

In this approach, the "engine" you expose internally is a richer platform than the raw library, but you still avoid reinventing low-level parsing and session semantics. This is often the sweet spot for firms that want control and extensibility without carrying the full burden of protocol implementation.

Key Engine Capabilities to Evaluate

Regardless of build-versus-buy, your engine must meet a set of functional and non-functional requirements. It helps to group these by theme.

FIX Version and Extension Support

Your engine should:

- Support the FIX versions you actually need (for example, 4.2 and 4.4 for many equities venues, FIXT 1.1/5.0SP2 for newer venues).

- Allow *configurable message dictionaries*: the ability to define which tags and message types are valid, which are required, and what their datatypes are.
- Handle custom tags and components gracefully, without forcing code changes for every venue extension.

In practice, version support is less about marketing checklists and more about whether you can express venue-specific rules declaratively rather than by patching code.

Order Flow and Drop-Copy Capabilities

Most firms run at least two broad categories of FIX sessions:

- **Order-entry sessions**, where you send NewOrderSingle, replace, and cancel messages, and receive ExecutionReports and rejects.
- **Drop-copy sessions**, where you receive post-trade or real-time copies of executions and other events, often for multiple accounts or sessions.

An engine should make it easy to:

- Distinguish these flows in configuration (for example, different session profiles or roles).
- Route messages from multiple order-entry sessions into a shared drop-copy consumer, and vice versa.
- Apply different performance and recovery characteristics: order-entry sessions may prioritize ultra-low-latency and minimal buffering; drop copy may prioritize completeness and persistence.

Well-designed engines treat order-entry and drop-copy sessions symmetrically at the transport level but offer configuration hooks to tune them differently.

Throughput, Latency, and Backpressure

Performance characteristics matter both for speed and for stability.

- **Latency** is the delay between your application submitting a message and that message leaving the host, or between a packet arriving and being delivered to your application.
- **Throughput** is how many messages per second the engine can process and route when under sustained load.
- **Backpressure** is how the engine behaves when downstream components cannot keep up (for example, slow venues, slow disks, or slow internal consumers).

You want an engine that can:

- Process bursts of traffic without dropping messages or violating sequence order.
- Expose queues and flow-control information so you can see where bottlenecks are.
- Apply backpressure in predictable ways: perhaps by queuing up to a limit and then rejecting or slowing new messages, rather than silently consuming memory until the process fails.

Session Recovery and Persistence Models

Sessions will drop. Processes will restart. Your engine's persistence model determines what happens next.

Common models include:

- **Full message store.** Every inbound and outbound message is written to disk or durable storage. Recovery can reconstruct the full conversation and support resends of any message since the start of the day (or longer).
- **Sequence-only store.** Only sequence numbers and minimal session metadata are persisted; messages themselves are kept in memory or not at all. Recovery is faster, but historical resends may not be possible.
- **In-memory with snapshots.** The engine keeps state in memory but periodically snapshots critical pieces to disk. After a

crash, it rolls forward from the last snapshot and may request resends from the counterparty.

For latency-sensitive order-entry flows, teams sometimes lean toward lighter-weight persistence to avoid disk I/O on the hot path, while using richer persistence for drop-copy or post-trade sessions where completeness is paramount. The key is to understand the trade-offs explicitly and, where possible, move heavy persistence work off the critical latency path (for example, onto background threads).

Operational Ecosystem

Finally, do not underestimate the value of tooling around the engine:

- **Configuration management.** Are sessions defined via files, a database, or an API? Can you templatize settings for dozens of similar sessions? Is there a safe, auditable way to roll changes to production?
- **Scriptability.** Can you interact with the engine from scripts or automation (for example, starting/stopping sessions, fetching runtime stats, triggering resends)?
- **Metrics and logs.** Does the engine expose the metrics you need for monitoring and capacity planning, and does it integrate with your logging infrastructure?
- **Vendor support SLAs.** If using a commercial product, how quickly can you get help during a production incident or exchange certification?

A technically elegant engine without good operational support is a liability in production.

Performance Configuration: Threading and Process Models

With an engine selected (or built), the next step is to configure it. A central decision is how to map work onto threads and processes.

Single-Threaded Reactor Versus Multi-Threaded Pipeline

Two broad patterns are common.

Single-threaded reactor. One thread handles reading from sockets, parsing messages, updating session state, and writing outbound data. This model:

- Minimizes context switches and locking overhead.
- Keeps processing strictly ordered and easier to reason about.
- Works very well up to a certain throughput threshold.

For many venues and small session counts, a single-threaded reactor can deliver excellent latency, especially if paired with careful CPU pinning.

Multi-threaded pipeline. Work is split across multiple threads or stages. For example:

- One thread per NIC or group of sockets for I/O.
- One or more threads for parsing and validating messages.
- Separate threads for application callbacks or business logic.

This model:

- Scales better when you have many active sessions or higher throughput.
- Allows isolating slow components (for example, logging, disk I/O) away from the critical path.
- Introduces complexity: you must manage queues, avoid head-of-line blocking, and be careful with locks and shared data.

In practice, many engines start with a mostly single-threaded core for session and parsing, with optional worker threads for callbacks, logging, or persistence.

CPU Pinning and Affinity

Latency-sensitive shops often *pin* engine threads to specific CPU cores. The idea is to reduce variability due to the operating system moving threads around.

Typical patterns include:

- Pin the main engine thread to a core local to the NIC handling market connectivity.
- Avoid placing other noisy processes (for example, monitoring agents, batch jobs) on the same cores.
- Reserve separate cores for disk or logging threads if they do heavy work.

On multi-socket machines, you may also consider NUMA locality: ensure that the engine's memory and NIC interrupts are tied to the same socket when possible.

Splitting Roles Across Processes or Hosts

The engine has two logical roles:

- **Acceptor**, where you host sessions that clients connect to (for example, you are the broker or venue).
- **Initiator**, where you connect out to venues or upstream brokers.

For small deployments, these roles may live in the same process. As you scale, it can be beneficial to:

- Run acceptor and initiator roles in separate processes, even on the same host, to isolate resource usage and failure domains.
- Place high-importance or ultra-low-latency sessions on dedicated hosts, minimizing interference from lower-priority flows.
- Shard sessions by asset class, venue, or client group across multiple engine instances for load distribution and operational independence.

The goal is to avoid a situation where trouble in one session (for example, a misbehaving client or choking venue) cascades into latency or outages for others.

Network and Transport Tuning

The FIX engine rides on top of TCP (and often TLS). Its behavior is strongly influenced by the underlying network configuration.

Socket Buffers and Nagle's Algorithm

Two TCP-level concepts are particularly important:

- **Socket buffers.** These determine how much data can be queued for sending or receiving before the application or kernel must catch up. Too small, and you risk drops or stalls during bursts. Too large, and you add latency due to queuing.
- **Nagle's algorithm.** This algorithm bundles small writes into larger packets to improve efficiency. Unfortunately, in trading we often care more about minimizing latency than maximizing bandwidth.

Most low-latency setups:

- Disable Nagle's algorithm (for example, via TCP_NODELAY) on FIX sockets so that messages are sent as soon as possible.
- Choose socket buffer sizes based on measured traffic patterns: large enough to absorb expected bursts, but not so large that latent backlogs hide problems.

TCP Keep-Alives and Heartbeats

FIX has its own heartbeat mechanism at the protocol level (the HeartBtInt interval and test request messages). The operating system also has TCP keep-alive settings.

You should think about these together:

- **HeartBtInt** should be chosen based on venue requirements and your tolerance for detecting dead connections. Shorter intervals detect failures faster but generate more traffic and state.
- **TCP keep-alives** can provide a safety net against silent middlebox timeouts, especially on long-lived but quiet sessions (for example, some drop-copy links outside trading hours).

The key is to avoid conflicting settings: if your FIX heartbeat suggests a link is healthy but network devices silently kill idle TCP connections, you may encounter surprising disconnects. Align your TCP and FIX-level liveness strategies.

TLS and mTLS Overhead

Transport encryption adds CPU cost and sometimes latency variability. At the same time, it is increasingly mandatory for both regulatory and commercial reasons.

When enabling TLS or mutual TLS:

- Prefer modern, efficient cipher suites that are widely supported, balancing security and performance.
- Use session resumption mechanisms where appropriate, so that repeated reconnects do not incur full handshake cost each time.
- Consider terminating TLS in a dedicated process or offload component if the engine itself becomes CPU-bound on cryptography.

The FIX heartbeats and session timers should be tuned with TLS in mind: initial handshakes and certificate checks may add seconds to connection establishment, and your retry logic should account for that.

Practical Tuning Recipes

Theory becomes useful when turned into concrete patterns. This subsection offers a set of starting configurations and scaling patterns.

Scaling from a Handful of Sessions to Dozens

Suppose you start with:

- Fewer than 10 order-entry sessions.
- A similar number of drop-copy sessions.
- Modest message rates (for example, hundreds of messages per second).

A sensible initial configuration might be:

- A single-engine process running both initiator and acceptor roles, using a single-threaded reactor core.
- Nagle disabled; socket buffers sized modestly but identically for all sessions.
- A full message store for all sessions to simplify troubleshooting and recovery.

As you add sessions and volume, monitor:

- CPU utilization of the engine process.
- Latency distributions across sessions (not just averages).
- Queue depths inside the engine, if exposed.

When you see sustained CPU pressure or latency degradation, consider:

- Splitting drop-copy sessions into a separate engine instance, so that heavy bursts of fills do not interfere with order-entry.
- Moving persistence for order-entry sessions to a lighter model (for example, sequence-only store) while keeping full message logging in a separate path.

Sharding by Client or Venue

At larger scales, you may run:

- Hundreds of client-facing sessions (if you are a broker).

- Dozens of venue sessions across asset classes and regions.

Two common sharding strategies are:

- **By client group.** Assign groups of client sessions to different engine instances or hosts. This contains the blast radius of any single client's misbehavior.
- **By venue or asset class.** Place all sessions to a given exchange or asset type on the same instance, simplifying tuning for that exchange's patterns and simplifying operational isolation by venue.

In both cases, think about:

- How to balance load so that no single instance becomes the bottleneck.
- How to route monitoring and logs so that operations can quickly see which shard is in trouble.
- How to fail over sessions in case an instance or host is lost.

Validating Configuration Under Load

Before you send real money through a configuration, you should test it with *synthetic load*. This typically involves:

- A replay tool that sends recorded historical flows (for example, a busy market open) through your engine toward a simulator.
- Synthetic order bursts targeted at worst-case scenarios: many clients sending at once, or a venue sending a storm of execution reports.
- Deliberately induced network issues: added latency, packet loss, or disconnects.

During these tests, observe:

- Whether sequence numbers remain consistent and resends behave as expected.

- How engine latency and CPU behave as you approach and exceed expected peak loads.
- Whether persistence and logging keep up without causing back-pressure or stalls.

The goal is not to eliminate all risk—markets are inherently unpredictable—but to ensure that your engine configuration behaves predictably under stress, and that you know how it degrades when overloaded.

Stability Versus Speed: Finding the Right Balance

There is a natural temptation to tune everything for minimal latency. In practice, your business needs a balance: orders must be fast enough to be competitive, but also reliable enough that a single glitch does not turn into a multi-hour outage or regulatory incident.

Key balancing decisions include:

- How much persistence you place on the hot path for order-entry sessions.
- How aggressively you disable protective features (for example, large buffers, conservative heartbeats) in pursuit of microseconds.
- How much you isolate critical flows (for example, primary venue sessions) from non-critical flows (for example, test clients, less-used venues).

A useful rule of thumb is to start from a conservative, stable configuration and then *measure* the impact of each optimization step. If disabling a layer of persistence saves little latency but greatly increases recovery complexity, it may not be worth it. Conversely, if a small adjustment to thread affinity yields a meaningful improvement with little downside, it is a good trade.

In the remainder of the chapter we will deepen this picture by overlaying security controls and observability on top of the engine configuration. A well-chosen, well-tuned FIX engine is the foundation; robust security and monitoring are what keep that foundation strong under real-world conditions.

7.2 Counterparty Onboarding & Certification Processes

In the previous section we treated the FIX engine as a long-lived, configurable infrastructure component. We looked at how to select and tune it so that sessions are fast and stable. That gave us the "machine" that can speak FIX reliably.

In practice, however, your FIX engine does not talk to an abstract counterparty. It talks to very specific exchanges, brokers, and clients, each with its own rules, conventions, and quirks. The question this section answers is: *how do you bring a new counterparty live through FIX without chaos or guesswork?*

We will turn counterparty onboarding from an ad-hoc exchange of emails and test trades into a controlled, repeatable engineering process. The goal is to:

- Capture each counterparty's custom demands in a structured way.
- Translate those demands into a certification test matrix.
- Automate as much as possible so every new session follows the same path to production.
- Produce clear evidence and sign-off for operations, risk, and regulators.

Why Onboarding Feels Chaotic in Real Life

Before we design a clean pipeline, it helps to name the sources of friction you will recognise from practice.

Shared Envelope, Different Dialects

The FIX protocol gives everyone a common envelope: standard message types, standard tags, and standard session behaviour. Within that envelope, each venue or broker defines its own:

- Required and optional tags for each message type.
- Allowed values and semantics for fields like OrdType, TimeInForce, or ExecType.
- Special rules for cancels and replaces (for example, which fields are allowed to change on a replace).
- Error and reject behaviour: when does a bad order get rejected immediately versus being passively ignored?
- Drop-copy content and timing: which events are echoed, and how soon after the actual execution.

All of this is often squeezed into a PDF or spreadsheet rather than a machine-readable spec. Humans must translate that informal description into FIX dictionaries, configuration files, and application logic.

Venue Versus Broker Versus Client Complexity

The type of counterparty also shapes onboarding complexity:

- **Exchanges and MTFs** usually have detailed rule books and formal certification processes, but also more rigid requirements and edge cases (auction orders, special session states, circuit breakers).
- **Prime brokers and clearing brokers** may reuse a venue's message style but layer on account structure, risk controls, and post-trade allocations.
- **End clients (if you are a broker)** often want tailored workflows: custom tags in NewOrderSingle, special treatment for certain accounts, or bespoke drop-copy feeds.

Without discipline, every onboarding becomes a bespoke project with its own shortcuts and undocumented decisions. That is risky, especially once you operate at scale.

From Ad-Hoc Testing to a Controlled Pipeline

To bring order to this chaos, we treat onboarding like any other engineered process: define clear stages, inputs, outputs, and ownership. A simple but robust pipeline has five main stages:

1. Requirements capture.
2. Environment and connectivity setup.
3. Definition of a certification matrix.
4. Execution of scripted conformance tests and evidence capture.
5. Final sign-off and controlled migration to production.

We will examine each stage in turn, always tying it back to your FIX engine and to the order-entry and drop-copy flows.

Stage 1: Requirements Capture

Requirements capture means turning "Here is our FIX spec" into precise, checkable statements.

Message Dictionaries and Session Profiles

Start by extracting and formalising:

- **Supported message types.** For example, NewOrderSingle, OrderCancelRequest, OrderCancelReplaceRequest, ExecutionReport, OrderMassCancelRequest, TradingSessionStatus, and any others specific to the venue.
- **Required tags per message.** For each message type, which tags are mandatory, which are optional, and which are explicitly forbidden.
- **Allowed values.** For example, which sides (Side), instruments, order types (OrdType), and time-in-force options are permitted.

- **Session parameters.** Heartbeat interval, expected daily schedule (logon/logoff windows), maximum message size, compression or sequence-reset rules.

Where your engine supports external FIX dictionaries, define or extend one specifically for this counterparty. Where it does not, this information may become validation code or configuration.

It is valuable to distinguish:

- A *global* or *house* dictionary that covers common FIX semantics across many venues.
- A *counterparty-specific overlay* that tightens or extends rules for this particular link.

This separation reduces duplication and keeps future changes manageable.

Order-Entry, Drop-Copy, and Other Flows

Next, clarify which flows will exist with this counterparty:

- One or more **order-entry** sessions for live trading.
- Zero or more **drop-copy** sessions providing fills and possibly orders for post-trade systems.
- Optional **administrative** sessions carrying reference data, risk alerts, or system status.

For each flow, capture:

- Expected message directions (who is initiator, who is acceptor).
- Expected message rates and peak bursts.
- Required delivery guarantees: for example, “all executions must appear on drop copy, even if the order-entry session drops and reconnects.”

This mapping informs both engine configuration and the later certification matrix.

Operational and Compliance Requirements

Finally, record the non-functional requirements that matter for operations and compliance:

- Log retention obligations, especially for regulatory reporting.
- Requirements for timestamps, unique IDs, and audit trails.
- Any mandated risk checks or cancel-on-disconnect behaviours.
- Support contacts and escalation paths at the counterparty during certification and production.

Think of this as building a *counterparty dossier* that combines technical and operational context.

Stage 2: Environment and Connectivity Setup

Once you know what you need to support, you set up where and how you will talk.

Test Versus Production Environments

Almost all serious counterparties provide at least a test or "UAT" environment and a production environment. These may differ in:

- Connection endpoints (hostnames, IPs, ports).
- Credentials and session identifiers (SenderCompID, TargetCompID, and passwords).
- Available instruments or symbol ranges.
- Rules about simulated executions versus real fills.

To avoid catastrophic mistakes, enforce strict separation in your engine configuration:

- Use distinct session IDs and logon credentials for UAT and production.
- Use distinct network segments or subnets where possible.
- Make it visually obvious in your tools and dashboards which environment is which.

Never reuse the same sender IDs or passwords across environments. That makes cross-wiring errors harder to detect.

Network, Firewalls, and Certificates

For each environment, coordinate with your network and security teams to:

- Reserve static IP addresses and open firewall rules for the relevant ports.
- Configure any required VPNs or private lines.
- Exchange and install TLS or mutual TLS certificates if the link is encrypted.

Record details such as:

- Which side initiates the TCP connection.
- Expected IP address ranges and any layer-7 filters (for example, IP allowlists).
- Certificate expiry dates and renewal procedures.

All of this should be automated or at least templated, so that every new counterparty does not require reinventing the wheel. Your FIX engine, as discussed in the prior section, should already support running with different credentials and TLS settings per session; onboarding plugs into that capability.

Smoke Tests

Before diving into functional testing, perform simple connectivity checks:

- Can you establish a TCP connection to the endpoint?
- Can you complete a FIX Logon/Logout cycle?
- Are heartbeats exchanged at the agreed interval?
- Does the counterparty's monitoring see your connection as expected?

These smoke tests validate the "plumbing" and reveal basic misconfigurations early, before you invest time in detailed scenarios.

Stage 3: Building a Certification Matrix

The certification matrix is the heart of a disciplined onboarding process. It is a structured checklist of behaviours that must be demonstrated before you go live.

From Spec to Test Cases

Start from the requirements captured in Stage 1 and systematically derive test cases. At minimum, cover:

Core order flow

- Submit a simple buy and sell NewOrderSingle with standard order types (for example, limit, market) and verify that execution reports match the spec.
- Submit orders with different time-in-force values (for example, day, IOC, FOK) and confirm they behave correctly.

Amendments and cancels

- Replace an existing order's quantity and price; verify the replace is accepted and the original order is retired as the venue defines.
- Attempt invalid replaces (for example, changing a field that is not allowed to change) and confirm that the venue rejects correctly.
- Cancel live orders, including edge cases such as already-filled or partially-filled orders.

Mass actions and special workflows

- Test order-mass-cancel behaviour under different filters (by symbol, account, or session).
- If supported, test auction orders, pegged orders, or other special types.

Error handling and rejects

- Intentionally send malformed messages: missing required tags, unknown symbols, or out-of-range quantities.
- Verify that you receive the expected reject messages, with correct reason codes.

Drop-copy and post-trade

- Verify that every fill on the order-entry session appears on the drop-copy session with consistent identifiers.
- Test cancels, busts (trade breaks), and corrections, confirming that drop-copy reflects the final state.

Positive and Negative Testing

It is important to distinguish:

- **Positive tests**: show that valid behaviour works. These tests ensure you understand and correctly implement the "happy path."
- **Negative tests**: show that invalid behaviour is rejected safely and predictably. These tests protect you against subtle bugs and mismatched assumptions.

Both types belong in the certification matrix. In many real-world failures, the happy path is fine; the incident arises from something slightly off-spec that was never tested.

Defining Pass/Fail Criteria

Each test case in the matrix should have clear pass/fail conditions, such as:

- Specific expected FIX messages and fields (for example, an ExecutionReport with OrdStatus = Rejected and a given Text or RefTagID).
- Timing expectations where relevant (for example, drop-copy fill within a certain delay of the primary execution).
- Logging and audit expectations (for example, presence of certain messages in your logs).

Ambiguous expectations lead to arguments during certification and, worse, to bugs in production.

Stage 4: Scripted Conformance and Evidence Capture

With a matrix defined, you need a way to execute it repeatably. This is where automation and your FIX engine's interfaces become central.

Driving the Engine Directly

Instead of testing via your full trading application from the start, consider building or using a simple test harness that:

- Connects to your FIX engine.
- Sends handcrafted FIX messages or structured requests representing the test cases.
- Listens for responses and records them.

Some commercial engines ship with such tools; otherwise, you can build a thin harness tailored to your environment. The benefit is control: you can precisely craft messages without interference from complex business logic or risk checks.

Once engine-level behaviour is verified, you can repeat the key scenarios end-to-end through your real trading stack. This two-layer approach (engine-only, then full stack) makes debugging easier.

Automated Test Suites

Turn your certification matrix into executable tests:

- For each scenario, define inputs (messages to send), expected outputs, and a timeout.
- Implement the scenario as a script or configuration object that your harness can run.
- Group scenarios into suites: basic connectivity, core order flow, special order types, drop copy, error handling, and so on.

You should be able to run:

- Individual tests when investigating a specific issue.
- A "smoke suite" for quick feedback.
- A "full certification suite" that you run before go-live and whenever major changes occur.

This is analogous to unit and integration tests in software development, but oriented toward FIX sessions and counterparty behaviour.

Evidence: Logs, Transcripts, and Metrics

Certification is not only about "we saw the right behaviour once." You need durable evidence that:

- Shows exactly which messages were exchanged.
- Ties those messages to the scenarios you declared.
- Can be audited later by operations, compliance, or regulators.

Typical evidence includes:

- **FIX message transcripts:** raw FIX logs or prettified renderings, tagged by test case ID.
- **Timestamps and latency measurements:** for example, time from order submission to first execution report, and from execution report to drop-copy confirmation.
- **Engine metrics snapshots:** counts of messages, sessions, rejects, and sequence-number gaps during testing.

Automate evidence collection as much as possible. For example, your harness could automatically:

- Save all relevant engine and application logs for the test window.
- Extract and annotate the specific message sequences per case.
- Produce a simple human-readable report that ties results back to the certification matrix.

This becomes your "packet of proof" that onboarding was done correctly.

Stage 5: Sign-Off and Controlled Migration

After you have run the certification suite and captured evidence, you need a clear path to production.

Formal Sign-Off

Define in advance:

- Who must sign off internally (for example, a representative from technology, operations, and risk).
- What exactly they are signing off on (for example, "All tests in the certification matrix passed in the counterparty's UAT environment on this date," with a reference to the evidence package).
- How any deviations or known limitations are documented (for example, "Order type X is not supported at launch; both sides acknowledge this.").

If the counterparty has its own certification team, they may provide a formal sign-off as well. Store both theirs and yours in a durable, searchable repository.

Migration Strategies: Parallel and Phased

When you move from test to production, avoid a "big bang" whenever possible. Safer patterns include:

- **Parallel sessions.** Run old and new sessions in parallel for a period. For example, keep sending live orders via an existing connection while mirroring a subset of flow or synthetic orders through the new session.
- **Account or symbol slicing.** Start by sending a small set of accounts or instruments through the new session, gradually expanding as confidence grows.
- **Drop-copy cross-checks.** Use drop-copy data to verify that the executions you see on the new session match those seen via the old session or via other sources.

Design the migration scenarios as extensions of the certification matrix, with planned checks and clear rollback criteria.

Decommissioning Legacy Sessions

Once the new connection has proven itself in production:

- Plan a controlled shutdown of the old sessions, including final reconciliation of any remaining open orders or positions.
- Retain logs and configuration for the legacy sessions according to your retention policies.
- Update documentation, runbooks, and operational dashboards to remove references to retired sessions.

Treat decommissioning with the same discipline as onboarding; rushed decommissioning is a common source of orphaned orders or confusing records.

Embedding the Pipeline into Your Organisation

A single well-run onboarding is good; a repeatable process embedded in your organisation is better.

Roles and Responsibilities

Clarify who owns each stage:

- Technology teams typically own FIX engine configuration, test harnesses, and execution of automated suites.
- Network and security teams own firewall rules, VPNs, and TLS setup.
- Operations teams own day-to-day monitoring and the practical aspects of go-live.
- Risk and compliance teams own sign-off thresholds and documentation requirements.

The certification matrix becomes the shared artifact around which these groups coordinate.

Continuous Improvement

Over time, you will discover:

- New edge cases that should be added to the matrix.
- Better ways to automate certain steps.
- Patterns in failures that suggest upstream improvements (for example, clearer internal standards for how your own system uses particular tags).

Treat the onboarding pipeline as a living system. After each major onboarding or incident, perform a brief review: what should be added or changed in the standard pipeline to prevent similar surprises?

Connecting Back to Engine Configuration

Notice how this disciplined onboarding process relies on and reinforces the decisions from the previous section:

- Your choice of FIX engine and its configurability determines how easily you can express counterparty-specific dictionaries and session profiles.

- Your thread and process model, and your sharding of sessions by venue or client, affect how you isolate test and production flows during migration.
- Your transport and TLS tuning affect how realistic your latency and failure scenarios are in certification.

Conversely, robust onboarding illuminates where the engine's configuration model might need refinement. If you repeatedly find yourself hand-coding exceptions for a venue, that is a sign your underlying configuration abstractions can be improved.

By turning onboarding and certification into a disciplined pipeline, you close the loop: you no longer have a fixed engine and ad-hoc connections, but an evolving platform where new counterparties are integrated consistently, tested rigorously, and brought to production with confidence. In the next section, we will add a further layer of protection by systematically applying security, authentication, and entitlements to these sessions.

7.3 Security, Authentication & Entitlements

The previous sections established two foundations. First, you now have a FIX engine that is selected and tuned to run stable, low-latency sessions. Second, you have a disciplined onboarding and certification pipeline that ensures each counterparty behaves as expected before going live.

We now layer security on top of that foundation. The goal is not to turn you into a cryptographer, but to translate common security jargon into concrete practices you can actually apply to FIX:

- How to secure the network transport with TLS and mutual TLS.
- How to manage FIX credentials and session identities safely over their lifetime.

- How to design entitlements so counterparties can only do what they are supposed to do, across both order-entry and drop-copy flows.

Throughout, keep one principle in mind: *make the secure path the normal path.* Security that relies on heroics, manual steps, or rare exceptions will not survive under production pressure.

Thinking Clearly About the Threat Model

Before choosing controls, you should be clear what you are defending against. For FIX connectivity, realistic threats fall into three broad categories.

Eavesdropping and Tampering on the Wire

FIX messages often contain sensitive information:

- Trading intentions (working orders, strategy behaviour).
- Client identities and account numbers.
- Executed quantities and prices.

If the network path between you and your counterparty crosses any shared or untrusted infrastructure (for example, the public internet, shared data-center fabrics, or even internal networks with many tenants), there is a risk that someone could:

- Passively listen to your traffic (eavesdropping).
- Actively modify messages in transit (tampering).

Even inside your own walls, it is usually safer to assume that any sufficiently large network is not fully trustworthy and to protect high-value flows accordingly.

Impersonation and Misuse of Sessions

Even if the network path were perfectly safe, an attacker or buggy system might:

- Log on to a FIX session using stolen or misplaced credentials.
- Connect from an unexpected location and send orders as if they were a legitimate client.
- Abuse a legitimate session to submit orders, cancels, or mass cancels beyond what was agreed.

Here the risk is not just someone seeing the data, but someone *acting as you* or as your client.

Overexposure of Data Through Drop Copy

Drop-copy sessions are often treated as "read-only" and therefore lower risk. That is a mistake.

A broad drop-copy feed can reveal:

- The full picture of a client's trading across multiple venues.
- Strategy behaviour (for example, how quickly positions are opened or closed).
- Aggregate order-book presence if it includes all working orders.

If a drop-copy feed is compromised or misrouted, an attacker or unauthorized internal user might not be able to place orders, but they could gain a highly sensitive view of your trading book or your clients' activity.

With this threat model in mind, we can build a layered defence: encrypt the transport, authenticate each session, and constrain what authenticated sessions can do.

Securing the Transport: TLS and Mutual TLS

At the lowest visible layer in your FIX stack sits TCP. On top of that you can run TLS (Transport Layer Security), which provides encryption and integrity protection.

TLS in Plain Language

TLS wraps your TCP connection in an encrypted tunnel. When correctly configured:

- Anyone observing network packets sees only ciphertext, not FIX tag–value strings.
- Any change to the data in transit is detected and causes the connection to fail, rather than silently delivering altered messages.

From a FIX engine's point of view, once the TLS handshake is complete, it simply reads and writes bytes to a secure socket. The FIX messages themselves do not change.

Server-Only TLS Versus Mutual TLS

In "ordinary" web browsing, only the server presents a certificate; the client authenticates the server but not vice versa. For FIX, you often want *mutual TLS* (mTLS):

- **Server-only TLS**: the server presents its certificate, and the client verifies it. The client proves its identity later using FIX Logon credentials (for example, username and password in the Logon message).
- **Mutual TLS**: both sides present certificates. The TLS layer verifies that each party holds a valid certificate issued by a trusted authority before the FIX session is even attempted.

Mutual TLS adds a strong extra factor of authentication:

- An attacker would need both the FIX credentials *and* the private key corresponding to a valid certificate.
- You can enforce IP and certificate-based access, making "random client on the internet" attacks far harder.

For high-value links—exchange gateways, prime broker connections, major clients—mutual TLS is a sensible default when supported by both sides.

Practical TLS Choices

You do not need to design your own cryptography, but you do need to make some practical choices.

Certificate types and key sizes

Work with your security team to:

- Decide whether certificates are issued by an internal corporate certificate authority (CA) or a commercial CA. For purely bilateral FIX links, internal CAs are common.
- Use key sizes and algorithms that meet current security standards and any regulatory requirements.

The main operational concern is not the exact algorithm but how you manage issuance and expiry, which we discuss later.

Cipher suites

Most modern TLS stacks can be configured to prefer stronger and more efficient ciphers. Your checklist should include:

- Align cipher preferences with your counterparties' requirements; many exchanges publish recommended settings.
- Avoid legacy or deprecated algorithms; these may be accepted by default but weaken security.

Remember that different sessions can use different TLS profiles. You might accept a broader set of ciphers on a low-sensitivity test link, but tighten them for production order-entry.

Handshake overhead and session resumption

TLS handshakes consume CPU and add latency. For FIX, this matters especially when:

- Sessions are frequently re-established (for example, daily logon/logoff windows).
- You have many concurrent sessions starting at the same time (for example, market open).

Mitigation strategies include:

- Using TLS session resumption features where compatible with your counterparties. This allows repeated connections to reuse cryptographic material from a previous handshake.
- Staggering logon times slightly across sessions to avoid a sharp spike in handshake load at, say, 08:00:00.
- Offloading TLS to dedicated processes or appliances if your engine becomes CPU-bound on encryption; in this case, the offload layer terminates TLS and passes plaintext FIX to the engine over a controlled internal link.

The aim is to keep transport security "always on" without destabilising your session behaviour or latency profile.

Session-Level Authentication: Identities and Credentials

Once the transport is secured, the FIX session itself still needs to know *who* is on each side. This is done via Logon messages and session identifiers.

Session Identities: CompIDs and Accounts

At a minimum, each FIX session is defined by:

- Your SenderCompID and the counterparty's TargetCompID.
- Sometimes additional fields such as SenderSubID, TargetSubID, or OnBehalfOfCompID to distinguish desks, systems, or clients.

Treat these identifiers as part of your security surface:

- Do not reuse the same IDs across multiple environments (UAT, production, disaster recovery).
- Avoid sharing IDs between conceptually different roles (for example, prop trading versus client agency flow).

Clear separation of identities makes misconfigurations and abusive behaviour easier to detect and contain.

Logon Credentials and Policies

In many deployments, the FIX Logon message carries:

- A username or session ID (sometimes the same as SenderCompID, sometimes separate).
- A password or authentication token.

Basic hygiene is essential:

- Generate strong, random passwords; avoid anything human-chosen or reused across systems.
- Store credentials securely, not in plain-text configuration files on shared drives.
- Implement credential rotation policies: passwords should change regularly and on staff changes, not remain static for years.

Rotation need not be painful if you plan for it:

- Build credential changes into your onboarding and change-management pipelines.
- Support "overlap windows" where both old and new credentials are valid for a short time while both sides update.
- Test Logon behaviour with new credentials in a non-production environment before flipping them live.

When combined with mutual TLS, Logon credentials provide a second layer of identity verification: even if a certificate is stolen, the attacker still needs the Logon password, and vice versa.

IP Allowlists and Network-Level Controls

An additional simple but effective control is to restrict which IP addresses may connect to a given FIX session:

- On your side, configure firewalls or engine acceptors to only allow connections from the counterparty's advertised IP ranges.
- Ask counterparties to apply the same restriction for your outbound connections.

This measure:

- Reduces the attack surface from "anywhere on the internet" to a few known addresses.
- Helps detect accidental cross-wiring: if a session unexpectedly originates from a new IP, that is a signal to investigate.

However, do not rely solely on IP allowlists. They are easy to misconfigure and may not be sufficient in cloud or dynamic environments. They should complement, not replace, proper authentication.

Credential Lifecycle Management

Security controls matter not just at a point in time, but over the life of the system. This is where lifecycle management enters: certificates and FIX credentials are born, used, rotated, and eventually retired.

Issuance and Initial Distribution

When you create new credentials or certificates:

- Use secure channels to transmit them to the counterparty or internal team; avoid email in clear text, chat messages, or ad-hoc file copies.
- Record who requested, approved, and received the credentials.
- Immediately add the new identities to your configuration management and monitoring systems, so they are visible and auditable.

For TLS certificates, define a simple, documented process:

- How certificate signing requests (CSRs) are generated.
- Who approves issuance.
- How the private keys are protected on your systems (for example, restricted file permissions or hardware security modules).

Monitoring and Renewal

Certificates have explicit expiry dates; passwords and tokens should have implicit ones via rotation policies.

You should:

- Maintain an inventory of all active FIX-related certificates and their expiry dates.
- Set automated alerts well before expiry (for example, 60, 30, and 7 days ahead).
- Periodically review unused or dormant credentials and consider revoking them to reduce attack surface.

Last-minute certificate renewals during trading hours are both stressful and risky. Align renewals with planned maintenance windows and rehearse the steps in a non-production environment.

Revocation and Incident Response

If you suspect that a certificate or FIX credential has been compromised, speed matters:

- Revoke the certificate in your CA and remove it from any accept lists on the engine or front-end components.
- Disable or change affected FIX passwords immediately, and coordinate with counterparties for matching changes on their side.
- Use your monitoring tools to identify sessions and messages that may have been affected during the suspected compromise window.

This is why the previous chapter's emphasis on observability is important: good logs and metrics make it possible to understand the impact of a compromised credential and to prove to stakeholders what did or did not happen.

Entitlements: Controlling What Sessions May Do

So far, we have focused on verifying *who* is on the other end of a session. Entitlements address a different question: *given that this session is authenticated, what is it allowed to do?*

Why Entitlements Matter

In many incidents, the attacker is not an outsider but a misconfigured internal system, a bug, or a legitimate user misusing their access. Without entitlements:

- A client session might trade instruments or markets they are not supposed to access.
- An internal tool could accidentally send drop-copy data for all clients to the wrong recipient.
- A single compromised session could submit orders or mass cancels across many accounts.

Proper entitlements ensure that even if a session misbehaves, the damage is limited to its authorized scope.

Designing an Entitlement Model

A useful way to think about entitlements is to break them into three questions:

1. **Which accounts and legal entities may this session act for?**
2. **Which instruments or markets may it trade?**
3. **Which operations may it perform?** (For example, new orders, replaces, cancels, mass cancels, post-trade allocations.)

For each FIX session or group of sessions, define:

Account entitlements

- A list of accounts, sub-accounts, or client codes that this session may reference in tags like Account or PartyID.
- Whether the session can trade for "house" accounts, client accounts, or both.

Instrument and market entitlements

- Allowed symbol lists or symbol patterns.
- Permitted venues or market segments (for example, specific exchanges, dark pools, or product lines).

Action entitlements

- Whether the session can submit new orders, replaces, single-order cancels, or mass cancels.
- Whether it can perform special operations such as firm-wide kill switches or credit limit changes (if exposed via FIX).

The entitlement model should be explicit and configurable, not scattered across informal documentation or embedded deeply in business code.

Where to Enforce Entitlements

Entitlements can be enforced in multiple layers:

- **At the FIX engine edge:** The engine inspects incoming messages, and if a session attempts an unauthorized action or account, it rejects the message before passing it further inside.
- **Within the trading application:** Additional checks ensure that even if a message passes engine-level validation, it is still consistent with business rules and risk limits.

A layered approach is strongest:

- The engine provides a fast "circuit breaker" at the perimeter.
- The application provides richer, context-aware checks (for example, combined position limits or dynamic credit checks).

When a message is rejected for entitlement reasons, ensure that:

- The counterparty receives a clear reject message with appropriate reason codes.
- Logs capture enough detail to reconstruct what was attempted and why it was rejected.

Special Focus: Securing Drop-Copy Flows

Drop-copy sessions carry information, not trading actions, but their security requirements are no less important.

Avoiding Over-Broad Feeds

It is tempting to create one giant drop-copy feed "for convenience," containing:

- All clients.
- All instruments.
- All venues.

Operationally, that may seem simpler, but it is dangerous:

- A single misrouted or compromised feed reveals everything.
- It is harder to prove to a specific client that they only receive their own data.

Instead, design drop-copy entitlements with the same care as order-entry:

- Partition feeds by client or legal entity where possible.
- Restrict each feed to the relevant accounts, instruments, and venues.
- Make exceptions explicit, documented, and approved (for example, a compliance monitoring feed that legitimately sees all flow).

Session Separation and Credentials

Apply the same identity and credential principles to drop copy:

- Use distinct session IDs and Logon credentials for drop-copy versus order-entry sessions, even if they connect to the same counterparty.
- Apply separate TLS certificates where appropriate; this allows you to revoke or rotate a drop-copy certificate without impacting order flow.

This separation:

- Limits the blast radius of any compromise: losing a drop-copy credential does not immediately allow order-entry, and vice versa.
- Simplifies monitoring, as you can treat drops in drop-copy connectivity differently from trading session events.

Monitoring for Information Leakage

Finally, treat suspicious patterns on drop-copy as potential security incidents, not just technical glitches. Examples include:

- A feed suddenly delivering data for unexpected accounts or instruments.
- A new session or IP address appearing for a sensitive drop-copy connection.
- Unexpected spikes in data volume or connection attempts on drop-copy ports.

Your observability stack should be able to flag these as anomalies and route them to both operations and security teams.

Checklists for Go-Live and Operations

To make security practical, distil it into checklists that can be followed before go-live and during operations.

Pre Go-Live Security Checklist for a New Counterparty

For each new or significantly changed connection, verify:

- Transport:
  - TLS or mutual TLS is enabled and tested in the relevant environments.
  - Cipher suites and protocol versions meet policy requirements.
- Identities and credentials:
  - Session IDs (SenderCompID, TargetCompID, etc.) are unique per environment.
  - Logon passwords or tokens are strong, stored securely, and recorded in the credential inventory.
  - IP allowlists or firewall rules are configured on both sides.
- Entitlements:
  - Account, instrument, and action entitlements are defined and configured at the engine and/or application layer.
  - Drop-copy sessions are scoped to the correct accounts and flows.
- Lifecycle:
  - Certificate expiry dates are recorded with alerts.
  - Procedures for rotation and emergency revocation are documented and rehearsed in a lower environment.

Ongoing Operational Checklist

On a regular cadence (for example, monthly or quarterly), and after any security-relevant incident, confirm that:

- No dormant or unused sessions still have active credentials without justification.
- Entitlement configurations still match business intent (for example, client offboarding is reflected in FIX access).
- TLS and credential inventories are up to date.
- Logs and monitoring continue to capture enough detail to support incident investigation and regulatory inquiries.

Bringing It All Together

Security for FIX is not an add-on; it is intertwined with the engine configuration and onboarding process:

- Your engine's support for TLS, authentication hooks, and session configuration determines how easily you can implement secure defaults.
- Your onboarding pipeline is the natural place to collect certificates, distribute credentials, and define entitlements as part of bringing a counterparty live.
- Your monitoring and observability layer (covered in the next section) is what lets you see when these controls are working, when they are under attack, or when they have drifted out of alignment with policy.

By translating jargon like "TLS," "authentication," and "entitlements" into concrete FIX practices, you create an environment where security is both strong and operationally manageable. Sessions remain fast and stable, but they are also well-defended: only the right parties can connect, and once they do, they can only do what they are supposed to do.

7.4 Monitoring, Alerting, and Observability

By this point in the chapter, you have a carefully chosen FIX engine, a disciplined onboarding pipeline, and layered security around your sessions. The remaining question is simple but crucial:

Can you actually see what is happening in production, in time to prevent bad things from becoming very bad?

This section answers that question by defining a practical observability model for FIX:

- Which metrics matter, and how to collect them.
- How to log FIX traffic in a way that is both useful and safe.
- How to tie these signals together into alerts and runbooks that guide real-time response.

The emphasis is not on a particular tool, but on what you should be able to observe and how to reason about what you see.

What Does It Mean to Observe a FIX Ecosystem?

A FIX environment is not just a few sockets; it is a living system made of:

- The FIX engine processes and their session state.
- Your trading applications and risk checks.
- Networks, firewalls, TLS termination, and external venues or clients.

Observability, in this context, means being able to:

- Answer basic health questions: Are sessions connected? Are messages flowing? Are sequence numbers in sync?

- Detect and localize problems: Is a slowdown due to your engine, your application, the network, or the venue?
- Explain and reconstruct events after the fact: What exactly happened during that incident at 10:05?

To do this, you need three kinds of signals:

- **Metrics**: numeric time series about rates, counts, and resource usage.
- **Logs**: detailed, timestamped records of individual events and messages.
- **Traces or correlations**: links between events across components, so you can follow one order through the ecosystem.

We will build up each of these, then show how to design dashboards and alerts, and finally how to test your setup before trusting it with real money.

A Minimal Metrics Contract for FIX Engines

Start with a "minimal contract" of metrics your FIX engine should expose. You can always add more later, but there is a core set you should not go live without.

Session State and Churn

For each FIX session, you want visibility into:

- **Connection state**: connected, disconnected, attempting logon, logged out by peer, logged out locally.
- **Logon and logout counts**: how many times the session has connected or dropped in a given period.
- **Disconnect reasons**: protocol error, TCP reset, timeout, administrative logout, or manual intervention.

Even simple charts of "number of connected sessions over time" and "disconnects per hour" can reveal:

- Patterns such as regular logon storms or recurring flaps at certain times.
- The difference between a single bad session and a systemic issue (for example, many sessions dropping together).

Message and Error Rates

Next, track message traffic per session and in aggregate:

- **Messages per second (MPS)**: inbound and outbound, broken down by type if possible (orders, cancels, execution reports, rejects, heartbeats, administrative messages).
- **Error and reject counts**: protocol rejects (bad messages), business rejects (invalid orders), and internal errors.
- **Resend and gap-fill counts**: how many resend requests you send and receive, and how many gap-fill messages are exchanged.

These metrics help you see:

- Normal intraday patterns (for example, spikes at market open, quiet mid-day).
- Abnormal behaviour such as a sudden surge in rejects or resends, which often signals a deeper problem (version mismatch, dictionary issue, application bug).

Sequence Number Behaviour

Sequence numbers are the backbone of FIX sessions. You should observe for each session:

- Current inbound and outbound sequence numbers.
- The rate at which they increase.

- Any detected gaps or rollbacks.

From this, you can derive:

- Alerts when sequence numbers reset unexpectedly (for example, due to Logon with reset flags or manual intervention).
- Evidence of missed or duplicated messages (a gap that is not followed by a resend or a jump backwards).

Monitoring sequence number health is essential for detecting silent data loss or misconfigured recovery.

Internal Queues and Backpressure

Inside the engine and around it, messages flow through queues: from sockets into parsers, from engines into applications, from applications back out.

You should track:

- Queue depths for key internal buffers (for example, per-session outbound queues).
- Dropped-message counters, if any queues are allowed to overflow.
- Backpressure signals, such as "session temporarily not accepting new sends."

Rising queues and backpressure often precede more visible problems:

- Latency increases as messages wait longer in queues.
- Eventually sessions may disconnect, or your application may start timing out.

Seeing backpressure early allows you to intervene (for example, throttling a chatty client) before things break.

Host-Level Resource Metrics

Finally, remember that the FIX engine runs on real servers. At the host level, you should monitor:

- CPU usage per engine process and in aggregate.
- Memory usage and growth over time.
- Network I/O: bytes and packets per interface, retransmissions if available.
- Disk I/O if you use persistent message stores.

These metrics connect application-level symptoms to underlying causes. For example:

- A spike in CPU may explain an increase in latency across sessions on the same host.
- Saturated network interfaces can lead to timeouts and disconnects that look like venue problems but are self-inflicted.

Latency as a First-Class Metric

Many trading incidents are not complete outages; they are slowdowns. Orders still flow, but too slowly to be competitive or to meet obligations. That is why latency must be a first-class citizen in your observability design.

Breaking Down Latency Components

Think of latency as composed of several stages:

- **Internal processing latency**: time spent inside your system (engine plus application logic).
- **Venue or counterparty round-trip time**: network transit plus processing on the other side.
- **Post-trade processing latency**: time from execution to appearance on drop copy or in downstream systems.

You do not need nanosecond precision to be effective, but you do need stable, comparable measurements over time.

Measuring Latency in Practice

Typical approaches include:

- Time-stamping when an order leaves your application and when the first related execution report arrives.
- Time-stamping when a venue or broker fill enters your system and when it appears on your drop-copy consumer or risk system.
- Using host clocks synchronized by NTP or PTP so that cross-component comparisons are meaningful.

From these measurements, build basic statistics:

- **Percentiles** (for example, median, 95th, 99th) rather than only averages. Rare but severe spikes often matter more than small shifts in averages.
- **Breakdown by session and by message type**: venue A versus venue B, order-entry versus drop-copy.

You can then define service-level objectives (SLOs). For example:

> 99% of NewOrderSingle messages to Venue X should receive a first execution report (or reject) within Y milliseconds during normal market conditions.

These SLOs become the basis for alerts and capacity planning.

Relating Latency to Other Signals

Latency never exists in isolation. Meaningful observability connects latency to:

- Message rates (did the slowdown coincide with a burst in traffic?).
- Resend volumes (are we seeing many resends that could indicate packet loss or engine overload?).
- Host resource metrics (is CPU or network saturated?).

To make these relationships concrete for operators, it helps to visualise them together, which we will do with an example shortly.

Designing Dashboards to See Risk at a Glance

Once you know which metrics matter, the next step is to present them so that an operator glancing at a screen for 10 seconds can answer:

> Is everything OK? If not, where should I look first?

This is where dashboards come in.

Core Dashboard Panels

A practical FIX operations dashboard often contains at least four panels:

- **Message rate**: inbound and outbound MPS per major session or venue.
- **Error and reject rate**: counts of rejects, disconnects, and failed logons.
- **Latency percentiles**: internal and external latency for key flows.
- **Sequence and resend health**: number of resends, detected gaps, and possibly a summary health indicator.

Additional panels can show CPU, memory, and network usage for the underlying hosts.

This mock dashboard shows a pattern that often appears in real life:

- A burst in message rate.
- A coupled spike in latency percentiles.
- A small burst of resends and errors at the same time.

Presenting these metrics together helps operators quickly see that "something happened around 30 minutes" and that it affected both performance and reliability.

Per-Session and Aggregate Views

It is useful to have both:

- **Aggregate views** across all sessions or all venues, to spot systemic issues.
- **Drill-down views** per critical session (for example, a primary exchange or a major client), to investigate and manage specific problems.

For example, an aggregate latency panel might show that "overall" things look fine, but a per-session view reveals that one venue is slow while another is normal. This distinction is vital when dealing with external partners.

Colour and Thresholds

Simple visual cues go a long way:

- Use colour or shading to distinguish normal ranges from abnormal ones. For instance, show latency bands in green up to the SLO limit, then yellow and red for higher values.
- Highlight panels when alerts are active; for example, a red border around a chart when a threshold is breached.

The goal is that someone new to the system can, within a week, learn to "read" the dashboard as easily as a pilot reads cockpit instruments.

Logging Strategy: Detail Without Chaos

Metrics tell you *that* something is wrong; logs tell you *what* happened in detail. For FIX, both message-level logs and higher-level application logs are important.

What to Log at the FIX Layer

At the FIX engine level, you typically want to log:

- Session lifecycle events: logons, logouts, disconnects, and their reasons.
- Administrative messages: heartbeats, test requests, sequence resets, resend requests, and gap fills.

- Business messages: new orders, cancels, replaces, execution reports, rejects, mass actions.

Each log entry should include:

- A precise timestamp.
- Session identifiers (SenderCompID, TargetCompID, and any sub-IDs).
- Direction (inbound or outbound).
- The full FIX string or a structured representation of all tags (subject to masking sensitive fields).

You can then:

- Reconstruct the history of a particular order or session.
- Diagnose interoperability issues with venues or clients.
- Provide regulators with detailed evidence if required.

Masking and Tokenizing Sensitive Fields

Raw FIX messages can contain highly sensitive data, such as client names, account numbers, and sometimes personally identifiable information.

To balance usefulness and privacy:

- Identify which tags contain sensitive information (for example, account identifiers, client names in free-text fields, or internal notes).
- Configure your logging to mask or hash these fields before writing them to log files.
- Where possible, use stable hashes so that the same real-world value always maps to the same token in the logs. This allows correlation without revealing the original value.

Be explicit in your design: decide at design time which tags are safe to log as-is and which must always be protected.

Correlating FIX Logs with Application Logs

Your trading application and risk systems will also produce logs: decisions, risk checks, state transitions.

You gain a lot by correlating these with FIX logs, using:

- A shared order identifier present in both layers.
- Consistent timestamp formats and time synchronization across systems.
- If available, a correlation ID that is carried through from the earliest point (for example, client request) all the way through FIX interactions and back.

This correlation turns a messy pile of logs into a coherent "story" for each order or incident.

Automated Gap Detection and Data Integrity Checks

One of the more subtle risks in FIX processing is silent data loss: missing or duplicated messages that do not immediately crash anything, but later show up as reconciliation breaks or regulatory issues.

Near Real-Time Sequence Gap Tracking

Using the sequence number metrics discussed earlier, you can build automated gap detection:

- Continuously compare expected versus seen sequence numbers for each session.
- When a gap is detected (for example, you receive 101, 102, 104), trigger a resend request if the session rules allow, and log the event.
- Alert if the gap is not resolved within a reasonable time window, or if gaps become frequent.

This should run both at the engine level and, where appropriate, at a higher level (for example, counting expected versus actual execution reports for a known set of orders).

Using Drop Copy as a Cross-Check

Drop-copy feeds are a powerful tool for cross-checking data integrity:

- For orders sent over order-entry sessions, verify that corresponding fills appear on drop copy as expected.
- For executions received via drop copy, verify that they map to known orders in your internal system.

Automated reconciliations can:

- Raise alerts when fills appear on drop copy without a corresponding local order, suggesting misrouting or missing data.
- Detect when some but not all expected drop-copy messages arrive, indicating a partial feed issue.

These checks may run with a slight delay (for example, every few minutes) but add a robust safety net against silent mismatches.

Alerting Patterns and Runbooks

Metrics and logs generate a huge amount of raw information. Alerting is about focus: deciding which conditions should trigger action from humans, and what they should do when that happens.

Defining Useful Alerts

Good alerts are:

- **Actionable**: there is a clear next step or investigation path.
- **Scoped**: they point roughly to where the problem is (for example, "Venue X initiator sessions" rather than "something somewhere is wrong").

- **Calibrated**: they avoid both constant noise and total silence.

Useful alert types for FIX include:

Session stability

- Multiple disconnects or failed logons for a session within a short window.
- Unexpected logouts or logon attempts outside normal trading hours.

Performance and latency

- Latency percentiles breaching SLOs for a venue or client.
- Sustainably high engine CPU or queue depths coupled with latency increases.

Protocol and security

- Surges in protocol rejects or parsing errors.
- Spikes in authentication failures (invalid Logon credentials, TLS handshake failures).

Entitlements and risk

- Repeated entitlement rejections for a session (for example, attempting to trade unauthorized instruments or accounts).
- Unexpected mass cancel requests or kill-switch events.

Data integrity

- Unresolved sequence gaps or frequent resends.
- Mismatches between order-entry executions and drop-copy confirmations.

Runbooks: What to Do When an Alert Fires

Every significant alert should have a short, concrete runbook entry, answering:

- What does this alert mean in plain language?
- What are the most likely causes (venue outage, internal bug, network failure, misconfiguration)?
- Which dashboards or logs should be checked first?
- Which teams or counterparties should be contacted, and how urgently?
- Under what conditions should trading be paused or sessions manually disconnected?

Runbooks turn on-call engineers and operations staff from "log readers" into effective responders, reducing the time from detection to mitigation.

Testing Observability Before You Need It

It is dangerous to wait for the first real incident to learn whether your monitoring and alerting work. You should test them in controlled ways.

Injecting Synthetic Failures

In non-production or low-risk windows, you can:

- Deliberately misconfigure a test session to cause Logon failures or rejects.
- Introduce artificial latency or rate limits to simulate a slow venue.
- Temporarily raise message rates to approach system capacity.

During these tests, verify:

- That the expected metrics move as anticipated.

- That dashboards make the situation visually obvious.
- That alerts trigger at the right time and with useful context.

Tabletop Exercises for Major Incidents

For higher-impact scenarios—such as suspected credential compromise, major venue outage, or widespread data corruption—you can run "tabletop exercises":

- Walk through an incident scenario step by step with representatives from technology, operations, risk, and compliance.
- Use real dashboards and past logs where possible to make the exercise concrete.
- Identify gaps in metrics, logging, or runbooks and update them accordingly.

The intent is not to rehearse every detail but to ensure that, when real stress hits, your teams and tools are familiar with each other.

Closing the Loop: From Visibility to Control

Observability is not an end in itself. It is valuable because it allows you to:

- Detect emerging risks in order flow and drop copy early.
- Attribute problems accurately to your systems, networks, or external counterparties.
- Respond quickly and confidently, limiting trading impact and regulatory exposure.

The pieces built across this chapter now fit together:

- A robust FIX engine, tuned for performance, provides the hooks for metrics and high-quality logs.

- A disciplined onboarding process and strong security controls ensure that sessions behave as expected and are well-defined.
- Monitoring, alerting, and observability make that behaviour visible, so you can operate FIX connectivity as a critical, well-understood part of your trading business rather than as a mysterious black box.

Once you reach this point, FIX stops being a source of surprises and becomes a reliable, measurable service in your trading stack—one that you can scale, secure, and manage with the same discipline as the rest of your infrastructure.

www.ingramcontent.com/pod-product-compliance
Lightning Source LLC
LaVergne TN
LVHW080530210926
848481LV00021B/1572